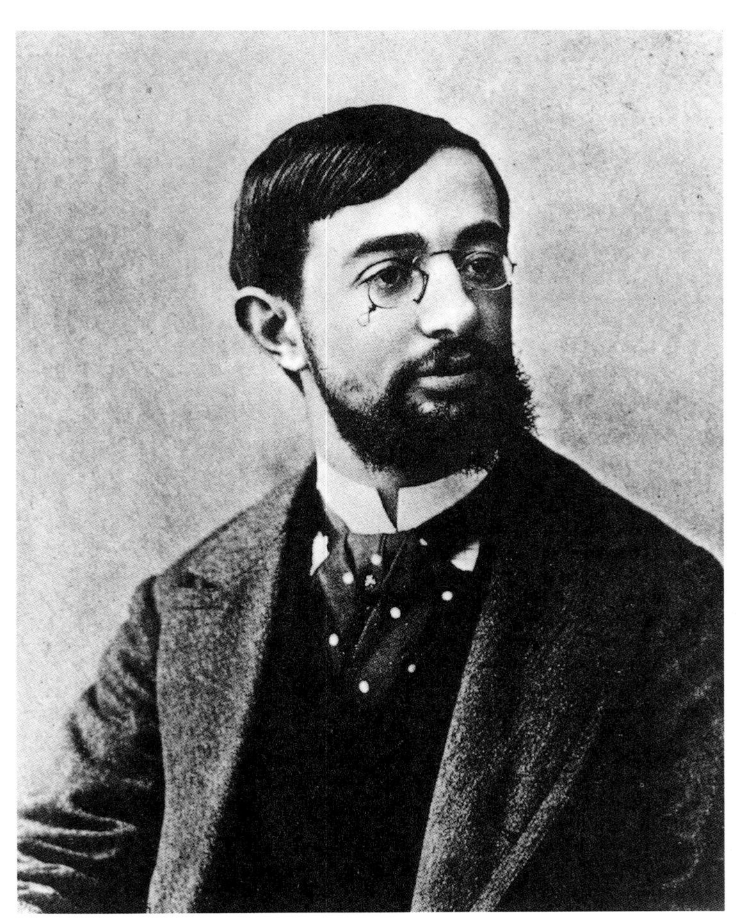

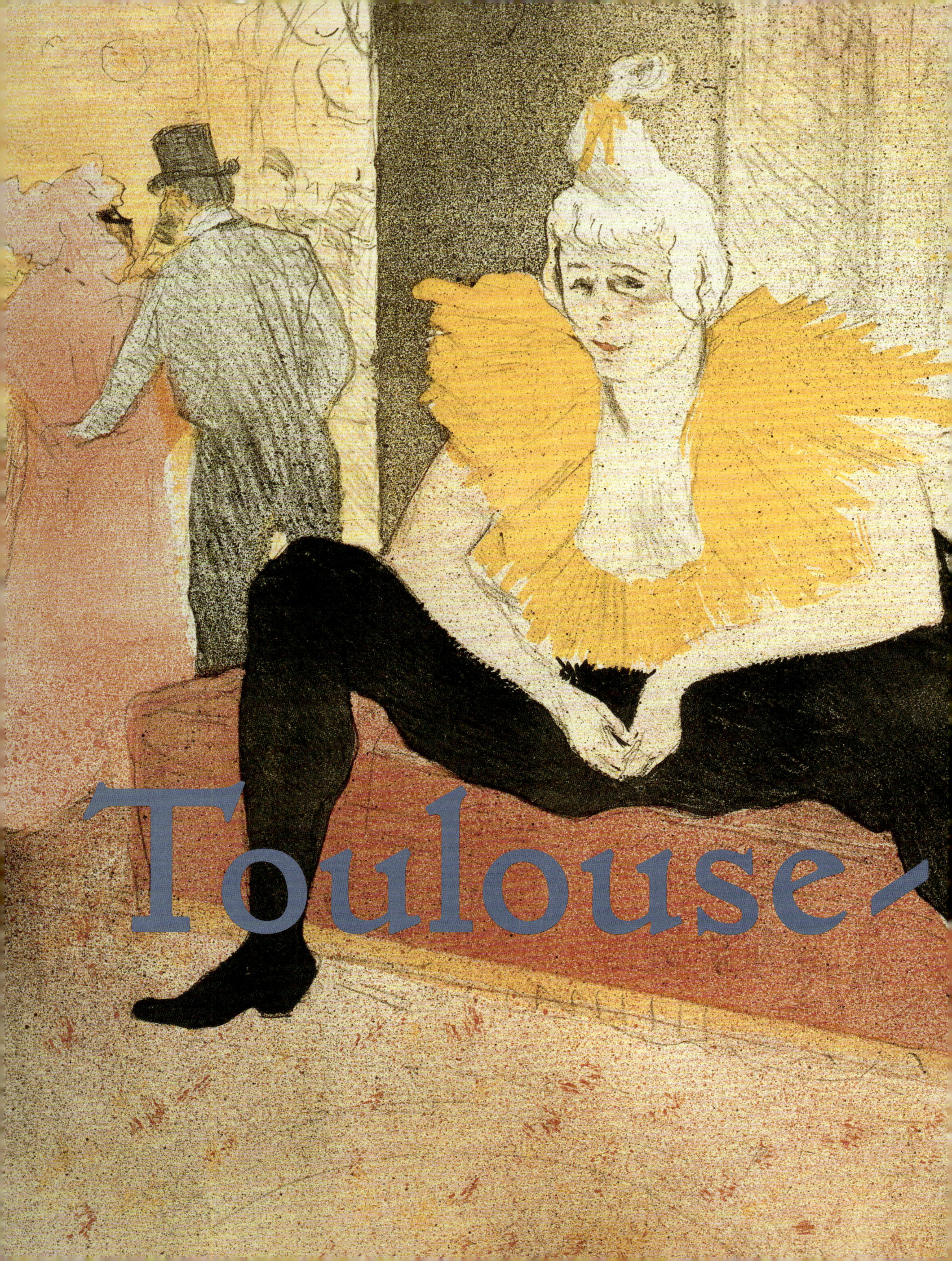

Toulouse

Lautrec

Riva Castleman

HIGH MUSEUM OF ART

*Toulouse-Lautrec: Posters and Prints from the Collection of
Irene and Howard Stein*
was on view at the High Museum of Art
Atlanta, Georgia
March 24–June 14, 1998
The exhibition was organized by the High Museum of Art.

Library of Congress Cataloging-in-Publication Data
Castleman, Riva.
    Toulouse-Lautrec : posters and prints from the
collection of Irene and Howard Stein / Riva Castleman.
       p. cm.
    Catalog of an exhibition held at the High Museum of
Art, Atlanta, Ga., Mar. 24–June 14, 1998.
    Includes bibliographical references.
    ISBN 0-939802-83-x (hard : alk. paper). —
ISBN 0-939802-84-8 (soft : alk. paper)
    1. Toulouse-Lautrec, Henri de, 1864–1901—
Exhibitions. 2. Stein, Irene, 1927– —Art collections
—Exhibitions. 3. Stein, Howard, 1923– —Art
collections—Exhibitions. 4. Posters—Private collec-
tions—Georgia—Atlanta—Exhibitions. 5. Prints—
Private collections—Georgia—Atlanta—Exhibitions
I. Toulouse-Lautrec, Henri de, 1864–1901. II. High
Museum of Art. III. Title.
NC1850.T6A4 1998
741.674'092—dc21   97-46141

Produced by Marquand Books, Inc., Seattle
Designed by Susan E. Kelly
Copyedited by Pamela A. Zytnicki

For the High Museum of Art
Kelly Morris, Manager of Publications
Anna Bloomfield, Associate Editor

Except for *Elles* series, photos of the Stein Collection
by Peter Harholdt, Baltimore

Printed and bound by Balding + Mansell, Norwich,
England

Cover: *L'Anglais au Moulin Rouge* (cat. 7).
Page 1: Paul Sescau, *Toulouse-Lautrec*, photograph.
  Musée Toulouse-Lautrec, Albi.
Frontispiece: *Elles: La Clownesse assise; Mademoiselle
  Cha-u-Kao* (cat. 46).

Contents

Collectors' Acknowledgments

Our thanks to Rosemary Uffner, who first introduced us to, and stimulated our interest in, the turn-of-the-century French poster. We wish to acknowledge Richard Reed Armstrong for his guidance and professionalism over the years. In addition, we are grateful to Mary Bartow of Sotheby's and to Ann Spink of Christie's for their knowledge and assistance in helping us acquire rare and important pieces at auction. We would especially like to thank David Brenneman of the High Museum of Art, whose invaluable assistance made this exhibition project an enjoyable and educational one for us.

We also wish to express our thanks and appreciation to our families and especially to our sister-in-law Hansi Fruchtman for her undying enthusiasm and tremendous support. Finally, we value and appreciate the love and support that our children, Cindy and Howard Goldberg, and Lisa and Bruce Stein, have given us through the years.

Irene and Howard Stein

Curator's Acknowledgments

My thanks go to Irene and Howard Stein for their patience and for the gracious hospitality that they showed to the High's staff. They have been ideal patrons. I would also like to thank Riva Castleman, Chief Curator Emerita of Prints and Illustrated Books, The Museum of Modern Art, for the meticulous and highly professional manner in which she went about cataloguing the Steins' collection. In preparing the catalogue for publication, thanks must also go to Kelly Morris and Anna Bloomfield for their outstanding editorial efforts; to Peter Harholdt for his photographs of the collection; and to Elisabeth Kaiser Schulte, who answered questions about the condition and printmaking techniques used in the creation of a number of works in the exhibition. Thanks also go to the Print Departments of Christie's and Sotheby's in New York and London, Richard Reed Armstrong in Chicago, Ianetti Gallery in San Francisco, and Belgis-Freidel Gallery in New York for their help in gathering information about works in the Steins' collection.

On behalf of Ms. Castleman, I would like to acknowledge the special help of Herbert D. Schimmel, and thank the following for their assistance: Colta Ives, Curator, Metropolitan Museum of Art, New York; the staff of the Department of Prints and Illustrated Books and the Library of The Museum of Modern Art; Mary Bartow of Sotheby's; and Jonathan Rendell of Christie's.

Many staff members of the High Museum of Art deserve thanks for making this catalogue possible. I would like to single out Jody Cohen, associate registrar, who oversaw the logistics of transporting the works to and from the Museum; Larry Miller and other members of the preparators crew helped to inventory the collection; and Lauren Levin and Catherine Holton, interns in the European Art department, assisted with research. Lastly, I would like to thank Phaedra Siebert, my curatorial assistant, who inventoried the collection and undertook the difficult task of procuring photographic material for the catalogue.

David A. Brenneman
Frances B. Bunzl Family Curator of European Art

Preface

The art of Henri de Toulouse-Lautrec, arguably the greatest draftsman of the past one hundred years, is important not only for its sheer linear mastery, innovative use of flat color planes, and acerbic commentary on his contemporary social milieu, but also because it reminds us that works of great value are sometimes not so obviously presented in art galleries or museums. Lautrec was gifted at taking his immediate environment of dance hall performers, flamboyant poets, and other denizens of the demimonde, and creating striking images for public consumption as advertisements, posters, and illustrations. This move into popular culture, always with a flair for economy and a robust love of character, is what marks this artist as one of the most important Post-Impressionists.

Collecting art is something that distinguishes people of significant accomplishment from others who are also successful in their professional pursuits. The development of a discriminating eye, one that recognizes nuances of style, has been a hallmark of sophistication and leadership for centuries in western civilization. Atlanta is a city and metropolitan area where habits of collecting art are not comparable to other major burgs and regions. Every so often, however, an exceptional individual or couple emerges, as if out of nowhere, to the attention of the High. Such is the case of Irene and Howard Stein.

The Steins' collection of prints and posters by Henri de Toulouse-Lautrec is striking for both its range and depth. Moreover, the Steins have prided themselves on having collected the finest examples available within an ever-shrinking supply of works by this master. This exhibition, which is the second in an ongoing series celebrating Atlanta collectors, pays tribute to their connoisseurship, as well as their tenacity. It is the rare collectors who are willing to make that extra sacrifice in order to upgrade an image that already exists in their collection. The Steins have done this repeatedly and have never balked at acquiring the occasional gem that they discover in their rigorous research.

The High is extremely grateful to Howard and Irene Stein, and to their entire family, for permitting us to present their exceptional collection as a special exhibition. I also wish to thank Dr. David Brenneman, the Museum's Frances B.

Bunzl Family Curator of European Art, for his inspired and diligent work on
this important project.

Finally, we extend the opportunity to our members and visitors to share in
the vision of this remarkable artist. While the world has changed considerably
in these past one hundred years, clearly human nature remains a constant.

Ned Rifkin
Nancy and Holcombe T. Green, Jr. Director

Foreword

Irene and Howard Stein's interest in the posters and prints of Henri de Toulouse-Lautrec began almost twenty-five years ago, when they purchased a poster by the fin de siècle artist Alphonse Mucha. That work depicted one of the artist's favorite subjects, the actress Sarah Bernhardt. This initial purchase was followed by the acquisition of several color posters by well-known artists of that period, including Jules Chéret, Fernand Louis Gottlob, and others. Though they did not acquire any works by Lautrec at the outset, their early collecting of works by Mucha, Chéret, and Gottlob established their taste for color posters.

In the early 1980s, the Steins bought their first Lautrec. The print was *Babylone d'Allemagne* of 1894 (cat. 23), one of the artist's most controversial works. This acquisition led them to focus solely on the work of Lautrec, a decision based in large part on their recognition that he was the absolute master of the poster. The Steins' exclusive commitment to the work of this one artist was strengthened by Howard's professional activities as the owner of a carpet mill. The bold colors and designs of Lautrec's posters mirrored Howard's approach to carpet design, and the mill's worldwide business interests enabled Irene and Howard to see important collections and exhibitions of the artist's works firsthand, which further fueled their interest. Their travels also brought them into contact with a small circle of private dealers and auction house representatives, who shared their enthusiasm for Lautrec and helped them sharpen their connoisseurship skills.

By the late 1980s, Irene and Howard had assembled a collection that included most of Lautrec's color posters, and they were then faced with the decision of how to continue their passion for collecting his work. They decided to focus on the exceptional color prints that Lautrec produced for private collectors. This new direction soon led to their greatest triumph, the acquisition at auction of an extremely rare trial proof of Lautrec's print *La Grande Loge* (cat. 61). Since then, Irene and Howard have continued to add rare color and black-and-white lithographs to their collection, thereby assembling a remarkably well-rounded representation of all aspects of Lautrec's printmaking oeuvre.

The Steins' many years of collecting have resulted in what is undoubtedly the best collection of Lautrec prints in the Southeast and, moreover, one of the best private collections of his work to be found anywhere in the United States. They attribute their success both to their focused collecting and to the sheer joy that collecting brings them. In recent years, the Steins' children and grandchildren have come to share in their enthusiasm, and, in staging this exhibition of their collection, it is their sincere wish to share their passion for collecting and for Lautrec with all visitors to the High Museum of Art.

David A. Brenneman
Frances B. Bunzl Family Curator of European Art

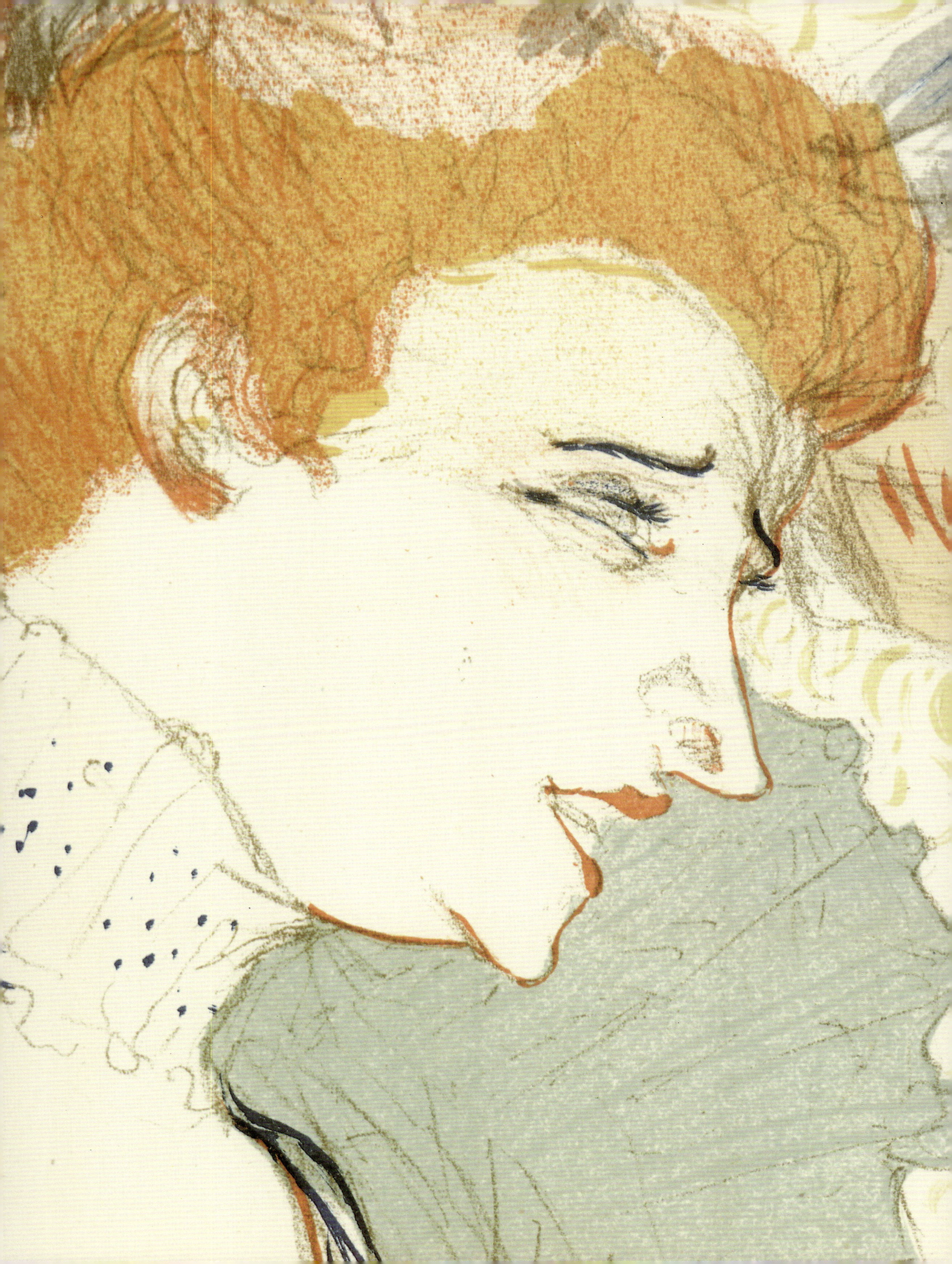

The Artist's Life and Work*Riva Castleman*

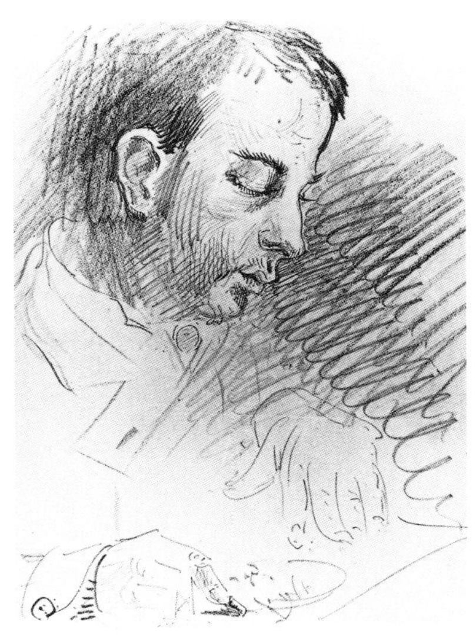

Alphonse de Toulouse-Lautrec, *Portrait of Henri Drawing*, ca. 1880, pencil on paper, 8⅞ × 7⅜ in. Private collection.

1. Edmond de Goncourt (*Journal*, vol. 4 [Monaco: Imprimerie nationale, 1956], p. 909), refers to "the ridiculous homunculus whose caricatural deformity is reflected in each of his drawings," quoted in Julia Frey, *Toulouse-Lautrec: A Life* (New York: Viking, 1994), p. 420.

2. Letter from Count Alphonse de Toulouse-Lautrec to M. de la Panouse, September 1901, quoted in Herbert D. Schimmel, ed., *The Letters of Henri de Toulouse-Lautrec* (New York: Oxford University Press, 1991), no. 4, p. 413.

The "homunculus," a pathetic error of nature whose gifts made up for his crippled form, died at his mother's estate on September 9, 1901.[1] Afterward his father, a member of one of France's oldest aristocratic families, a man who favored hunting over parenting for most of his son's thirty-six years, wrote to a friend, "Who suffered more, the father or the son? He with his physical disabilities, distressing misfortunes made all the more painful for him by the fact that he would have liked the elegant, active life of all healthy, sports-loving persons, or I, the 'author' of days so sad, numbered, discounted, cut short."[2] Perhaps he felt his son's fate would have been different had he not married his first cousin.

Henri de Toulouse-Lautrec Monfa was born on November 24, 1864, in the provincial town of Albi, the only surviving son and heir of Count Alphonse-Charles de Toulouse-Lautrec Monfa and his wife, Adèle-Zoë Tapié de Céleyran. Henri was a dwarf in appearance, his legs, unlike his torso, stunted after being broken in childhood, while his gross facial features may have been due to a genetic mistake. Throughout his life, his defects frequently caused him both physical and emotional pain. Nevertheless, Lautrec's spirited vision of fin de siècle Paris, depicted in his paintings and prints, still echoes the era's dazzling vitality.

Ironically, the Count believed his son had wasted his artistic gifts. He had sought to nurture what he saw as a talent that ran in his family (particularly in one of the Count's brothers) and had placed Henri in the hands of René Princeteau, a family friend since the boy was nine years old and a painter of hunting scenes. Around the age of sixteen, "Henry" (as he was known *en famille*) began to study in earnest with the painter and assiduously copied Princeteau's work, enhancing his precocious ability to draw animals.

Before his studies with Princeteau, Lautrec had been a day student in the Lycée Fontanes in Paris with his cousin Louis Pascal and Maurice Joyant, a lifelong friend who eventually became the executor of his artistic estate in 1901. After various sicknesses and accidents that left the teenaged Henri stunted in growth and freakish in appearance, he managed to pass his baccalaureate on his second attempt in November 1881. Nearly every winter since he was eight years old, he had lived with his mother in hotel rooms in a suitably fashionable part of Paris. Now, seventeen years old and ready to embark on his formal art education, he was obliged to continue this arrangement, beginning the conflicted existence that led to his alcoholism and, ultimately, to his early death.

With the advice of Princeteau and the maneuvers of well-connected friends, he began his studies in 1882 in the Montmartre studio of Léon Bonnat, a society portraitist and one of Paris's most prominent artist-teachers. Although Henri started out armed with what his family considered a knack for representation, he now had to calm his enthusiasm for the amusing or characteristic moment as he pursued the path to academic perfection. Only half a year later, Bonnat closed his studio. Henri, along with several of Bonnat's other students, entered the atelier of Cormon (Fernand Piestre), a painter of historical scenes, with whom he was to study for almost five years.

The informal atmosphere of Cormon's studio helped to foster friendships among the young painters, which often resulted in pranks. Soon, some of Lautrec's less family-bound fellow artists became his drinking buddies. They frequented the cafés, bars, and brothels of the amusement district of Montmartre, which had been a working class village of dirt streets and gardens until artists and writers began to move there in the late 1870s.

In the spring of 1883, during his second year as a student, Henri moved into his own rooms in a neighborhood acceptable to his family, but his obligation to spend the summer with them in the south ended this first step toward independence. Although his allowance enabled him to rent a studio in Montmartre, he still was expected to dine and spend the night with his mother, or sometimes his father, in their hotel. Finally, in the summer of 1884, instead of returning to a family residence or vacation spot, he moved into the Montmartre apartment of fellow student René (Albert) Grenier and his live-in girlfriend, Lili (Amélie Sans).

Henri's new situation broadened his palette and his vision. Grenier lived on the same courtyard as Edgar Degas. Lautrec certainly must have encountered the older artist, whose work so influenced him at this time. While he enjoyed René, Lili, and their bohemian friends, Henri began to feel the difficulties of life on his own. At Cormon's, some students railed against the weak academicism purveyed there; simultaneously, all were full of anxiety about the studio competition that would determine their chances of entering the École des Beaux-Arts. Henri's first commission—to create illustrations for a sumptuous edition of Victor Hugo's works—fell through. For a time, an epidemic of cholera closed down all social activity in Paris. Lautrec's wit and spirit made him welcome in the Grenier circle. He became infatuated with the theatrical, red-headed Lili, who seems to have established his preference for models with red tresses. Gradually Lautrec

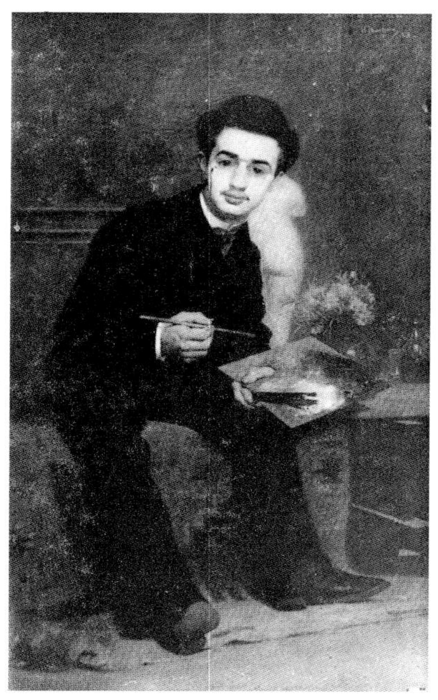

Henri Rachou, *Toulouse-Lautrec*, 1883, oil on canvas, 28½ × 10½ in. Musée des Augustins, Toulouse.

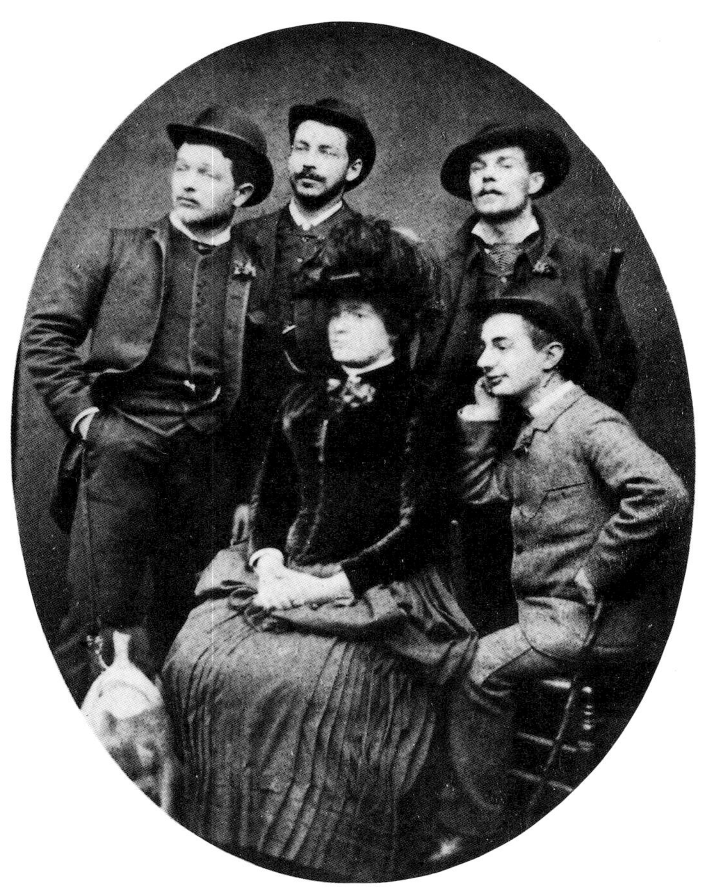

Lautrec with Friends in Paris, René Grenier, M. Rabache, Lucien Métivet, and Lili (Amélie) Sans, ca. 1884, photograph. The Museum of Modern Art, New York.

embraced the lifestyle that within five years empowered him to explore and portray a layer of Parisian life that his parents would never know.

In 1886, Vincent van Gogh entered Cormon's studio. His passion for Japanese prints undoubtedly influenced Lautrec's use of their distinctive compositional elements in his work. Also in that year, some of Lautrec's drawings were published in *Le Courrier français,* an illustrated magazine that had become the mouthpiece for a group of artists of liberal (if not outlandish) persuasion, called the Incohérents. Under the pseudonym Tolav Segroeg, Henri exhibited for the first time in their Salon in October. In that same year, he increased his familiarity with the more notorious members of the Montmartre community, including the well-known entertainer at the Chat Noir, Aristide Bruant, who took over the lease of the café when it moved in 1885, renaming it the Mirliton. In addition to hanging the works of young local artists, including Lautrec, and singing his street-smart songs at the Mirliton, Bruant also published a magazine, *Le Mirliton*. One of Lautrec's drawings appeared on the cover of the December 29, 1886, issue.

Lautrec had found his quintessential subject: the performers and their audiences in the bars and cabarets where he himself found diversion and acceptance. Like some of his fellow students, they had no problem embracing this strangely well-bred dwarf who made clever sketches amidst the smoke and

15

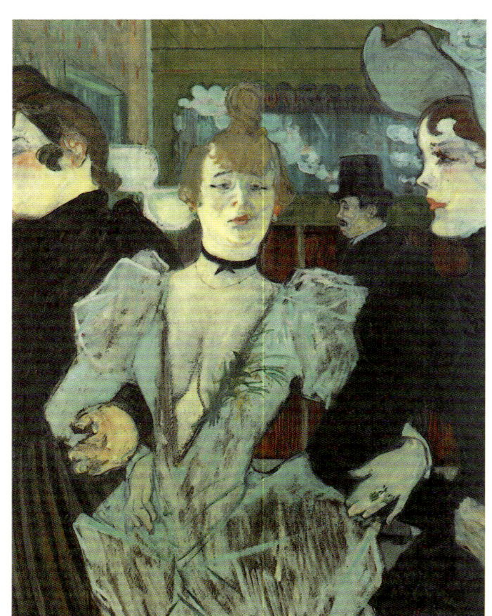

Henri de Toulouse-Lautrec, *La Goulue at the Moulin Rouge*, 1891–92, oil on cardboard, 31¼ × 23¼ in. The Museum of Modern Art, New York, gift of Mrs. David M. Levy.

pandemonium. His friends probably did not know that Henri's father had forbidden him to use the family name on his art. As a result, the young artist signed his works Treclau, an anagram of Lautrec, or simply placed his initials in a monogram that echoed the Japanese seals on the prints he traded his own work for with Van Gogh's neighbor, Alphonse Portier.

Lautrec captured the substance and spirit of Montmartre's cafés, dance halls, and bars mainly through depicting the people who worked there. Frenzied performances of the wild dance called the *chahut*, or cancan, and human oddities who lent a circus atmosphere to the mélange of entertainment attracted patrons of all social classes to drink, dance, and mingle without prejudice in places like the Moulin de la Galette, a neighborhood spot built around some old windmills. In the mid-1880s, Lautrec also frequented a dance hall near the Mirliton called the Élysée-Montmartre, where he discovered a particularly wild, red-blond dancer called La Goulue (Louise Weber), who had begun her career at the Moulin de la Galette. In 1889, the year that Lautrec painted his version of *Au Bal du Moulin de la Galette* (Renoir's 1876 painting of the same place was well known), a new cabaret called the Moulin Rouge opened. One of many Parisian enterprises that celebrated or took advantage of the centennial of the French revolution (the most famous of which was M. Eiffel's tower), the Moulin Rouge in many ways resembled a circus. In its garden, donkey rides, monkeys on chains, and a huge papier-mâché-and-wood elephant contributed to this effect. Charles Zidler, the director of the cabaret, snagged La Goulue, her partner, and several other popular entertainers from the Élysée-Montmartre. They brought with them the custom, originally a ruse to fool the police, of performing in street

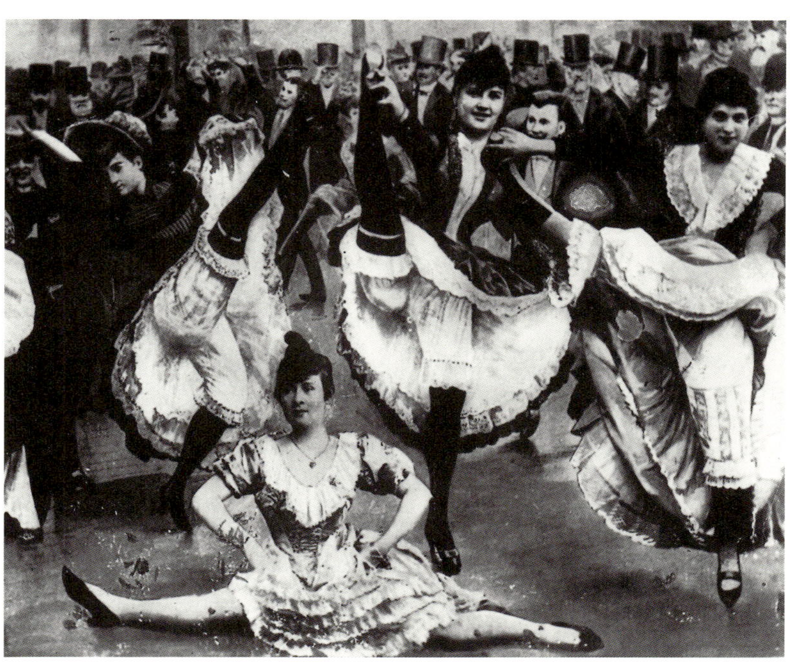

La Goulue Dancing the Quadrille at the Moulin Rouge, ca. 1894, retouched photograph. Private collection.

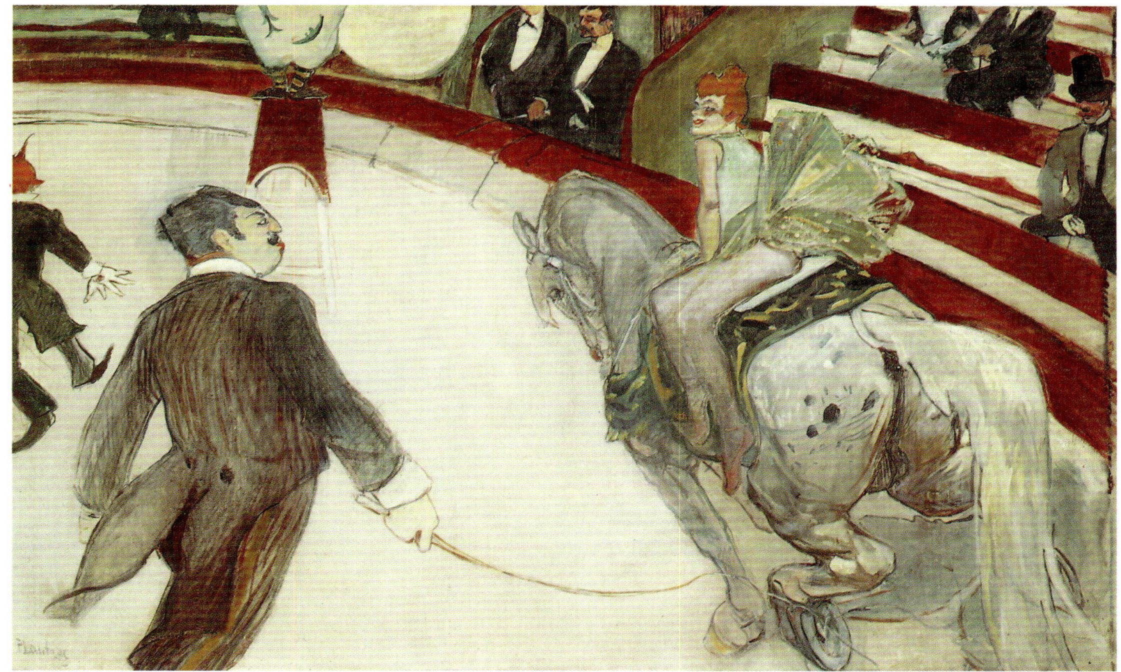

Henri de Toulouse-Lautrec,
Ecuyère (Au Cirque Fernando),
1887, oil on canvas, 39½ × 63½ in.
The Art Institute of Chicago,
Joseph Winterbotham Collection.

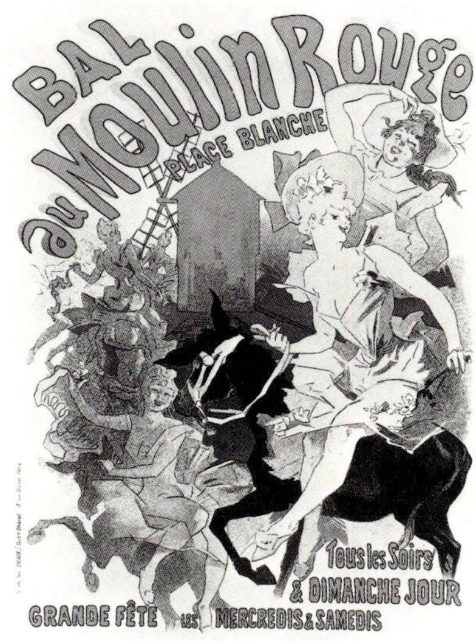

Jules Chéret, *Bal au Moulin Rouge*, 1889,
color lithograph, 23½ × 16½ in. Private
collection.

3. The technique of making prints by
drawing on special stones that, after
processing, retain the drawn image. The
stones then are inked and the image is
printed on paper.

clothes on the dance floor. Around 1889–90, Lautrec painted his view of
the interior of this establishment, and the original way he communicated the
ambiance of the popular dance hall undoubtedly led Zidler to commission a
poster from the artist in 1891.

In the entrance hall of the Moulin Rouge hung *Ecuyère (Au Cirque
Fernando)*, a wonderfully spirited painting and one of several works Lautrec
did of human and animal performers in the local circus during 1887. On one
side, the figure of the ringmaster frames the movement of a horse and female
rider (posed for by Lautrec's girlfriend of that year, the artist-model Suzanne
Valadon). For his Moulin Rouge poster (cat. 1), his first attempt at lithography,[3]
Lautrec framed the high-kicking La Goulue with the imposing male figure of
Valentin le Désossé (Jacques Renaudin), a loose-jointed amateur dancer who not
only accompanied La Goulue but also taught the other performers. Unlike the
first posters for the Moulin Rouge, created in 1889 by Jules Chéret, whose images
of sparkling, doll-like girls had hung on walls all over Paris since 1869, Lautrec's
composition depicted a new world, the tumultuous atmosphere of Montmartre
where not-so-nice women entertainers could be viewed by Parisians of every
class except middle- and upper-class ladies.

The Moulin Rouge poster was a success. Its size (over six feet high) and
boldness of design made it stand out on walls already plastered with other
posters. Other poster commissions followed. Publishers used Lautrec's posters
to advertise their journals and books; performers used them for their personal
publicity. In nearly every case, the selective use of solid black or single-color
passages within lightly but decisively outlined figures, usually contained within

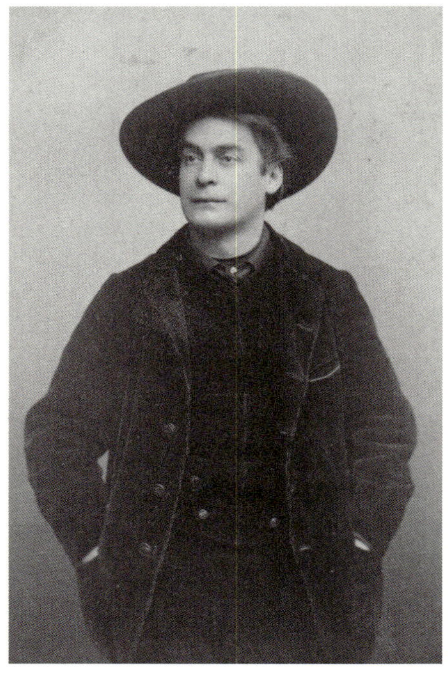

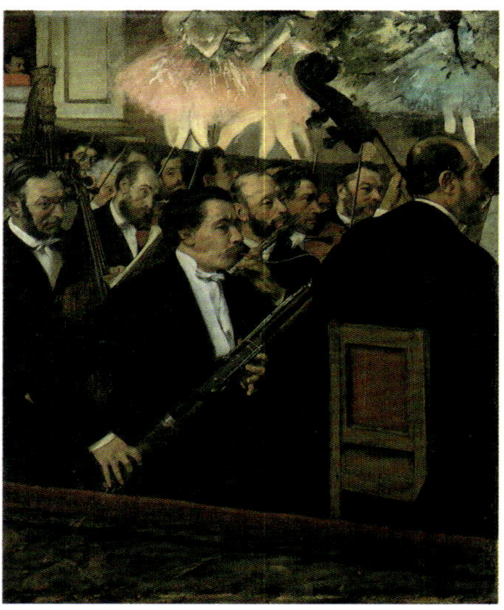

Nadeau, *Aristide Bruant*, ca. 1890s, photograph. Bibliothèque Nationale, Paris.

Edgar Degas, *The Opera Orchestra*, 1868, oil on canvas, 20⅞ × 17¾ in. Musée d'Orsay, Paris.

4. "My latest little work will go on display tomorrow. Please mention it. *Jane Avril au Jardin de Paris*. Published by Kleinmann. Let it be talked about. . . ." Letter from Henri de Toulouse-Lautrec to Roger Marx, Friday [June 2, 1893], quoted in Schimmel, *Letters*, no. 297, p. 211.

a diagonal composition that drew the viewer's eye into the scene, was an inventive formula that gave Lautrec's work its persuasive properties.

The singer Aristide Bruant was quick to see that Lautrec's distillation of a person's essential characteristics in the graphic arts was akin to the way he had refined his own role as a "personality." He ordered two posters (one the mirror image of the other) to advertise his appearances at the Ambassadeurs in 1892 (cat. 4) and at the Eldorado (cat. 5) sometime later. The performer's well-known rakish hat, supplemented by his outdoor garb of a red scarf and colossal coat, adorn a dynamic figure that, in bulk and attitude, appears like the heroic prow of a great sailing ship. The backgrounds of these posters and the one for the Moulin Rouge share a motif that, for Lautrec, had two sources: the shadow plays that he had seen at the Chat Noir, where he probably met Bruant for the first time, and the silhouettes in Japanese prints. In the Moulin Rouge poster, the crowd of onlookers form a staccato black fence behind La Goulue, while in Bruant's posters, a figure of a ruffian silhouetted against the night gloom evokes the theme of Bruant's songs.

Before these and other posters he did of Bruant dominated Paris walls, Lautrec had become involved with another *artiste*, Jane Avril, known as La Mélinite (an explosive). In 1893, she commissioned a poster of herself to publicize her debut at the Jardin de Paris. The composition is based upon a publicity photograph of the dancer and a motif of the neck of a bass viol silhouetted by stage footlights, derived from several Edgar Degas pictures of the ballet and the *café concert*. In *Jane Avril* (cat. 11), the bass viol is accompanied by the hand and face of the player, which repeats Lautrec's idea of a figurative frame, but this time it is extended into a real frame around the dancer. Lautrec promoted the poster by writing to critics shortly after its publication.[4] He also depicted Avril in other paintings and posters: as a patron of the *café concert* Divan Japonais (cat. 8, published four months before the Jardin du Paris poster); as a member of the dancing group Troupe de Mlle Églantine (cat. 40); and as a single figure in one of his last works (cat. 68). Avril appears in her street clothes on the cover of the print album *L'Estampe originale* (cat. 9). There she is, looking at a just-pulled lithograph from the handpress of Père Cotelle, the printer at Édouard Ancourt & Cie, where many of Lautrec's best lithographs were achieved. Although Lautrec made more lithographs of the singer Yvette Guilbert (whose cut-off figure appears on the stage in *Divan Japonais*) than of Avril, the popular chanteuse and some of the other women he depicted did not particularly appreciate the way he exaggerated their features and, unlike Avril, never became his friends.

Throughout the 1890s, Lautrec continued to create posters for the entertainers of the *cafés concerts* and for various publications and products. Simultaneously, he produced other commercial work, notably covers of sheet music. His skill at delineating a known personality or type was an elevation of caricature in

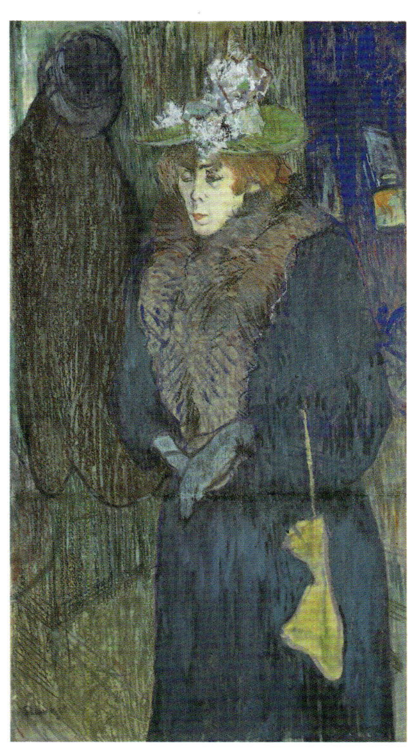

Henri de Toulouse-Lautrec, *Jane Avril in the Entrance to the Moulin Rouge*, 1892, pastel and oil on millboard, laid on panel, 40⅛ × 21⅝ in. Courtauld Gallery, London.

5. "Paris is dark and muddy, which doesn't prevent me from trotting in the streets after the musicians of the Opéra, whom I am trying to charm so as to sneak into the temple of the arts and of boredom. . . ." Letter from Henri de Toulouse-Lautrec to his mother [Paris, Autumn, 1885], quoted in Schimmel, *Letters*, no. 117, p. 95.

which his humor and wit imbued every subject, from the poster for *L'Artisan moderne* (cat. 42), showing a lady in bed with her dog being visited by a craftsman, to a lithograph of the sick President Carnot, the unlucky target of a contemporary satire (cat. 15).

Lautrec was also interested in performers in the legitimate theatre who, like the singers and dancers in the cafés, had not acquired the boring patina of respectability.[5] In the company of the playwright Romain Coolus (René Weil) or other close friends, such as the amateur painter and photographer Maurice Guibert, Lautrec attended both classical and experimental plays, where he enjoyed many of the respected actors of his day in their stellar roles. Several series of black-and-white lithographs of these personalities, including the divine Sarah Bernhardt, occasionally drawn from publicity postcards, appeared in journals such as *L'Escarmouche* and were also issued in limited editions on better paper for collectors. Lautrec and some of his contemporaries—mainly artists such as Édouard Vuillard, who had studied at Académie Julien and were known as Les Nabis—also created pictorial covers for programs of the more literary theatres, namely the Théâtre Libre and the Théâtre Lugné-Poë.

The last decades of the nineteenth century were the golden age for printing and publishing lithographs. In the nearly one hundred years since its invention, lithography had been primarily a black-and-white medium. Once color could be printed efficiently by exploiting the techniques of chromolithography and photomechanical processes, and by mechanizing some of the presses so that lithographic posters could be printed by the thousands, color prints became abundant. The new processes were used mostly for cheap reproductions of paintings, advertisements, and popular images. They depended more on *chromistes* (craftsmen in the print shop who could copy every color nuance of a painting or drawing onto lithographic stones so that the finished print looked "just like" the original) than on artists. Only a few painters made color prints before the 1890s. Then entrepreneurs such as André Marty and Ambroise Vollard encouraged Lautrec, Pierre Bonnard, and other artists to reinterpret their paintings or create new compositions for lithographs to be printed in small, collectible editions. After Lautrec made his first lithographic poster in a commercial shop, he began working directly and harmoniously with the printers Cotelle and Henri Stern, with whom he continued to work for most of his career. Such close associations produced daring color balances and effects in both his limited-edition prints and his posters.

Lautrec's first single prints, *La Goulue et sa soeur* (cat. 6) and *L'Anglais au Moulin Rouge* (cat. 7), both done in 1892 for Boussod, Valadon et Cie (Goupil & Cie), were again set in the dance hall. Soon afterward, in other color prints, he captured personalities at music halls and theatres. One of the most colorful dancers, Loïe Fuller, appeared at the Folies Bergère in Montmartre beginning in

19

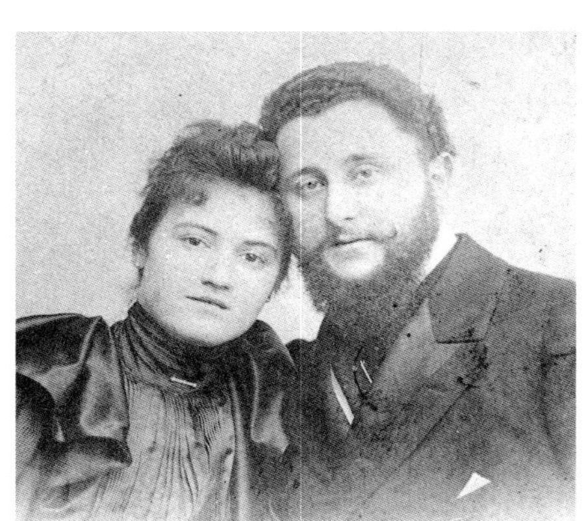

C. Klary, *Misia and Thadée Natanson*, carte de visite (detail), 7 × 9⅜ in. Private collection.

1892, and within a short time Lautrec created a print that simulated the luminescent effect produced by electric lights shining on her flowing costume (cat. 10). He was also entranced by the stage actress Marcelle Lender, who had appeared in plays at the Théâtre des Variétés since 1889. In 1895, when she danced the bolero in the final scene of the operetta *Chilpéric*, Lautrec was inspired to paint that moment. For wider circulation he made a color lithograph of Lender's head that was printed in the German arts magazine *Pan* (cat. 29).

Lautrec's circle of friends expanded as he became known. In January 1893, he and Charles Maurin had side-by-side solo shows at the Boussod et Valadon gallery, where his friend Maurice Joyant had become manager, succeeding Theo van Gogh after his breakdown in 1890. This exhibition included prints (some published by the gallery) and posters, as well as paintings and pastels—an unusual assemblage commented upon by most critics. Among those who admired the posters was Thadée Natanson, who published *La Revue blanche*, an artistic and literary journal, with his brothers Alfred and Alexandre. Its office, where many writers gathered, became one of Lautrec's habitual stops during the day. Misia Godebska, who married Thadée in 1893, soon became the alluring hostess of a salon of avant-garde writers and artists. Along with the writer Stéphane Mallarmé, the painter Édouard Vuillard, and the playwright Tristan Bernard, Lautrec was a frequent, and often outrageous, guest at the Natanson's country home. After drawing Misia on one of his song sheets, he made a poster for *La Revue blanche* which shows her in a skating costume (cat. 32). Despite Thadée's Jewish background, the Natansons were among the few friends Lautrec felt might be socially acceptable to that other, aristocratic part of his life.

One pervasive element in Lautrec's work is the viewpoint of the observer, and he often depicted people watching other people. The viewer of the picture itself becomes, more or less, another of the observers. Lautrec, being shorter than most, was always looking around those who blocked his view. The viewpoint of the observer, then, was determined by the unusual one of the artist, and it may well be a key to the novel attraction of his work. Among his compositions that emphasize viewing are the paintings and lithographs that depict audiences watching concerts or plays from their loges (or boxes). From the poster *Divan Japonais* (cat. 8) and the cover for a Théâtre Libre program, *La Loge au mascaron doré* of 1893 (cat. 22), to the single poster he designed for American distribution, *Au Concert* of 1896 (cat. 60), to one of his lithographic masterpieces, *La Grande Loge* of 1897 (cat. 61), we are able to imagine what those depicted are hearing or seeing from how they are shown.

Looking at people who are attracting the viewer and at those who are being attracted was a concept sharpened by Lautrec's interest in photography. Two photographers played important roles in his life: his buddy Maurice Guibert

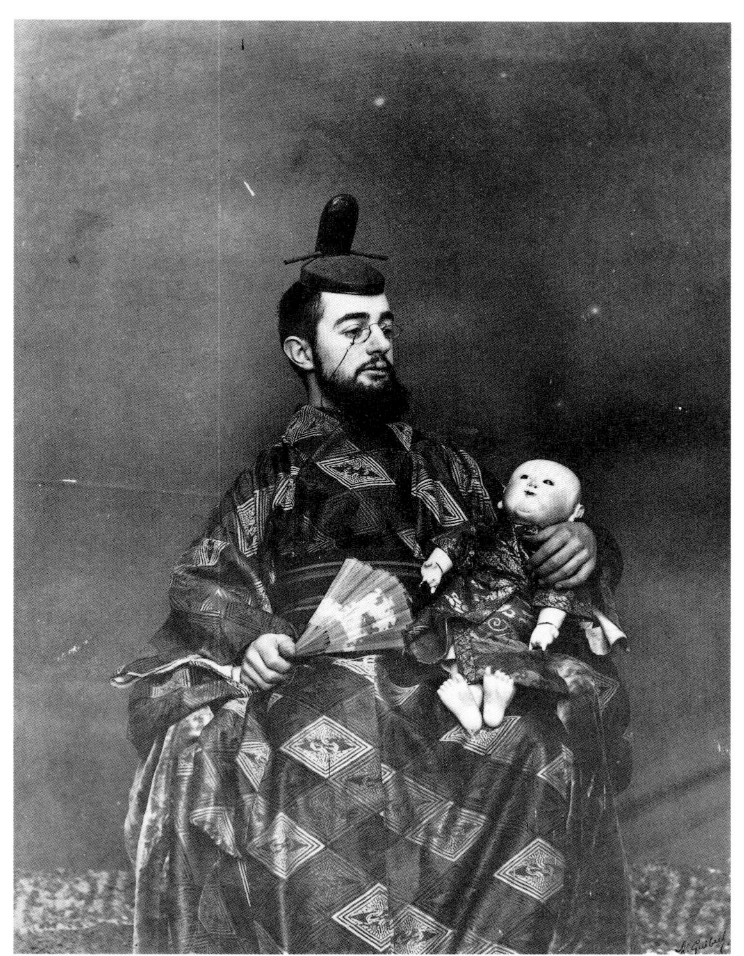

Maurice Guibert, *Toulouse-Lautrec Dressed in Japanese Costume*, ca. 1892, gelatin-silver print. The Museum of Modern Art, New York, anonymous gift.

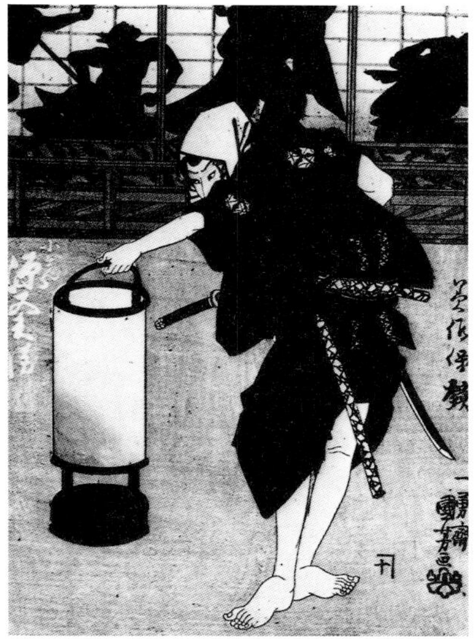

Utagawa Kuniyoshi, *Evening Gathering (Theater Scene)*, ca. 1843–46, color woodcut, 14¼ × 9⅝ in. Private collection.

documented Lautrec's hilarious costume and cross-dressing episodes as well as the goofy antics of their many shared vacations, and Paul Sescau photographed both Lautrec's friends and his paintings. Lautrec also studied and appropriated the poses of his subjects from photographs. His poster of 1896 advertising Sescau's photography studio (cat. 41) shows the draped photographer aiming his camera at the backside of a masked woman, exemplifying Lautrec's notion of the voyeuristic nature of that medium.

Nothing could have better demonstrated Lautrec's determination to reveal what attracted his eye than the series of lithographs titled *Elles* (literally "Them," but idiomatically "The Girls"), which he made in 1896 (cats. 44–55). Long before, he had found the Parisian brothels to be havens, not only as places to relieve what seems to have been a keen sex drive, but also where he was not critically eyed. The women whose lives were centered within these houses were charmed by his wit, happy to let him sketch them in all sorts of circumstances, and tolerant of his habitual drunken state. It was inevitable that Gustave Pellet— whose collection of erotica and publications of pornographic prints by Félicien Rops were significant markers of fin de siècle mores—commissioned Lautrec to create *Elles*. Lautrec was given the liberty to include any subject. Although

21

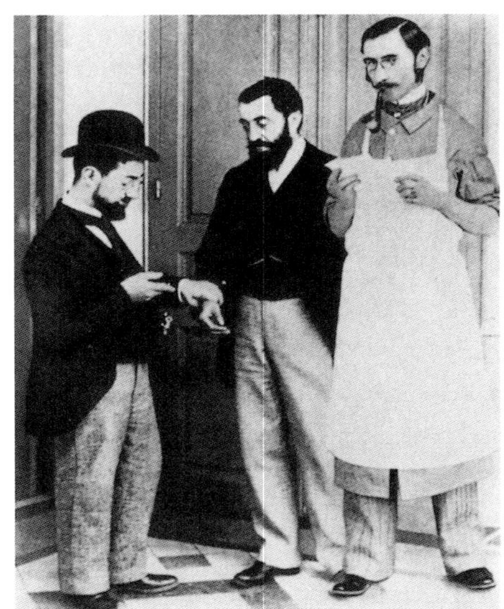

Lautrec with Maurice Guibert and Gabriel Tapié de Céleyran, photograph. Private collection.

6. "My cousin Gabriel having cared for me day and night during the nervous breakdown caused by Mother's unexpected departure, I ask my family to give him a magnificent commemorative gift." Letter from Henri de Toulouse-Lautrec to his family sent on January 16, 1899, after his mother left Paris, quoted in Schimmel, *Letters*, no. 558, p. 346. Gabriel Tapié de Céleyran was one of Lautrec's most frequent companions in Paris after he came there to study medicine. On the same day as this letter, Berthe Sarrazin, the housekeeper Lautrec's mother had asked to watch her son, wrote to her, "Now he doesn't want to see Monsieur Gabriel anymore. He told me that if he came I should throw him out, that he was a spy," quoted in Schimmel, *Letters*, no. 14, p. 396.

intimate bedroom scenes dominate the series, a seated portrait of a well-known cabaret contortionist, the lesbian clowness Cha-u-Kao, is the most vivid, memorable, and ambiguous print (cat. 46).

In 1897, Lautrec continued to produce color lithographs for Pellet, completing six between January and July. One of them, a version of his 1895 painting *La Clownesse au Moulin Rouge*, shows Cha-u-Kao strutting into the dance hall (cat. 62). His mature mastery of spattered ink and design is obvious when this work is compared to his first single print, *La Goulue et sa soeur* (cat. 6) of only five years earlier. His final color print of 1897 was *Partie de campagne* (cat. 64), made for an album issued by Ambroise Vollard and printed by the master lithographer Auguste Clot. There, in the fresh air, a horse-drawn cart chased by a collie moves down a country road. In the context of Lautrec's printed work, this scene is unusually idyllic, evocative of a part of his life that he rarely documented. The collie was one of many dogs that Lautrec had known and drawn since his childhood. His representation of them is affectionately canny and adds an unusually personal element to dozens of his late prints.

Most of Lautrec's adult life was split between his fairly disciplined professional work, his frenetic, often overindulgent social life, and traveling. In his youth he traveled between family homes, spas for his health, and diverse vacation spots. Beginning in 1888, he went to Brussels nearly annually to participate in the exhibitions of Les Vingt and Libre Esthétique and to shop. As Holland was close by, he occasionally included stops there on his trips to Brussels. The opportunity to see famous paintings there, later in London, and when he toured Spain and Portugal with Maurice Guibert in 1895 was one of the rewards of traveling abroad. Business and pleasure brought him to London several times between 1892 and 1898. There he indulged his anglophilia, cultivated in his childhood by his mother and, later, by many associations with the British in France. Lautrec wanted to go to Japan, where the images he had collected would become reality, but if other trips are any indication, he seemed incapable of spending extended periods away from France.

The artist's last years, from 1898 to his death in 1901, were troubled by a worsening of the debilities he had been born with or had accumulated during his short but intemperate life. After a period of extremely destructive behavior and bouts of paranoia, he was put into a private clinic by his distraught mother in March 1899.[6] There he stayed, drying out from the alcoholism that he could never fight alone, and calming down his sometimes violent temper. Within two weeks he was making great efforts to prove that he was well enough to resume a normal existence. At his request, lithographic stones were brought to his room, and he embarked on a series of circus drawings that were tours de force of observation and imagination. He finally was released on May 17 and almost immediately left Paris for Albi, his birthplace. He had been able to visit his printer during his confinement, so that some of the twenty lithographs initiated in 1899 were produced while he was at the clinic.

Soon after his discharge, Lautrec was asked to make a series of prints about the racetrack. His innate love of horses and their habits, which he had acutely observed since childhood, and the disciplined drawings that he did at the clinic served him well, although only one of the four compositions, *Le Jockey* (cat. 66), was completed and published. Lautrec's creative drive was diminishing rapidly as the new century dawned, and with the exception of two posters and miscellaneous black-and-white lithographs, his artistic production had nearly ceased. He spent less and less time in Paris, where he had resumed drinking, and after trips to Normandy and the familiar beach of many summers at Taussat-les-Bains, he finally arrived in Bordeaux in October 1900. He took a studio, where he painted throughout the winter and into spring, despite having suffered a small stroke. Though weak, Lautrec returned to Paris, where he painted for a few weeks, and then he left the City of Lights forever on June 15, 1901. He returned to Taussat-les-Bains where, in August, he had a second stroke that left him paralyzed. Lautrec was taken to the Château de Malromé, where he died two weeks later.

Despite his physical impairments and alcoholism, Lautrec was able, in only ten years, to produce over three hundred fifty lithographs. The numerous sketches that preceded most of them and the finished paintings of the same subjects, and many others, are focal points of some of the world's great art collections and of the museum dedicated to Lautrec's work in Albi. Many have tried to comprehend and analyze the formidable creative and intellectual energy, more audacious than heroic, that produced such a concentrated mass of memorable images. While the popular notion of Henri de Toulouse-Lautrec caricatures the man, the artist's work remains forever the captivating lens through which we glimpse a tantalizing way of being.

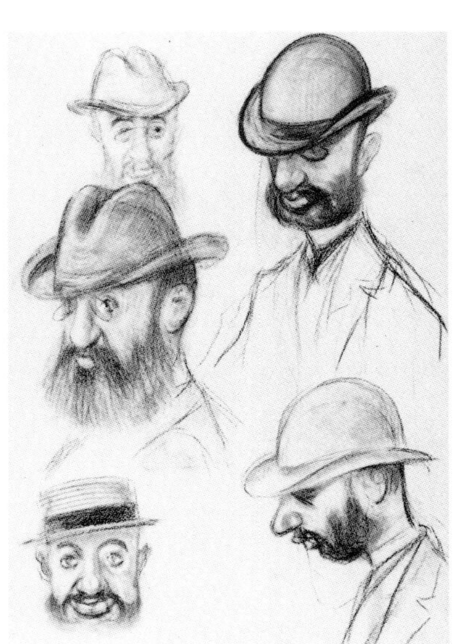

Michel Manzi, *Five Studies of Henri de Toulouse-Lautrec*, ca. 1890s, black chalk on paper, 16⅜ × 11⅜ in. Collection of Irene and Howard Stein.

Catalogue of the Collection

Note

The titles, subtitles, alternate titles, and former titles are listed as consistently as possible. The titles given at time of publication are listed first, even when this does not agree with the catalogues raisonnés.

The order of the works is chronological, intermixing prints and posters, and is based on documented publication and/or announcement dates. In some cases, confirming documentation is lacking but there is general agreement on the dates. The printing and publication dates of many other works are the subjects of dispute. I discuss these issues in the entries, and have placed the prints in what I regard as the most plausible order.

The dimensions for each lithograph are given in inches and centimeters, height before width. Where applicable, the dimensions of the image, as defined by the plate margins, are given first, followed by the dimensions of the sheet. State numbers (for example, first state, second state, etc.) are indicated only where there are multiple states. The state number assigned to each print by the four major catalogues raisonnés is indicated by a roman numeral following the catalogue raisonné number. Identified collection marks are indicated by their reference numbers in Frits Lugt, *Marques de Collections (Dessins-Estampes)*, 1921, and *Marques de Collections (Dessins-Estampes) Supplément*, 1956. Each print is also identified by the number assigned by the four major catalogues raisonnés: Wolfgang Wittrock, *Toulouse-Lautrec: The Complete Prints*, 1985; Götz Adriani, *Toulouse-Lautrec, the Complete Graphic Works*, 1988; Löys Delteil, *Le Peintre-graveur illustré, X–XI: H. de Toulouse-Lautrec*, 1920; and Jean Adhémar, *Les Lithographies et pointes sèches de Toulouse-Lautrec*, 1965. See Selected Bibliography for complete citations.

R. C.

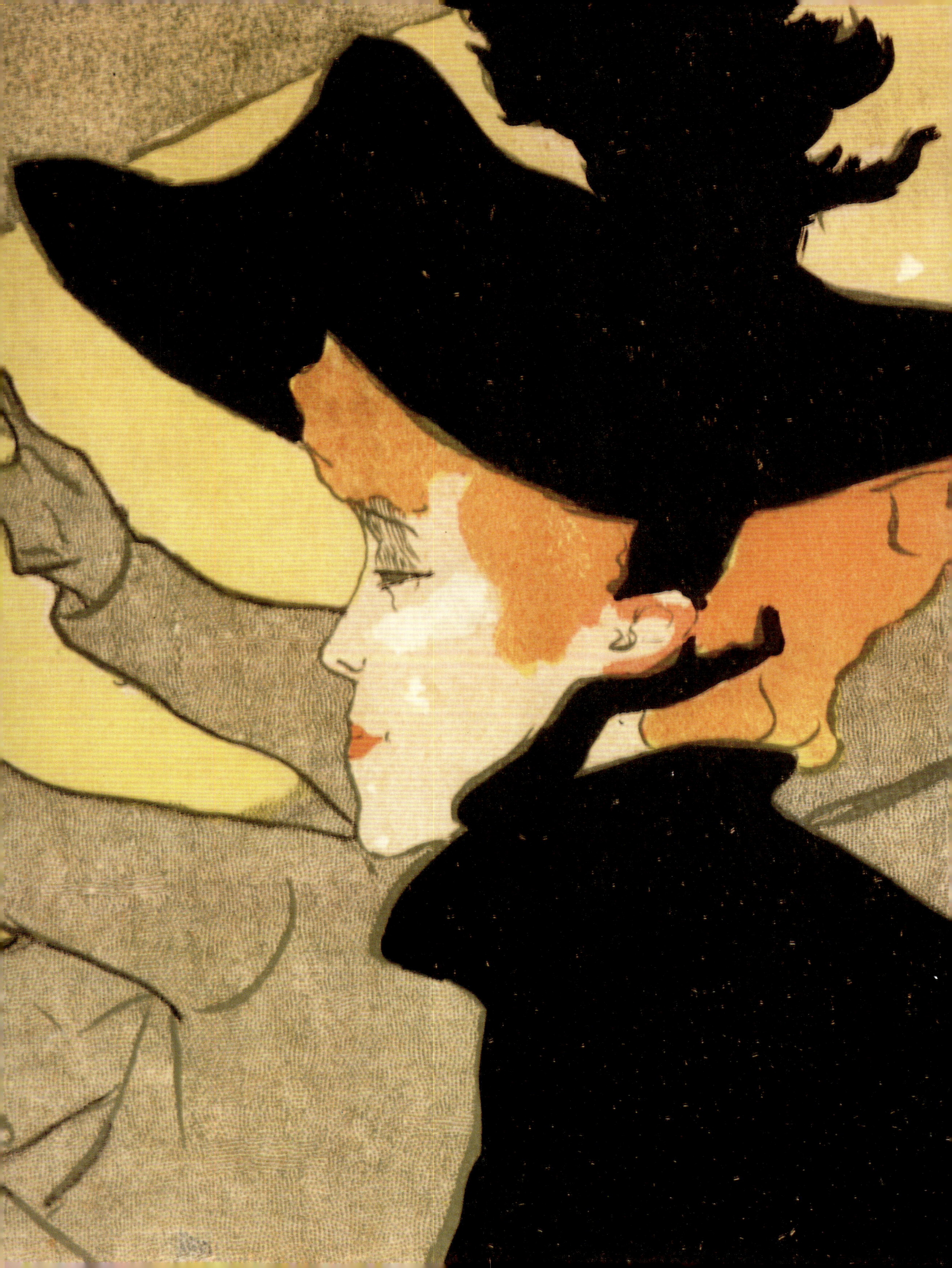

1

Moulin Rouge: La Goulue

1891
Brush and spatter lithograph in four
  colors on three sheets of wove paper
Image: 75¼ × 46 in. (191.1 × 116.8 cm)
Sheet: 76¾ × 48 in. (194.9 × 121.9 cm)
Printed by Affiches Américaines,
  Ch. Lévy, Paris
Commissioned by the Moulin Rouge
  (Charles Zidler)
Tax stamp lower right
Wittrock P1/A; Adriani 1/I; Delteil 339;
  Adhémar 1

Lautrec's first attempt at printmaking was astonishingly inventive. The composition was unconventional in one sense because, although an advertisement for a dance hall, the figures do not beckon the viewer to join them. Nevertheless, the ambiance of the place was clearly attractive, and its name was repeated three times to accentuate the excitement of the Moulin Rouge. Noted, too, were the types of entertainment: "concert" for the *café concert* performances of singers; "bal" for dancing under the globes of light shown. As with almost all of his subsequent lithographs, Lautrec first prepared a full-scale maquette of the poster. Most probably, a craftsman copied the outlines of the figures onto the lithographic stone. After this keystone was drawn, etched, and proofed, the artist corrected the drawing and organized the color passages—normally, in commercial printing, made from three separate stones carrying red, blue, and yellow inks. In this earliest work, Lautrec used spattered ink that produced veils of tone, notably on the figure of Valentin le Désossé (The Boneless, born Jacques Renaudin) looming in the foreground. The purple-gray of his body was produced from black, red, and blue. The central focus of the poster is La Goulue (The Glutton, born Louise Weber), the star of the Moulin Rouge, dancing the cancan. In contrast to the solid areas of bright red, yellow, and pitch black, the focal point, her exposed underclothing, has been left unprinted, the white paper producing a spotlit effect on the dancer. Discernable within the silhouetted frieze of onlookers are Lautrec's cousin Gabriel Tapié de Céleyran, shown in profile, and William Tom Warrener (later depicted as *L'Anglais au Moulin Rouge,* cat. 7), the moustached, top-hatted figure in the center.

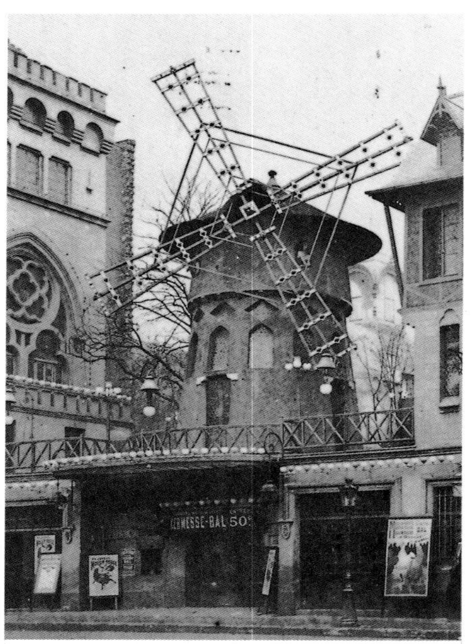

Le Moulin Rouge, ca. 1891, photograph.
Bibliothèque Nationale, Paris.

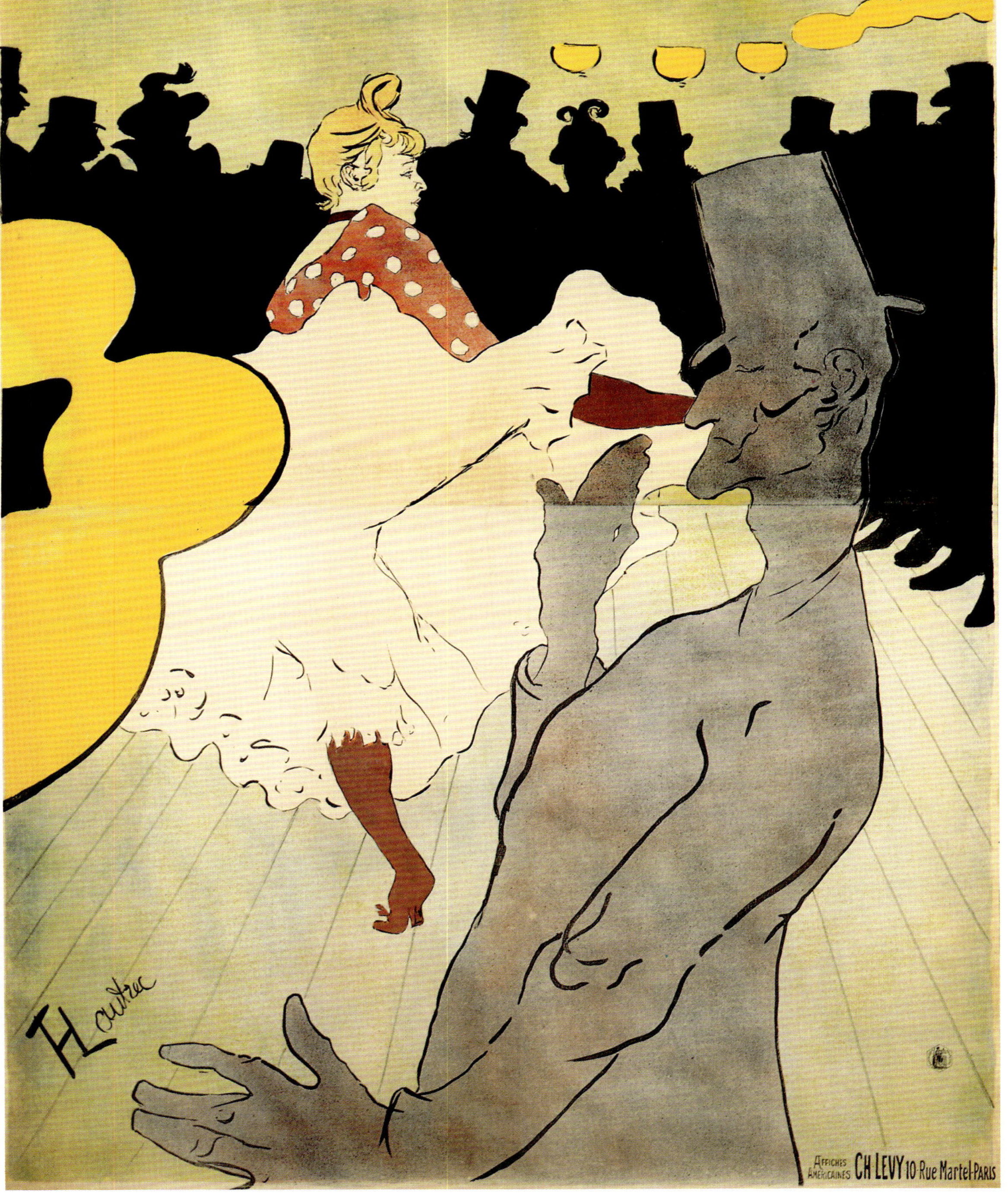

Moulin Rouge
Moulin Rouge
Moulin Rouge
LA GOULUE
CONCERT
BAL
TOUS LES SOIRS
HTLautrec
AFFICHES
AMÉRICAINES CH LEVY 10 Rue Martel-Paris

2

Le Pendu

1892

Crayon, brush, and spatter lithograph
  with scraper in two colors on wove
  paper mounted on wove poster paper
Mounted image: 27¾ × 18¾ in. (70.5 ×
  47.6 cm)
Poster text: 46⅞ × 34⅜ in. (119.1 ×
  87.3 cm)
Sheet: 49⅝ × 36½ in. (126 × 92.7 cm)
First state
Printed by R. Thomas & Co., Toulouse
Commissioned by the newspaper
  La Dépêche, Toulouse
Tax stamp upper left
Wittrock P2/A; Adriani 2/I; Delteil
  340; Adhémar 4

This duotone lithograph, printed in gray-green and black, is a composition that originally appeared as an illustrated portion of a traditional, lettered poster, as seen here. It advertises *Les Drames de Toulouse* by A. Siegel, a three-part novel that was serialized in *La Dépêche*, the Toulouse newspaper. The story Lautrec depicted is from the first volume, which recounts the Calas affair, an eighteenth-century tragedy in which a man was unjustly tortured to death on the rack for the presumed murder of his son. Anti-Protestant officials believed that the Protestant father had opposed his son's plan to convert to Catholicism. The print shows the father discovering his hanged son, who had committed suicide. The spotlighting of the body by the father's illuminating candle produces an aura of drama, evoking the title of the novel. Arthur Huc, the editor of the Toulouse-Lautrec family's local newspaper who commissioned the lithograph, exhibited works by Lautrec and some of Les Nabis in the office of *La Dépêche* in 1894. A year later Lautrec had an edition of thirty copies of *Le Pendu* printed without advertising.

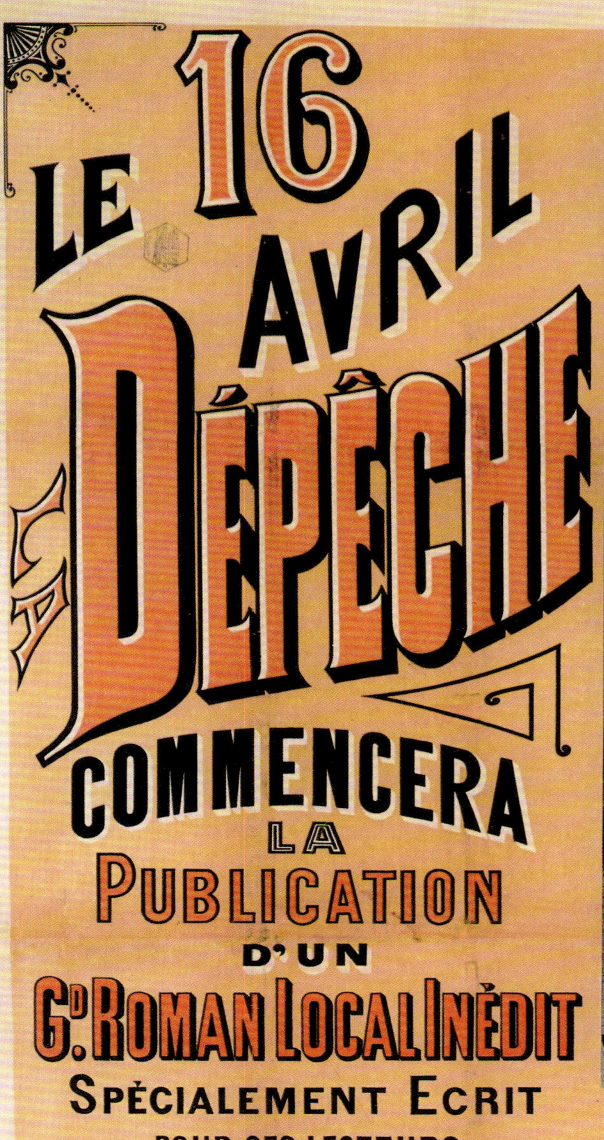
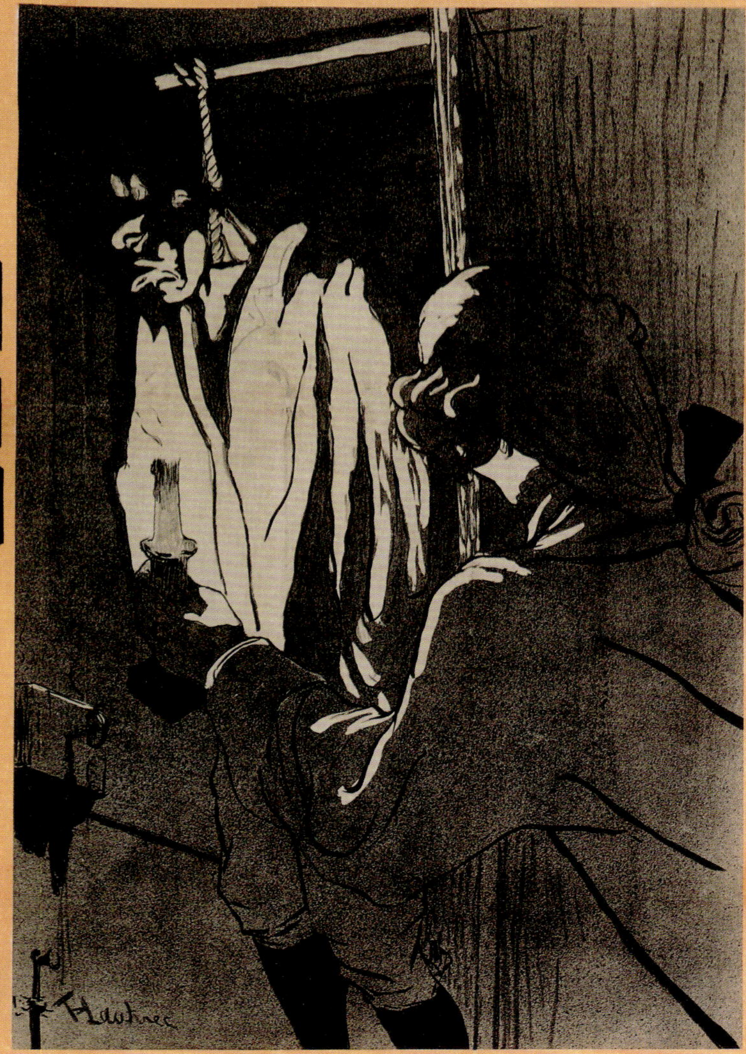

LE 16 AVRIL
LA DÉPÊCHE
COMMENCERA
LA
PUBLICATION
D'UN
Gd ROMAN LOCAL INÉDIT
SPÉCIALEMENT ÉCRIT
POUR SES LECTEURS.
PAR A. SIÉGEL
LES DRAMES DE TOULOUSE
CE ROMAN
FORMERA
3
PARTIES.
1ère PARTIE : CALAS LE MARTYR, (1761)
2me ......„....: LA BATAILLE DE PECH-DAVID, (1799)
3me ......„....: L'ASSASSINAT DU GÉNÉRAL RAMEL (1815)
R. THOMAS & Co TOULOUSE.

Reine de joie

1892

Brush, spatter, and transferred screen
  lithograph in four colors on wove paper
Image: 53⅝ × 36⅞ in. (136.2 × 93 cm)
Sheet: 58¼ × 38⅞ in. (148 × 98.7 cm)
Printed by Edw. Ancourt & Cie, Paris
Commissioned by Victor Joze
Wittrock P3; Adriani 5; Delteil 342;
  Adhémar 5

Victor Joze (Joze Dobrski de Jastzebiec), the author of the book *Reine de joie, moeurs du demi-monde,* asked Lautrec to create this poster. The book appeared in serialized form in the periodical *Fin de siècle,* beginning on June 4, 1892. Its subject was the alliance between a banker, Olizac, Baron de Rosenfeld, and a demimondaine, Hélène Roland. After the first episode appeared, Baron Alphonse de Rothschild, believing that he had been slandered, attempted to prevent the anti-Semitic novel from being printed. Even before the first part of the book was published, Lautrec's poster had already been mounted on walls all over Paris, and during the uproar many were torn down and other, unmounted examples were bought and undoubtedly destroyed. Lautrec was in London during this period, having completed the proofing of the poster and its reduced print for the book's frontispiece before his departure, so he was in for a surprise when he returned to Paris on June 10. The book finally appeared on July 10 with a cover designed by Pierre Bonnard, and the collector's edition of Lautrec's poster was put up for sale in Édouard Sagot's catalogue. In the poster, the model for Olizac, on the left, was Georges Lasserre and for the man on the right was Luzarche d'Azay. Lautrec showed the poster in several exhibitions, and its subtle and not-so-subtle allusions to sex were appreciated as "exquisitely perverse."[1]

1. Thadée Natanson refers to "the delicious *Reine de joie,* bright, pretty and exquisitely perverse" in *La Revue blanche* 16 (February 1893), p. 146, quoted in Phillip Dennis Cate, "The Popularization of Lautrec," in *Henri de Toulouse-Lautrec* (New York: The Museum of Modern Art, 1983), p. 83.

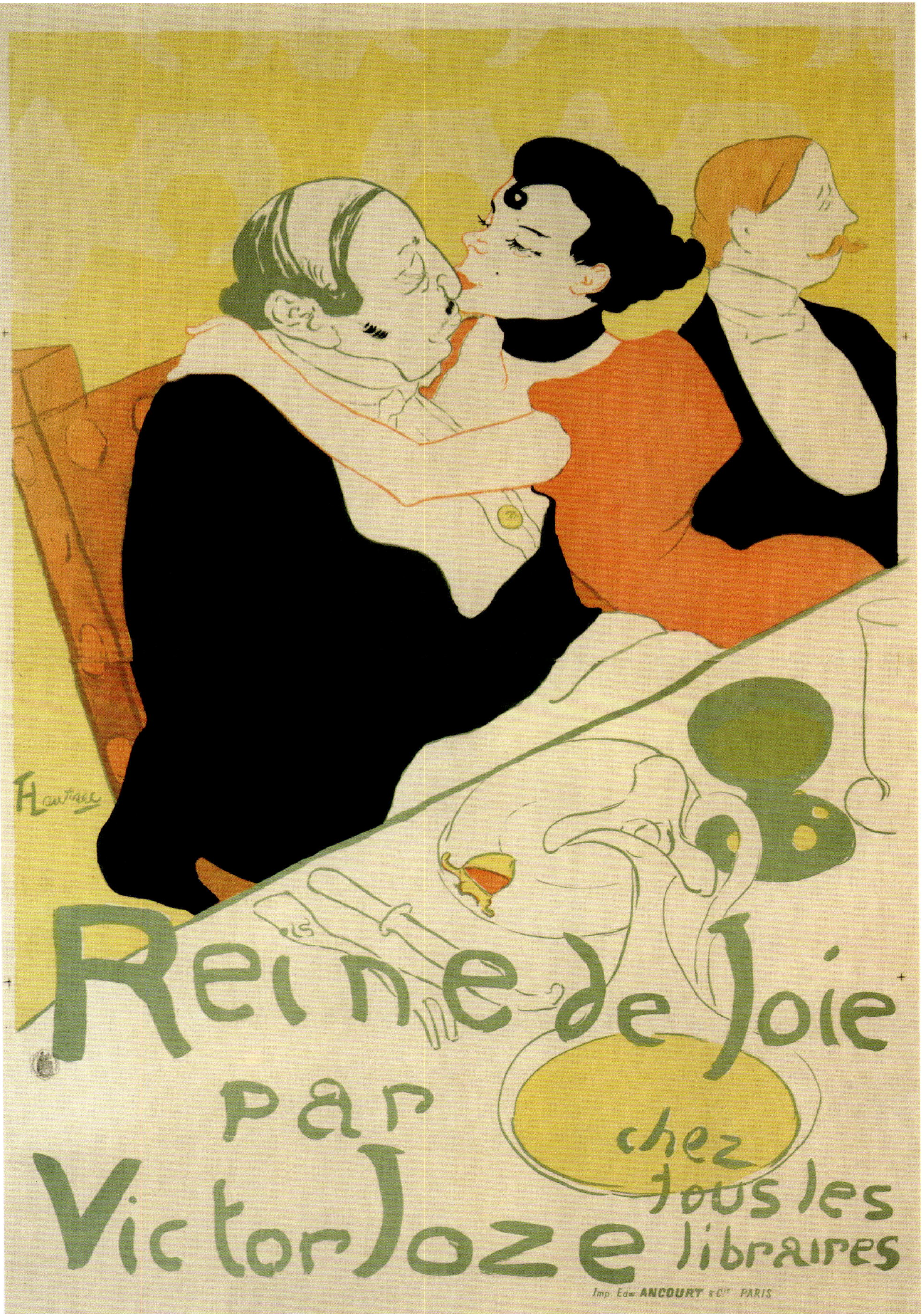

Reine de Joie
par
Victor Joze
chez
tous les
libraires
Imp. Edw ANCOURT & Cie PARIS

4

Ambassadeurs: Aristide Bruant

1892

Brush and spatter lithograph in five
  colors on two sheets of wove paper
Image: 52½ × 36¾ in. (133.4 × 93.3 cm)
Sheet: 58⅞ × 39¾ in. (149.5 × 101 cm)
Printed by Edw. Ancourt & Cie, Paris
Commissioned by the Ambassadeurs,
  M. Ducarre
Tax stamp upper left
Wittrock P4; Adriani 3; Delteil 343;
  Adhémar 6

On June 3, 1892, Aristide Bruant began a limited engagement at the Ambassadeurs, a major *café concert* in the Champs-Élysées. For his performance he recreated an approximation of his Mirliton cabaret on the stage. Bruant asked Lautrec to produce a poster for this important production, but after it was printed, Ducarre, the Ambassadeurs manager, seems to have hated the design and would not pay for it. Instead, he commissioned Charles Lévy (whose firm had printed Lautrec's first poster) to make a different one, based on a photograph of Bruant by Benque, in which the name of the café was not partially covered by Bruant's hat. Nevertheless, it was Lautrec's work posted around Paris that attracted attention. As he had done in designing the lettering for his Moulin Rouge poster, Lautrec used a variety of informal letters that worked in harmony with his figures. Outlined or surrounded by dark grounds, in the manner known as *cloisonniste*, the letters were fully integrated into the composition. Bruant emerges from the background of a dark night inhabited by the silhouette of a gesturing male, arm in the air. Holding a rough wood staff—one of his trademarks together with his broad-brimmed hat and red scarf—the singer and his point of view are immediately recognizable.

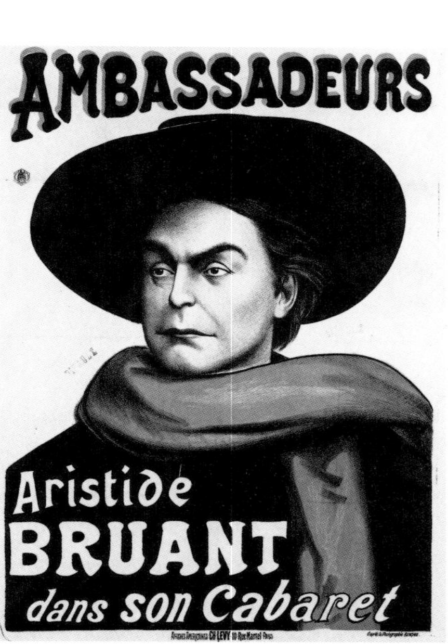

Charles Lévy, *Ambassadeurs, Aristide Bruant*, 1892, color lithograph, 49⅝ × 36⅛ in. Bibliothèque Nationale, Paris.

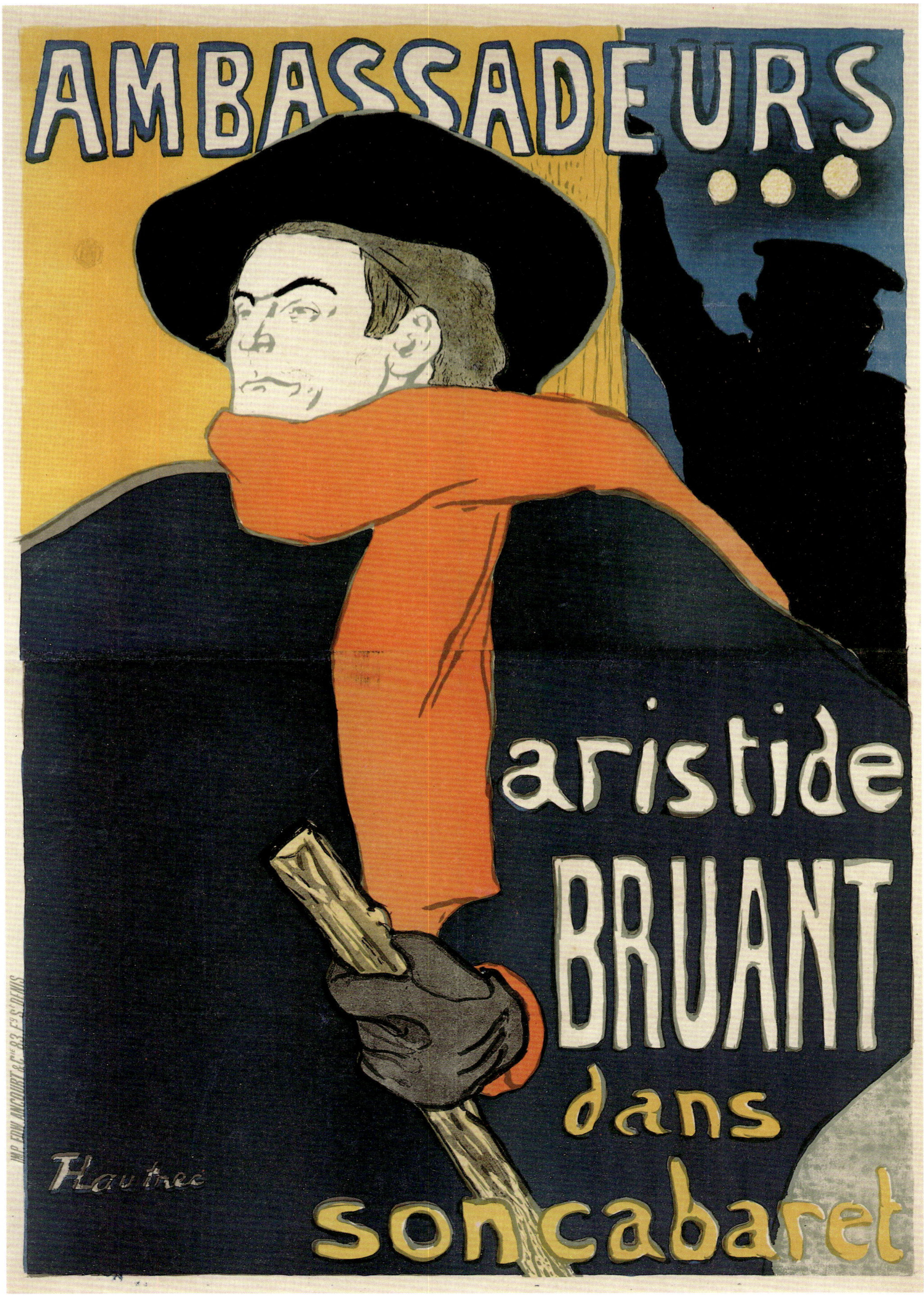

AMBASSADEURS...
aristide
BRUANT
dans
son cabaret
TLautrec

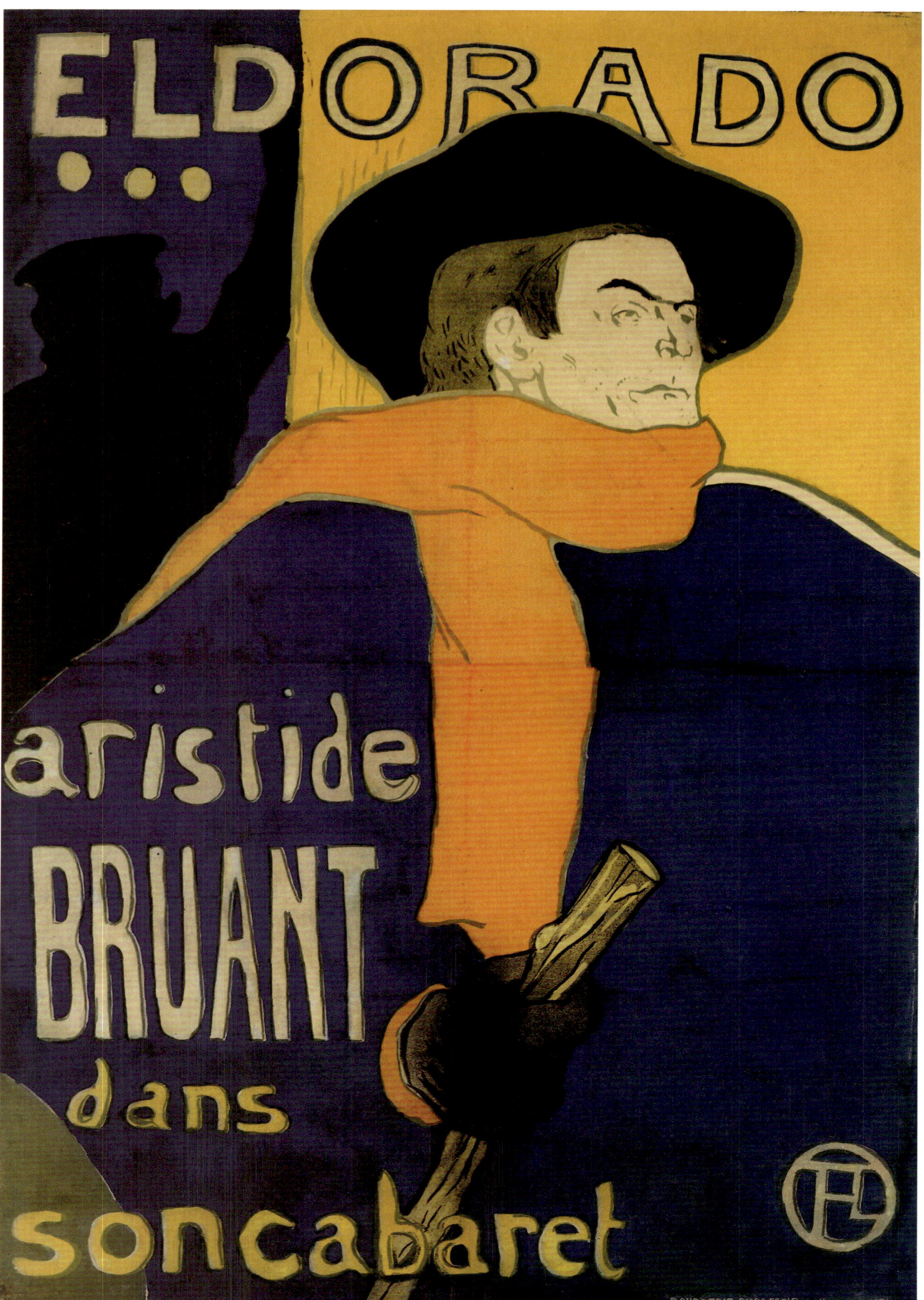
ELD•••ORADO
aristide
BRUANT
dans
son cabaret
Imp BOURGERIE & Cie 83, Fg S Denis (Affiches ANCOURT)

Eldorado: Aristide Bruant

1892

Brush and spatter lithograph in four
   colors on two sheets of wove paper
Image: 54⅛ × 38¾ in. (137.5 × 98.4 cm)
Sheet: 59¾ × 38⅞ in. (151.8 × 98.7 cm)
Printed by Bourgerie & Cie (Affiches
   Ancourt), Paris
Commissioned by the Eldorado(?)
Wittrock P5; Adriani 4; Delteil 344;
   Adhémar 7

This is a redrawing of the *Ambassadeurs* poster, reversing the image, for another engagement of Bruant's at the *café concert* Eldorado, at 4, boulevard de Strasbourg. The lettering is identical in style to that on the earlier poster, with only slight changes in placement due to the words starting at the left edge of the poster rather than at its center. There are few other differences, but one, a vertical line detailing a fold in Bruant's scarf that does not continue to the bottom sheet, appears to have been an oversight. Because of the large size of the composition, two sheets were used so that the upper half was printed from one set of stones, and the lower half from a second set. It is possible that a technician drew the two keystones, which were printed separately. This example is a proof made before the final edition and lacks the stones that would finally print a brown line on the shoulder and Lautrec's brown monogram. In addition, the colors have not been corrected, and Bruant's scarf is orange, not red as it would appear in the published version. The poster was printed by Bourgerie & Cie at Ancourt's address, and it may not have been printed until some years after the *Ambassadeurs* poster.[1]

1. Herbert D. Schimmel, ed., *The Letters of Henri de Toulouse-Lautrec* (New York: Oxford University Press, 1991), p. 262 n. 2 and 3. According to Schimmel, there is no record of Bruant's appearance at the Eldorado during the period 1892–94. Bruant retired in 1895.

La Goulue et sa soeur OR La Goulue et La Môme Fromage au Moulin Rouge

1892

Brush and spatter lithograph in five
  colors on wove paper
Image: 18⅛ × 13½ in. (46 × 34.3 cm)
Sheet: 23½ × 18⅜ in. (59.7 × 46.7 cm)
Second state, number 65
Printed by Edw. Ancourt & Cie, Paris
Published by Boussod, Valadon et Cie,
  Paris
Stamped lower left in red ink, 65; also
  signed in pencil, HTLautrec; stamp
  lower right of Edw. Ancourt (Lugt 12a)
Wittrock 1/II; Adriani 6/II; Delteil 11;
  Adhémar 2

Michel Manzi was in charge of the print department at the gallery of Boussod, Valadon et Cie (formerly the Goupil Gallery), and the gallery's new director, Maurice Joyant, was an old friend of Lautrec. Although the artist had not yet been featured in a one-man exhibition there, he had been included in group shows, so on the basis of his exciting images of the Moulin Rouge, Manzi asked Lautrec to make a few prints. This lithograph and *L'Anglais au Moulin Rouge* (cat. 7) were the results. It is related to Lautrec's painting of the year before, *La Goulue au Moulin Rouge* (The Museum of Modern Art, New York), which shows La Goulue arm in arm with two women, one of whom was supposedly her sister and the other a dancer. Lautrec painted the exact prototype, *La Goulue et sa soeur* (National Gallery of Art, Washington, D.C.), which views La Goulue from the back, as a maquette for the print in 1892. La Goulue (The Glutton) is shown on the floor of the Moulin Rouge with one of the women who appears in the earlier painting, usually identified as her sister, Jeanne (or Victorine) Weber, or as La Môme Fromage (The Cheese Kid), a dancer with whom La Goulue had a sisterly relationship. As this was his first attempt to work in the smaller size of a portfolio print, it was a fairly cautious and somewhat careless effort. The space around La Goulue's waist, for example, is filled with scratchy black areas that refer neither to the trousers of men in the background nor to the wainscotting of the hall, which is red. The edition was completed around October 14, when Lautrec wrote to Roger Marx asking him to review his first collector's edition. He also wrote to his Belgian friend, the poet and critic Émile Verhaeren, "I hope that this will be only the first in a series that I am doing and which will at least have the merit of being very limited and consequently rare."[1]

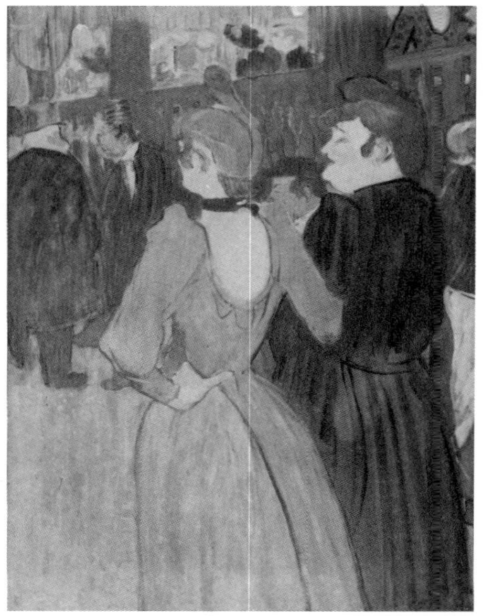

Henri de Toulouse-Lautrec, *La Goulue et sa soeur*, 1892, oil and gouache on cardboard, 18⅝ × 14⅜ in. National Gallery of Art, Washington, D.C., Chester Dale Collection.

1. Letter from Henri de Toulouse-Lautrec to the poet and critic Émile Verhaeren: "The [print] is by me, based on my picture, or rather, it's a highly transposed interpretation of the picture. . . . The price is one louis. The proofs are numbered from 1 to 100, the stones were obliterated in my presence. I hope, . . ." quoted in Herbert D. Schimmel, ed., *The Letters of Henri de Toulouse-Lautrec* (New York: Oxford University Press, 1991), no. 246, p. 185.

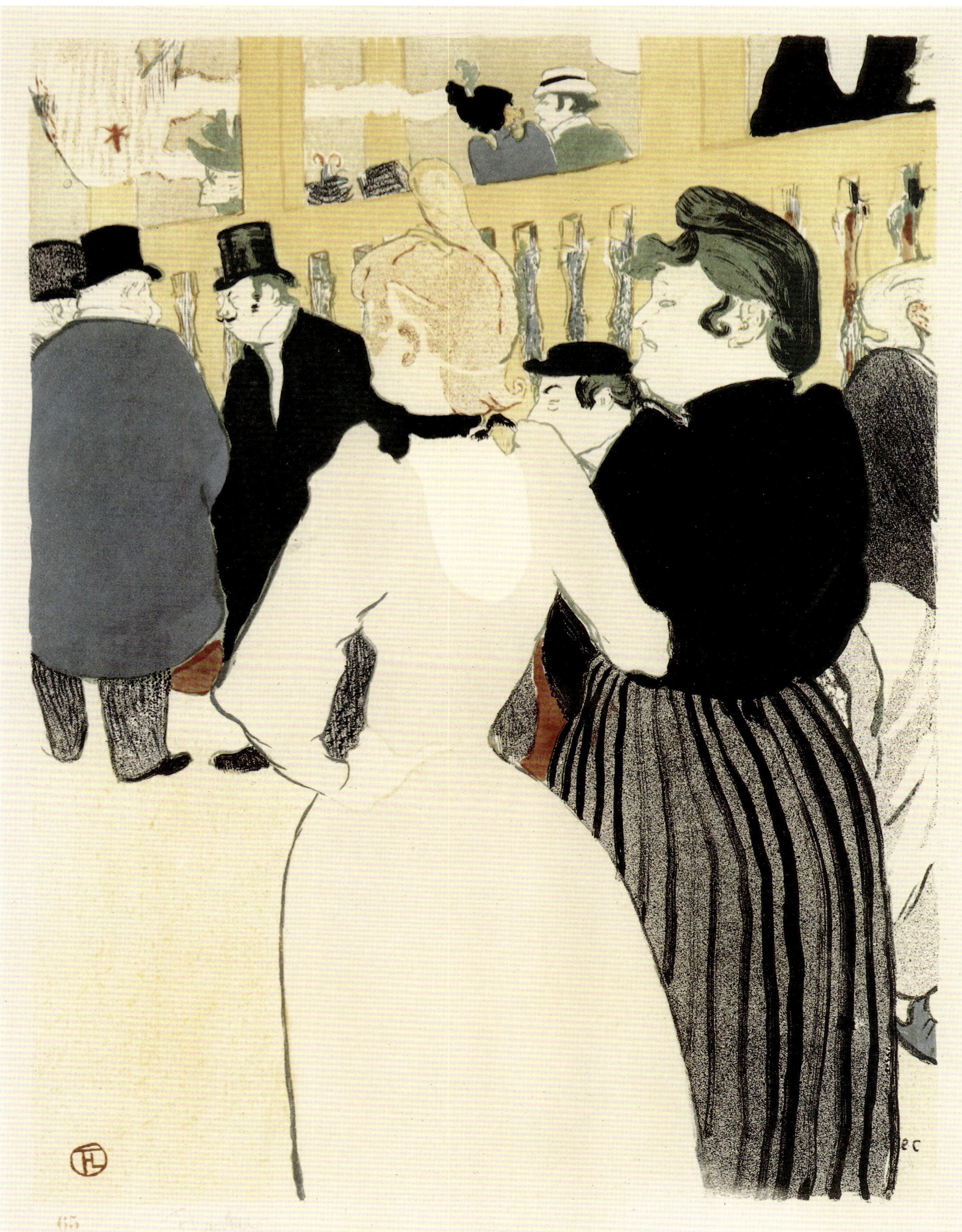

7

L'Anglais au Moulin Rouge

1892

Brush and spatter lithograph in seven
  colors on laid paper
Image: 19⅜ × 14½ in. (49.2 × 36.8 cm)
Sheet: 20⅜ × 16⅛ in. (51.7 × 41 cm)
Second state, number 10
Printed by Edw. Ancourt & Cie, Paris
Published by Boussod, Valadon et Cie,
  Paris
Signed lower left in pencil, *HTLautrec
no. 10*
Verso: Metropolitan Museum of Art
  stamp in brown ink and Metropolitan
  Museum of Art duplicate stamp (Lugt
  1808h)
Wittrock 2/II; Adriani 7/II; Delteil 12;
  Adhémar 3

The second and last of the prints Lautrec completed for Manzi in 1892 represents a British artist whose appearance must have seemed typically gentlemanly to Lautrec, the epitome of the English tradition that he admired. William Tom Warrener, born in Lincoln, England, had been a student at the Académie Julien, which, like Cormon's, included a few ambitious British painters. Warrener had already exhibited his impressionist paintings at London's Royal Academy for some years before moving into a Montmartre apartment formerly occupied by other English painters. With his gold-headed cane, mustache, and debonair carriage, he was a fine subject for Lautrec, who found amusement in the encounters of males and females in the dance halls. The oil sketch after which the print was designed was once titled *Flirt*, an allusion to Warrener's red ears "blushing at the risqué remarks of two of the nightclub's dancers."[1] Because Warrener's entire figure is rendered in one color in the print, this detail is not apparent. As he had in his first poster (cat. 1), Lautrec again used a purple for the framing character in this composition. The charming women were known as Rayon d'Or and La Sauterelle, whose proper bonnets and clothing disguise their professional status in the dance hall.

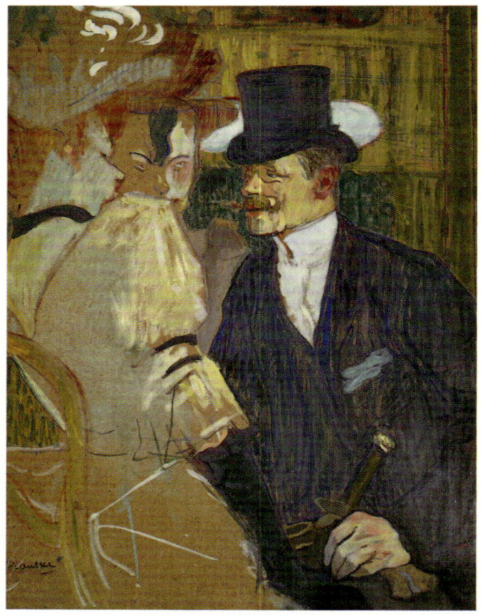

Henri de Toulouse-Lautrec, *The Englishman at the Moulin Rouge*, 1892, oil and gouache on cardboard, 33¾ × 26 in. The Metropolitan Museum of Art, New York, bequest of Miss Adelaide de Groot.

1. Colta Ives, *Toulouse-Lautrec in the Metropolitan Museum of Art* (New York: The Metropolitan Museum of Art, 1996), p. 32.

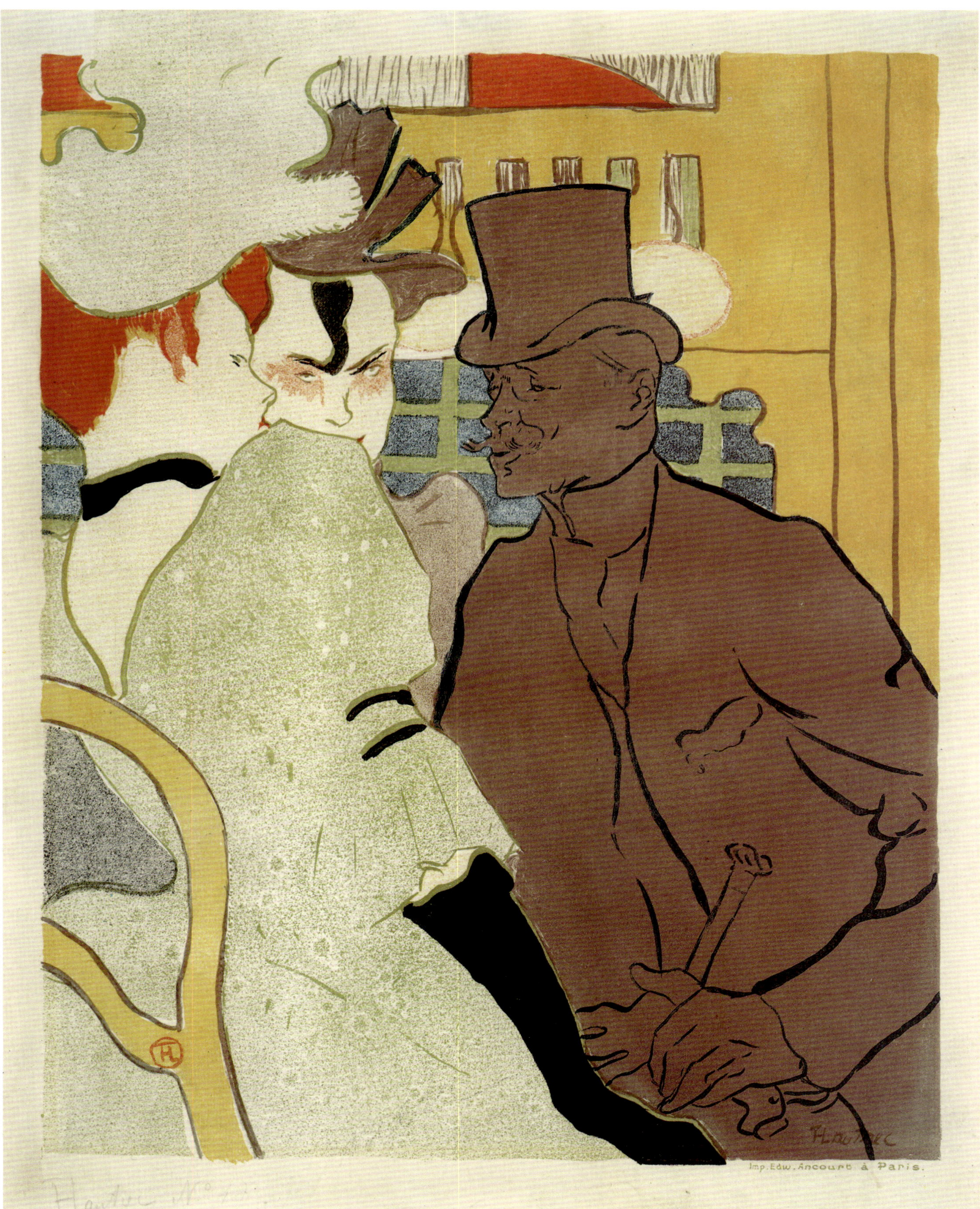

Imp.Edw.Ancourt à Paris.

8

Divan Japonais

1893
Crayon, brush, spatter, and transferred
 screen lithograph in four colors on
 wove paper
Image: 30¾ × 23¼ in. (78.1 × 59 cm)
Sheet: 31⅛ × 23½ in. (79 × 59.8 cm)
Printed by Edw. Ancourt & Cie, Paris
Commissioned by Ed. Fournier, owner
 of the Divan Japonais
Blindstamp lower left, "Bowinkels
 Gallery / Beverly Hills, Calif."
Wittrock P11; Adriani 8; Delteil 341;
 Adhémar 11

The dancer Jane Avril, seated as a respectable customer, dominates this handsome publicity poster created for the reopening, under new management, of the *café concert* Divan Japonais in 1893. Like a silhouettist who can only give a face its unique identity by showing it in profile, Lautrec often used his subject's profile as a means of relaying the strongest imprint of his or her character. In this case, he has emphasized this approach by showing Avril totally clothed in black so that her figure dominates the entire sheet. Fitted in behind her is the music and theatre critic Édouard Dujardin, and on the stage Yvette Guilbert, the clever *diseuse* identified by her familiar long black gloves, is partly visible. Guilbert was undoubtedly included by the artist as an evocation of the Divan's past, in order to remind those who had patronized it before of its probable attractions. Guilbert, however, never reappeared there after her performances two years earlier. As in his other early posters, Lautrec evokes Japanese formal arrangements with a composition consisting of an imposing flat area of black and several accents of color and black connected by lightly colored passages. The slightly patterned gray-green background of the balcony's railing, orchestra, and stage was produced by transferring a prepared screen of repeated motifs to the lithographic stone.

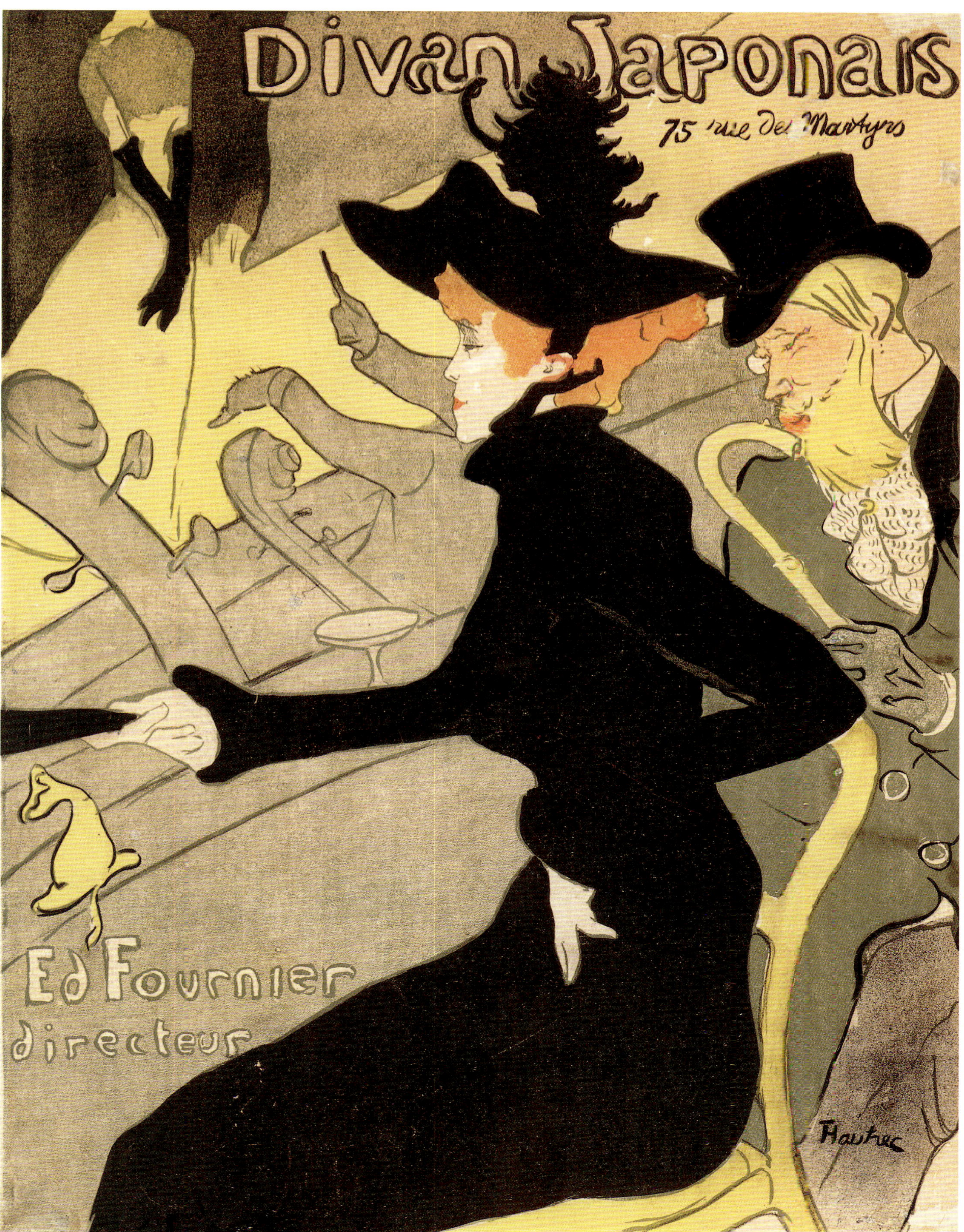

Divan Japonais
75 rue des Martyrs
Ed Fournier
directeur

9

La Lithographie: Couverture de L'Estampe originale

1893
Brush and spatter lithograph in six colors
  on wove paper
Image: 22 × 25½ in. (55.9 × 64.8 cm)
Sheet: 22⅞ × 32 in. (58.1 × 81.3 cm)
Only state, number 82
Printed by Edw. Ancourt & Cie, Paris
Published by *Journal des artistes* (André
  Marty) as the cover for the first album
  of *L'Estampe originale*, Paris
Signed lower left-center in pencil,
  HTLautrec No. 82
Wittrock 3; Adriani 9; Delteil 17;
  Adhémar 10

One of the ways to sell prints in the 1890s was to gather new prints by artists of similar stylistic inclinations into portfolios or albums. Often the criterion for inclusion was simply friendship or acquaintance. In 1893, André Marty published the first of nine portfolios titled *L'Estampe originale* (March 30), as well as a dozen other prints by Lautrec. In the case of *L'Estampe originale*, the artist was responsible for the wrapper of the first portfolio, which appropriately represents the printing process by which many of the works it included were produced. Lautrec also contributed a color lithograph, *Aux Ambassadeurs,* for the sixth portfolio in 1894 and a cover depicting Misia Natanson (the subject of his poster for *La Revue blanche* of 1895, cat. 32) for the final portfolio in 1895. On the cover for the first portfolio, he shows his friend Jane Avril seriously examining a proof just pulled on the Bisset lithographic press by Père Cotelle, the master printer at Edw. Ancourt et Cie. It is possible that the print she is looking at is the black-and-white print of herself that would appear shortly afterward in another of Marty's albums, *Le Café concert.* The economy of means in this print is outstanding: the keystone was printed in the olive-green that Lautrec favored for this purpose, to which were added black and four other colors. The weight of the planes of color and unprinted paper was carefully calculated against that of spattered areas (such as Cotelle's clothing), which demand less attention.

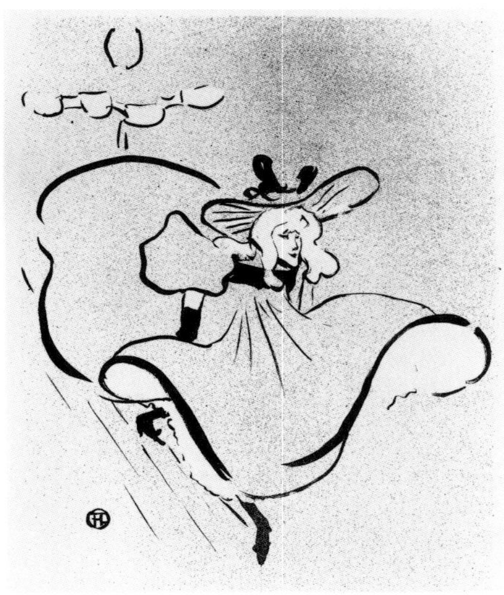

Henri de Toulouse-Lautrec, *Jane Avril*, 1893, lithograph printed in black, 10½ × 8⁷⁄₁₆ in. The Museum of Modern Art, New York, purchase fund.

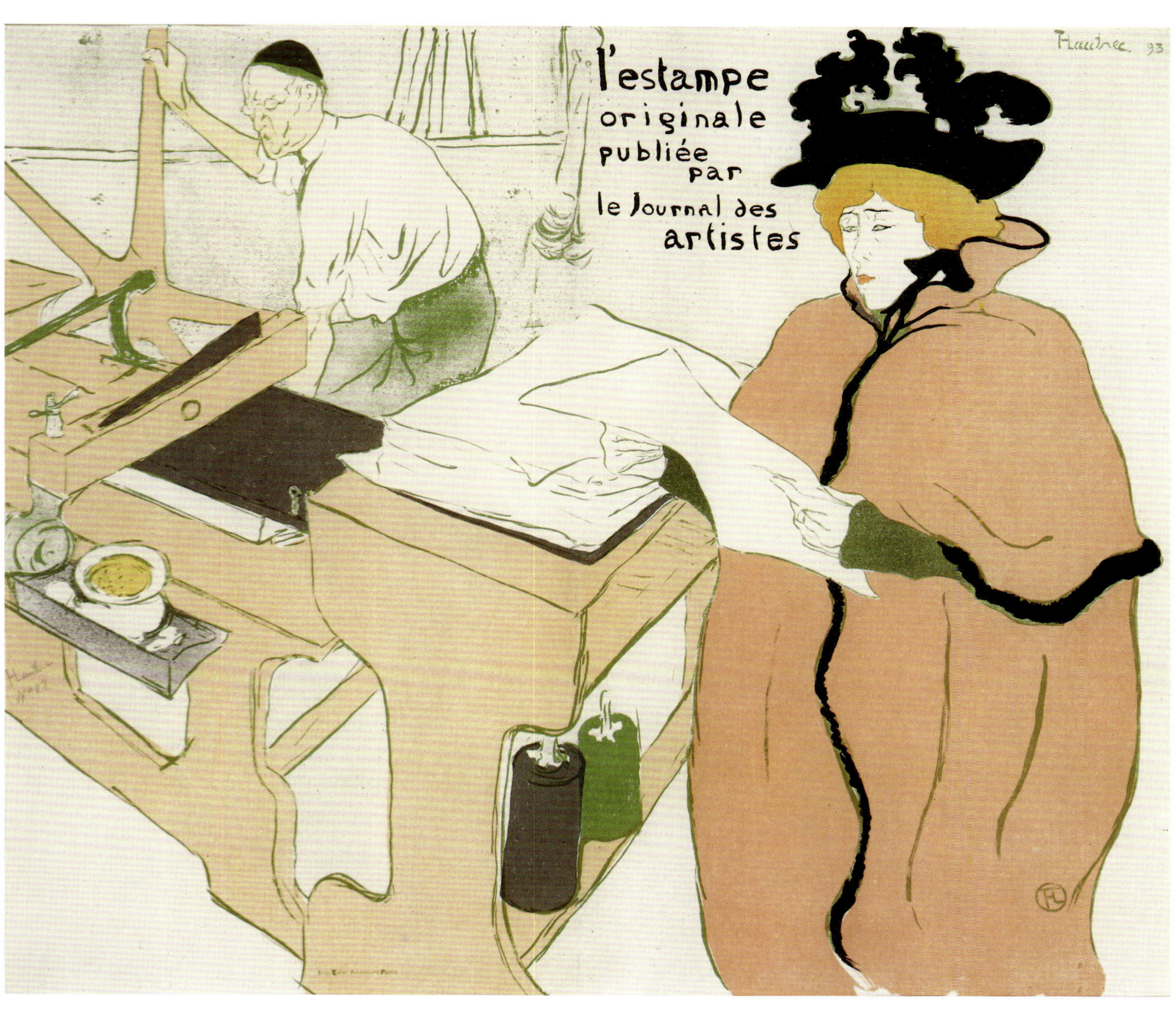

l'estampe
originale
publiée
par
le Journal des
artistes

10

Miss Loïe Fuller

1893
Brush and spatter lithograph in various
 colors and powdered gold, on wove
 paper
Image: 14½ × 10⅜ in. (36.8 × 26.4 cm)
Sheet: 14⅞ × 11 in. (37.8 × 27.9 cm)
Only state
Printed by Edw. Ancourt & Cie
 (H. Stern), Paris
Published by André Marty, Paris
Wittrock 17; Adriani 10; Delteil 39;
 Adhémar 8

An American dancer from Chicago was the sensation of the Parisian stage in
1893 when she appeared at the Folies Bergère. Loïe Fuller combined the baroque
histrionics of a Sarah Bernhardt with the latest fad of the time: electric light. No
one would have given her a prize for her dancing skill, but by assembling yards
of gossamer-thin fabric into a costume which she could manipulate into waves
and clouds that rose high above her head while she moved, she created an apparition that seemed supernatural. This effect was made totally ethereal by the
colored spotlights that illuminated the constant swirling and fluttering of Fuller's
costume. Lautrec was only one of many whose imaginations were enchanted
enough to put this fantasy into concrete form. The many bronzes of Fuller by
François Rupert Carabin and Pierre Roche, as well as posters of her by Jules
Chéret and Manuel Orazi, became popular collectibles at the turn of the century.
Among the interpretations of Fuller's exotic dances was Lautrec's lithograph,
commissioned by André Marty. It is possible to appreciate Lautrec's innovative
contribution to the visual language of art by contrasting one of Chéret's posters
of Fuller's spectacle with Lautrec's small print. The always cheerful Chéret girl
has not been transformed at all by the veils of Fuller's dance, while Lautrec
presents a haunting specter of nearly abstract form, dark but made luminescent
through the application of metallic powder. Lautrec's lithograph has its roots in
an intense observation of Japanese woodcuts, which typically combine economy
of form with luxury of surface.

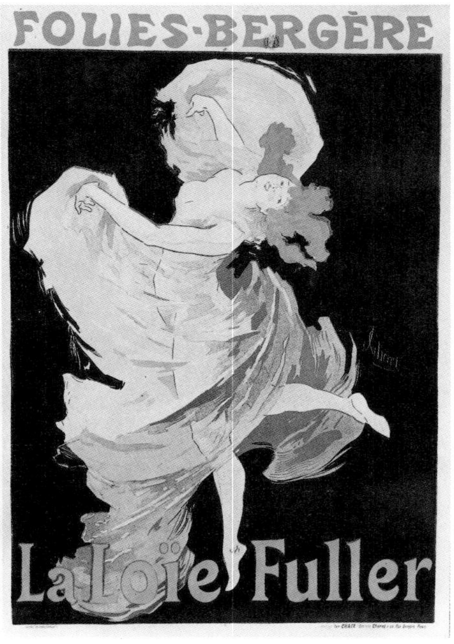

Jules Chéret, *Folies Bergère, La Loïe
Fuller*, 1893, color lithograph, 48½ ×
34½ in. The Museum of Modern Art,
New York, acquired by exchange.

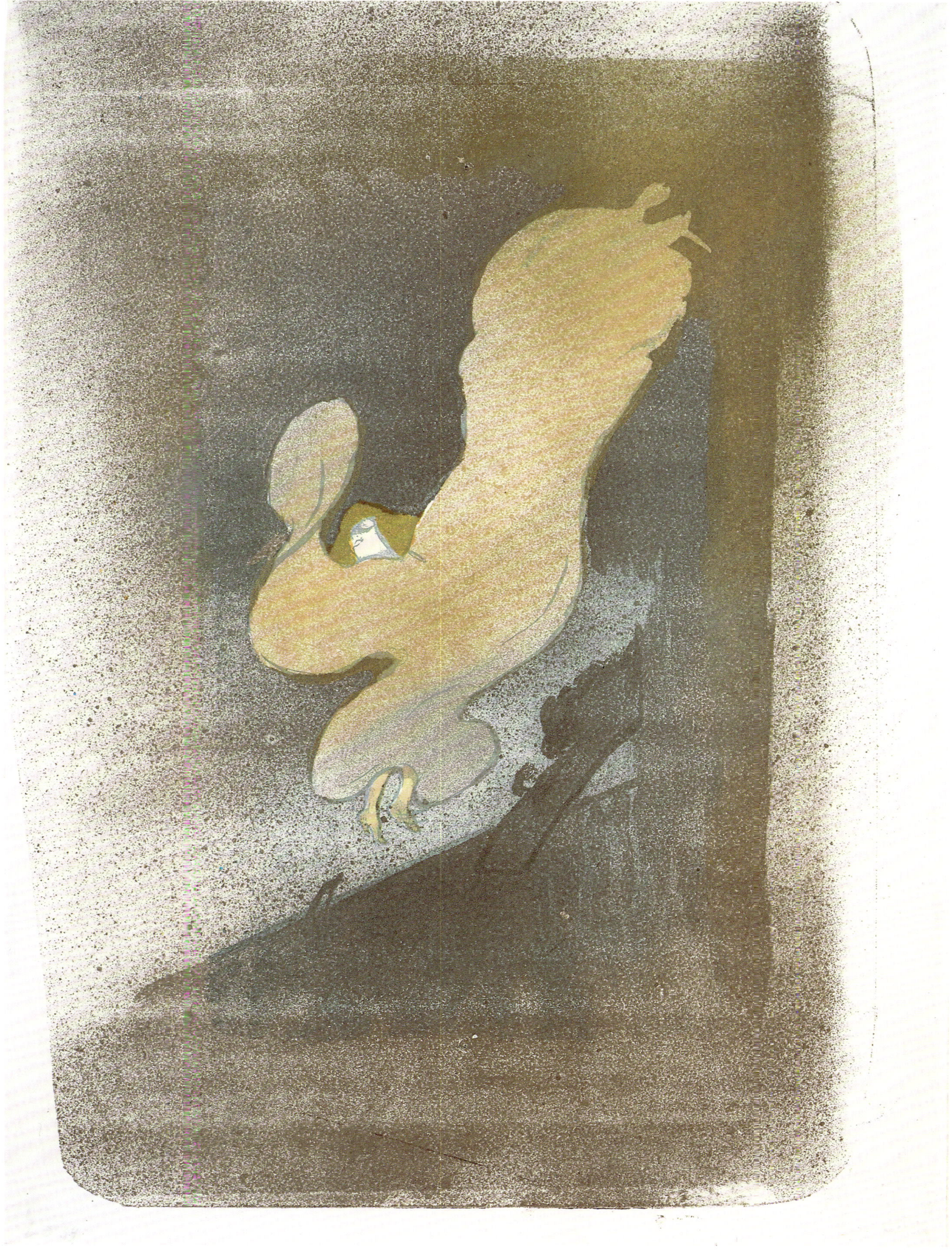

11

Jane Avril

1893

Brush and spatter lithograph in five
  colors on wove paper
Image: 49¼ × 35¼ in. (125.1 × 89.5 cm)
Sheet: 51¼ × 37⅜ in. (130.2 × 94.9 cm)
Printed by Chaix, Paris
Commissioned by the Jardin de Paris
Distributed by Ed. Kleinmann, Paris
Wittrock P6/C; Adriani 11/II; Delteil
  345; Adhémar 12

Jane Avril's family background was similar to that of many female performers of the time: her mother was a prostitute and her father an aristocrat—an Italian count, in Avril's case. Her career was circumscribed by her apparently manic-depressive nature, suggested by the sobriquet La Mélinite, characterizing her explosive dance performances, which were periodically interrupted by withdrawal from the stage altogether. The two previous works in which she is featured, *Divan Japonais* (cat. 8) and the cover for *L'Estampe originale* (cat. 9), may have been created during one of these periods of withdrawal. For her reappearance on the stage, she asked Lautrec to make this poster. The Jardin de Paris, a *café concert* in the Champs-Élysées, was a big step away from the Moulin Rouge, where Avril also appeared. The dancer in the poster is shown throwing up her foot in the cancan manner, an action previously caught in a photograph that was undoubtedly a model for Lautrec's poster. The clothing is different from that in the photograph, however, and Lautrec discarded details of the draping, curls, and strapped-on shoes. Exuberant movement is caught in unmodulated areas of black and color, applied to a light spattering of olive-green that represents the stage. Avril is framed by an extension of the neck of the bass viol in the foreground, held by a wavy-haired musician who is playing the repetitive notes of the score placed between him and the stage. A granular spattering rather than a solid black fills this frame, a treatment like that of the stage that does not overwhelm its main subject, Jane Avril. The poster went up on June 3, 1893.

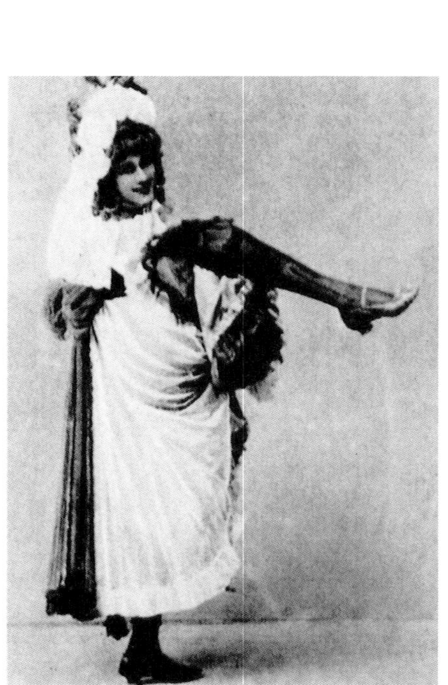

Jane Avril, ca. 1893, photograph. Private collection.

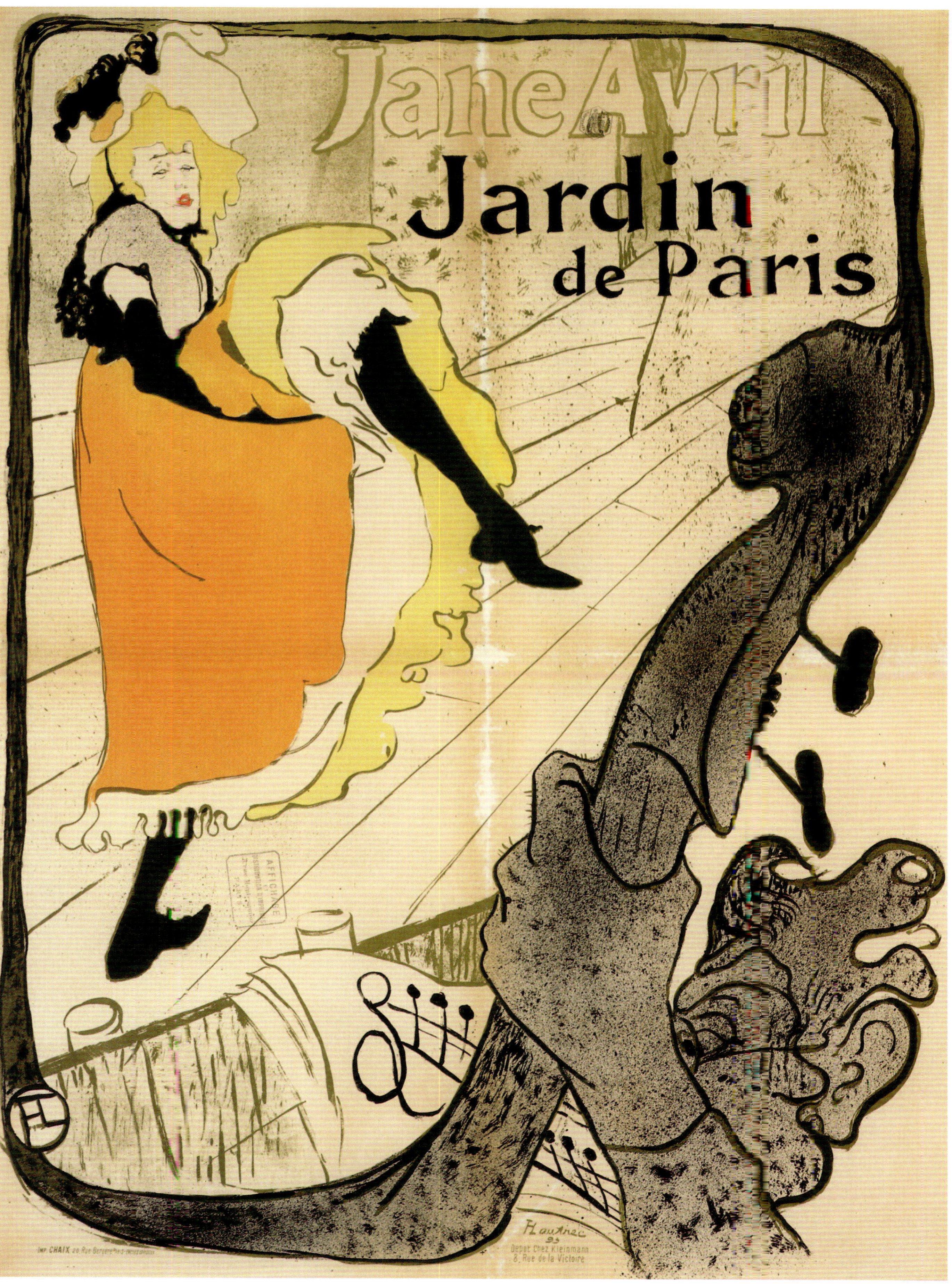

Jane Avril
Jardin
de Paris

12

Aristide Bruant dans son cabaret

1893
Brush and spatter lithograph in four
  colors on wove paper
Image: 51½ × 37⅛ in. (130.8 × 94.3 cm)
Sheet: 52¾ × 38 in. (134 × 96.5 cm)
Printed by Charles Verneau, Paris
Commissioned by Aristide Bruant
Wittrock P9/A; Adriani 12/I; Delteil
  348; Adhémar 15

This is an example of one of the best known of Lautrec's posters and the
boldest in economy of form before the letters were added, a stage which often
was issued in a limited edition for collectors of Lautrec's and other poster
makers' images. Many extant posters with letters were ripped off walls. In its
determined simplicity, the composition of this poster provides an important
example of how Lautrec transformed the already exciting medium of public
advertising. In his two earlier posters for Aristide Bruant's appearances
(cats. 4, 5), the background offered additional information about the event
advertised. Large unprinted spaces had been illegal on all but official govern-
mental posters until Lautrec's time, so that while Chéret and others often
composed their earlier works around central figures, they had to fill the backgrounds with a variety of incidental motifs. When Charles Lévy made his
portrait poster for Bruant's appearance at the Ambassadeurs (see fig., cat. 4),
which its proprietor preferred to Lautrec's, it showed the performer against an
unprinted background. In this poster of a year later, Lautrec showed his subject
with his back turned and left no room above the head for a banner printing of
the name of any café. When lettering was added, he used the black of the coat
as a background for "Aristide Bruant dans son cabaret," just as he had in his
Ambassadeurs poster. Bruant's profile and the texture of his staff are the only
areas of detailed drawing. Like the pale olive-green passages in other works,
these details are secondary to the main thrust of the black coat, red scarf, and
black hat, instantly recognizable symbols of Bruant. However, now these
components are rendered in total flatness and partly outlined, like the cloissoné
enamels from which some of Lautrec's contemporaries, such as Émile Bernard
and Paul Anquetin, derived their inspiration.

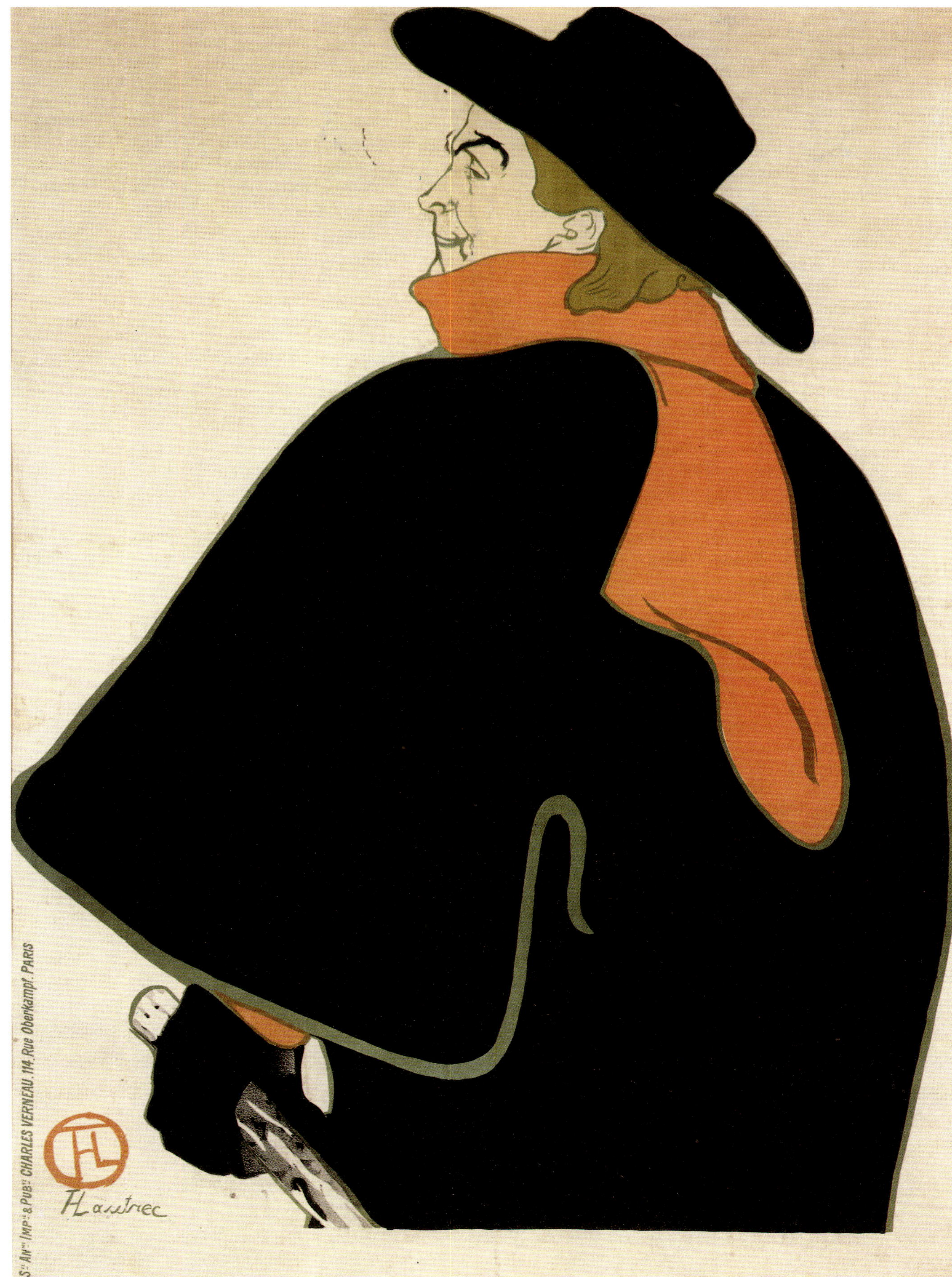

Sté Anme Impte & Pubté CHARLES VERNEAU. 114. Rue Oberkampf. PARIS
HTLautrec

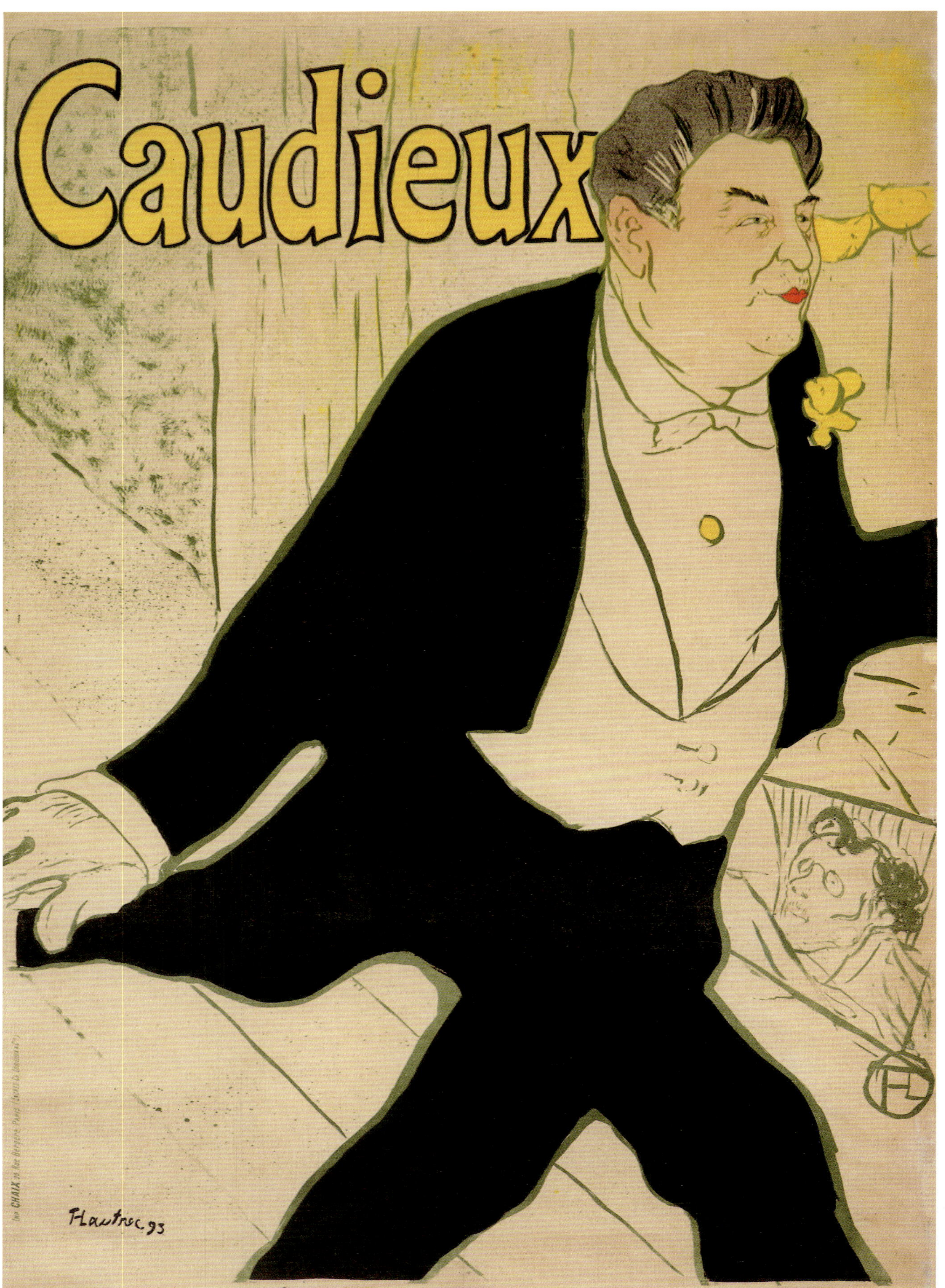

Caudieux
Imp. CHAIX 20 Rue Bergère, PARIS (Ateliers Cheret)
HTLautrec 93

13 Caudieux

1893
Brush and spatter lithograph in four
  colors on wove paper
Image: 48¾ × 35 in. (123.8 × 89 cm)
Sheet: 50½ × 35⅝ in. (128.2 × 90.5 cm)
Printed by Chaix, Paris
Commissioned by Caudieux
Wittrock P7; Adriani 15; Delteil 346;
  Adhémar 13

The comedian Caudieux appeared on the stage of the Petit Casino in 1893, and
Lautrec captured one aspect of his antics in a black-and-white lithograph for
Le Café concert, André Marty's album of twenty-two prints of entertainers. In
this poster, most likely commissioned by the performer, Lautrec shows Caudieux
striding across a stage. The slightly portly Caudieux (Le Bambocheur or liber-
tine) determinedly puts his face forward, arms outstretched and coattails flying.
In an unrelated oil sketch, Lautrec showed Caudieux powdering his face in his
dressing room, indicating that he used the traditional makeup of the comic:
white face and red lips. In the poster, Caudieux's makeup, stiff hair, and well-
defined hairline evoke the appearance of Japanese actors. Below the boards of
the stage is the head of a man, probably a prompter, peering up from the depths
of his booth between the performer and his unseen audience. The paraphernalia
of the stage, all lightly drawn, tend to emphasize through contrast Caudieux's
formidably exhilarating stage presence.

14

Au Pied de l'échafaud

1893
Crayon, brush, and spatter lithograph
  in five colors on wove paper
Image: 32⅝ × 23¼ in. (82.9 × 59 cm)
Sheet: 32⅝ × 24 in. (82.9 × 61 cm)
Printed by Chaix, Paris
Commissioned by the newspaper
  Le Matin, Paris
Tax stamp upper center
Wittrock P8; Adriani 14; Delteil 347;
  Adhémar 14

This is the third poster that Lautrec designed for a literary publication. Like *Le Pendu* (cat. 2), which was made to advertise the serialization of a novel, this work announced the appearance in parts of the memoirs of Abbé Faure, which recounted his experiences "at the foot of the scaffold" as the chaplin of La Roquette prison. Commissioned by Alfred Edwards, the director of *Le Matin*, the newspaper in which the serial appeared, the poster shows a green-faced prisoner about to join the thirty-seven others whose executions Faure had attended. The Abbé stands, prayer book in hand, behind the top-hatted executioner and in front of a silhouetted frieze of figures reminiscent of the crowd in Lautrec's first poster (cat. 1). This time the frieze is a band of mounted soldiers that forms a living fence in front of the barely visible prison wall. The faces of the principal figures are drawn in a shorthand that conveys their character in a way similar to the linear, black-and-white prints of peasants in Japanese books of the time. Unfortunately, *Le Matin*'s gothic lettering, clearly not by Lautrec, diminishes the impact of the artist's design, as the blood-red scaffold and black soldiers envelop their awaiting victim.

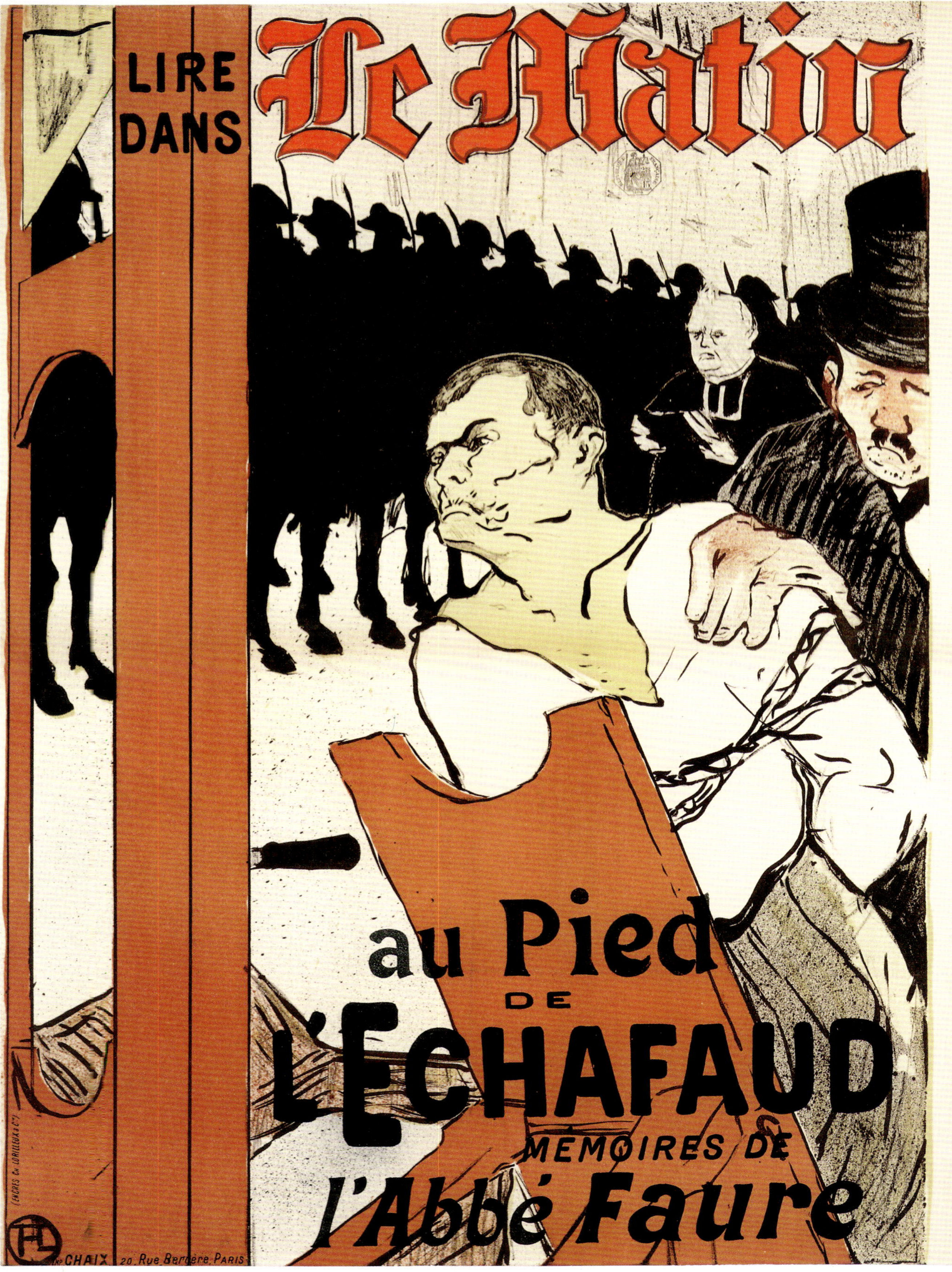
LIRE
DANS
Le Matin
au Pied
DE
L'ECHAFAUD
MEMOIRES DE
l'Abbé Faure
Imp. CHAIX, 20, Rue Bergère, PARIS

15

Carnot malade!

1893
Brush and spatter lithograph on mounted
  wove paper
Image: 9⅜ × 7¼ in. (23.8 × 18.4 cm)
Sheet: 13½ × 10¾ in. (34.3 × 27.3 cm)
First state, number 29
Published by Ed. Kleinmann, Paris
Signed lower left in pencil, *HTLautrec
No. 29*; stamped with Kleinmann
  blindstamp (Lugt 1573)
Wittrock 12; Adriani 34/I; Delteil 25/I;
  Adhémar 24

In the summer of 1893, Sadi Carnot, who had become fourth President of the Republic in 1887, was suffering from a liver ailment, the French national disease. Eugène Lemercier's monologue, for which this lithograph was the cover, compared Carnot's sickness with that of his government. Some copies of the print were colored, yellow on the patient's jaundiced face and red, white, and blue—the French tricolor—on his bedding. The ministrations of a doctor taking Carnot's pulse, a nun bringing him a bowl of nourishment, and the ignored official papers on the bed would have been recognized as a commentary on the weakness and disarray of the President's government. Less than a year later, in the midst of burgeoning incidents of anarchic disturbances, Carnot was assassinated. This version of Lautrec's print, without the words that indicated that the monologue, for which it was the cover, was performed at the Chat Noir, was sold by Kleinmann, the artist's print publisher from 1893 through 1895.

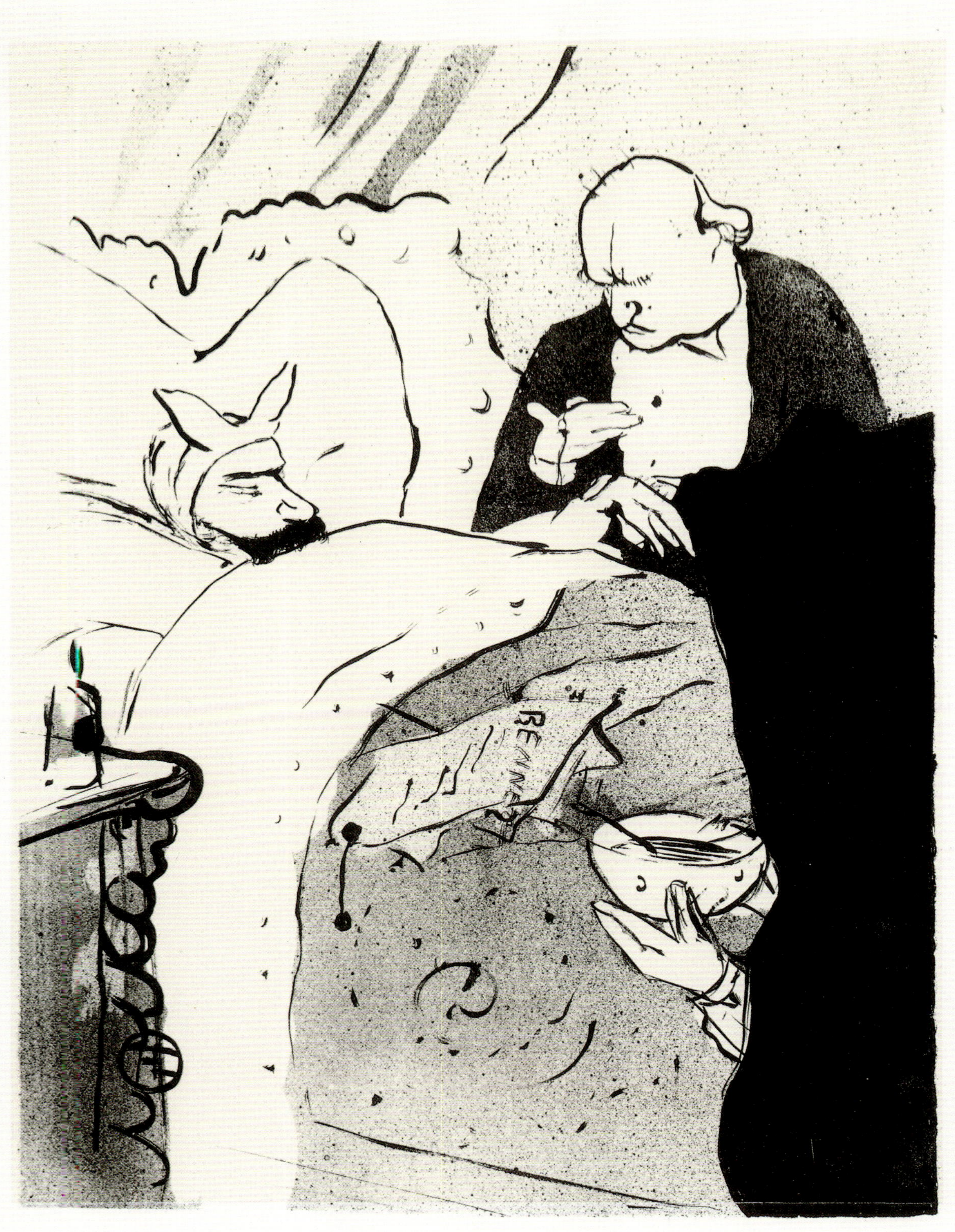

16

Le Petit Trottin

1893
Brush lithograph printed in olive green
  with stencil coloring on wove paper
Image: 11 × 7½ in. (27.9 × 19 cm)
Sheet: 13⅝ × 10 in. (34.6 × 25.4 cm)
Second state, third edition, after 1901
Printed by Joly, Paris
Published by A. Fourquet, Paris
Wittrock 14; Adriani 36/II; Delteil 27/
  II; Adhémar 18/II

The little errand girl with her big box or basket was a common sight in nineteenth-century Paris. Always among the poorest young women, these hard workers had to traverse streets on their own, trying to get to their destinations through a maze of obstructions, one of which was the lascivious attentions of men. In Lautrec's lithograph for Achille Melandri's song, set to music by Desiré Dihau, the girl looks back at a dandy whose monocled eye winks at her. Behind them is a public urinal, no doubt a possible hideaway for quick seductions. Color has been added through a stencil. The model for Lautrec's caricature of a man with something on his mind may have been his friend Maurice Guibert. The composer Dihau was a distant cousin of Lautrec's from Lille, for whom the artist created prints for two series of his musical settings for poems: *Les Veilles Histoires* in 1893 and *Melodies* in 1895–96. Dihau is better known today from paintings by his neighbor Edgar Degas, who depicted him several times playing his bassoon in the Paris Opera orchestra.

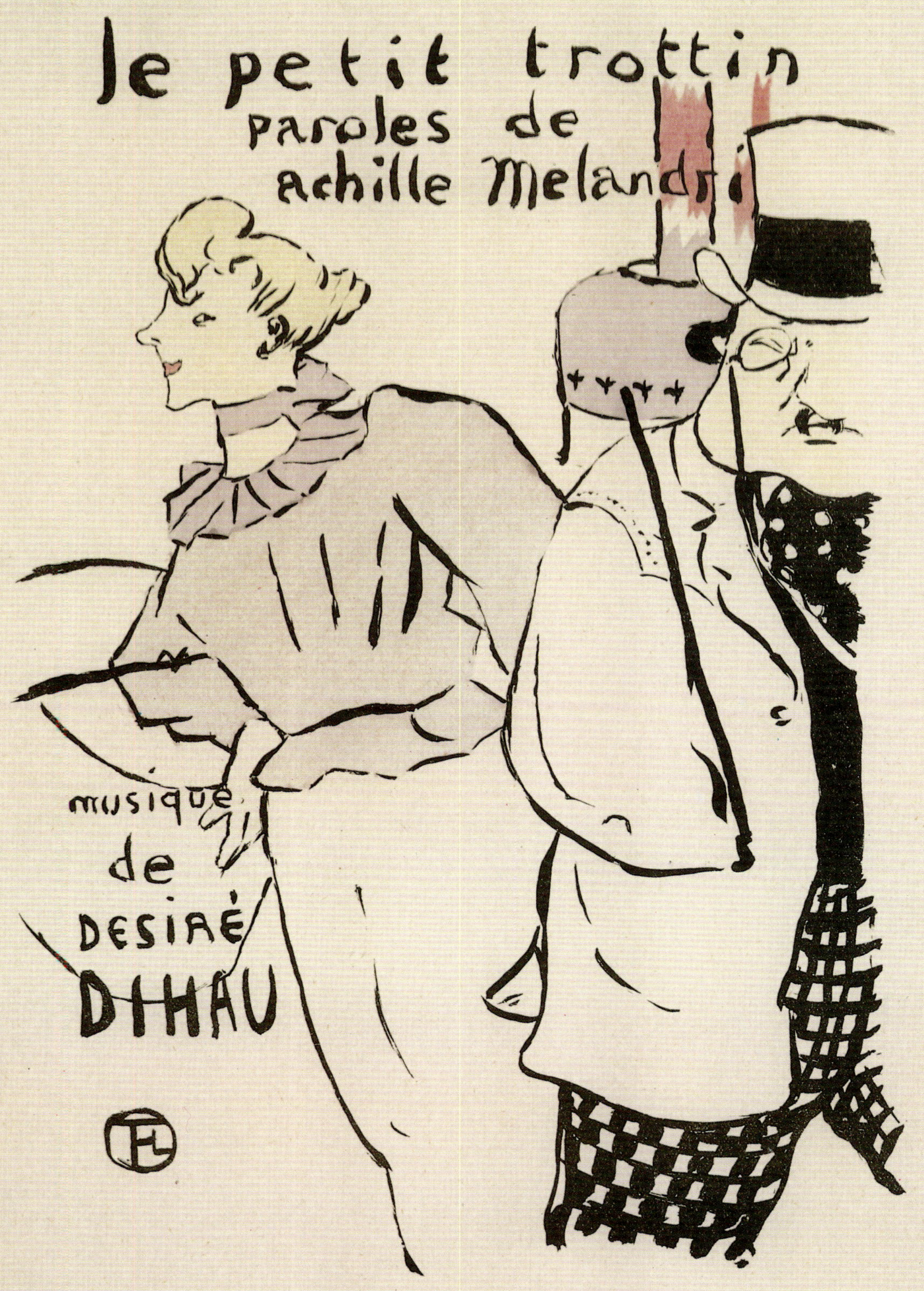

Je petit trottin
paroles de
achille Melandri
musique
de
DESIRÉ
DIHAU

17

Prochainement au théâtre: A. Bruant

1893
Crayon, brush, and spatter lithograph
  on wove paper
Image: 31½ × 22⅛ in. (80 × 56.2 cm)
Sheet: 31½ × 22⅞ in. (80 × 58.1 cm)
Third state
Printed by Chaix, Paris
Commissioned by Aristide Bruant
Tax stamp lower right
Wittrock P10/B; Adriani 57/III; Delteil
  349; Adhémar 71

The earliest dated appearance in print of Lautrec's only full-length representation of Aristide Bruant was a reduced version of this poster for the cover of Oscar Méténier's biography of Bruant, illustrated with drawings by Théophile Steinlen and published by *Le Mirliton* in 1893. In its poster size it was printed four ways: without text; with two different texts (one printed in red for Bruant's appearances "au Mirliton" and advertising beer for thirteen sous, and the other, shown here, "prochainement au théâtre"); and as an advertisement for *Dans la rue,* the second volume of Bruant's songs, published by *Le Mirliton* in 1895 with Steinlen's drawings, the first volume of which had appeared in 1888. The final appearance of the poster coincided with Bruant's retirement. The figure of Bruant, now seen in his corduroy suit and boots, stands on cobblestones *(dans la rue),* his hands in his pockets, with his trademark broad-brimmed hat but without his red scarf, so that only at his wrists and neckline are there hints of his red shirt. Unlike Lautrec's earlier posters, this one of more modest size presents Bruant as less fiercely heroic. Perhaps because the poster was intended for multiple uses, the familiar signs of the artist's persona were enough.

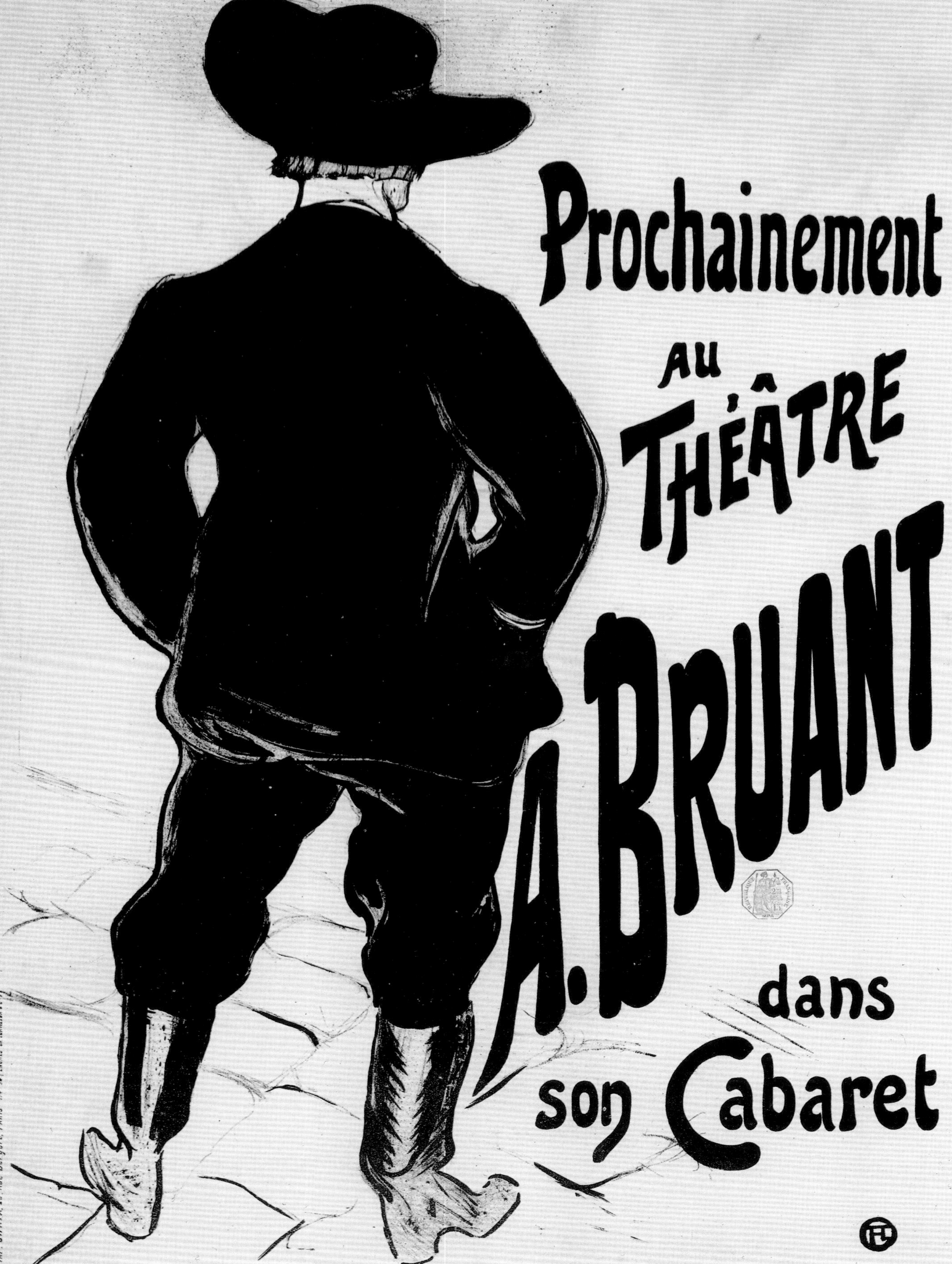

Prochainement
au THÉÂTRE
A. BRUANT
dans
son Cabaret
Imp. CHAIX, 20, Rue Bergère, PARIS

18

Truffier et Moreno
dans Les Femmes savantes

1893
Crayon, brush, and spatter lithograph
  with scraper on wove paper
Image: 14¾ × 10¼ in. (37.5 × 26 cm)
Sheet: 15 × 10⅞ in. (38.1 × 27.6 cm)
Distributed by Ed. Kleinmann, Paris
Stamped lower right with Kleinmann
  blindstamp (Lugt 1573)
Wittrock 46; Adriani 38; Delteil 54;
  Adhémar 60

During the 1893–94 season, Lautrec's friend Romain Coolus (René Weil)
accompanied the artist to many of the countless theatrical presentations offered
in Paris. Kleinmann, Lautrec's print publisher, may have suggested that scenes
from popular theatrical performances might be good subjects for prints. This
was the probable beginning of Lautrec's plan to create *L'Escarmouche*, an illustrated journal reproducing his theatrical prints. Molière's *Les Femmes savantes*
played at the Comédie-Française only three times, in August and September
1893, with Charles Jules Truffier as Trissotin and Marguerite Monceau (Moreno)
as Armande. Although this may have been one of the first performances Lautrec
chose to depict, it was not included in Kleinmann's sales catalogue until February 1894.

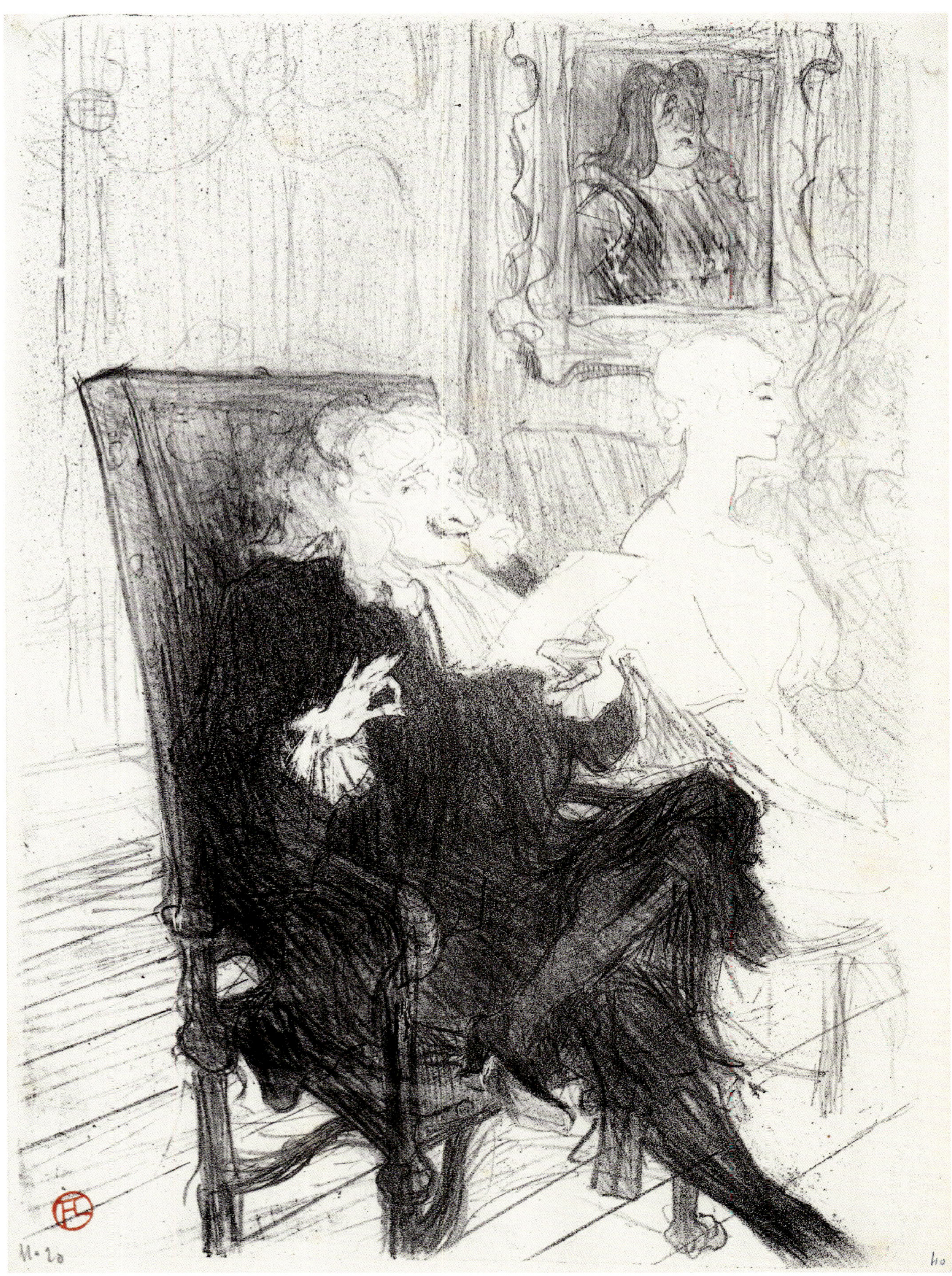

19

Judic

1893
Crayon, brush, and spatter lithograph
  on Japan paper
Image: 14⅞ × 10½ in. (37.8 × 26.7 cm)
Sheet: 18¾ × 12¾ in. (47.6 × 32.4 cm)
Only state, one of only five examples
  printed on Japan paper
Published by Ed. Kleinmann, Paris, 1894
Signed lower left in pencil, *HTLautrec*
Wittrock 54; Adriani 43; Delteil 56;
  Adhémar 39

Anna Judic, born Anna Maria Louise Damiens in 1849, was a well-known operetta singer who began her career at the age of seventeen. Although a high soprano, she was also a *diseuse,* speaking songs as early as 1868. She appeared in most of the Parisian theatres devoted to musical events and was notable for her performances in the premieres of Jacques Offenbach's operettas *La Roi carotte, Mme L'Archiduc,* and *La Créole* well before she was portrayed by Lautrec. She was the prima donna of the Théâtre des Variétés for a decade and a star of the *cafés concerts* in the 1890s. Lautrec shows her being laced into her corset, while a man (Desiré Dihau) waits at her side. (See *Elles: Femme en corset; Conquête de passage,* cat. 54, for a similar scene in a different setting.)

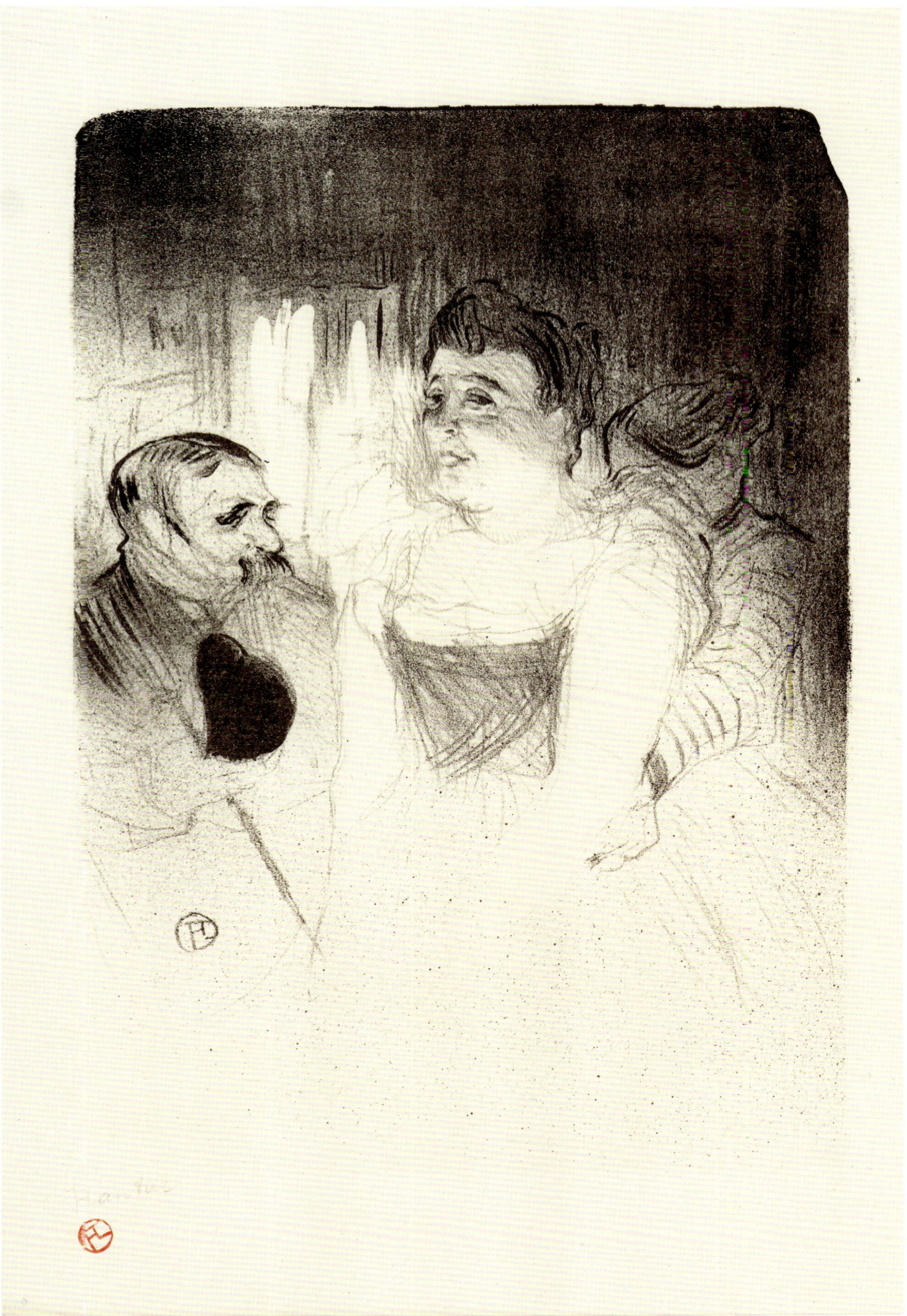

20

Répétition générale aux Folies Bergère: Émilienne d'Alençon et Mariquita

1893
Crayon, brush, and splatter lithograph
 with scraper on wove paper
Image: 14⅝ × 10⅛ in. (37.1 × 25.7 cm)
Sheet: 15 × 11⅛ in. (38.1 × 28.3 cm)
First state, number 89
Printed by Edw. Ancourt & Cie, Paris
Published by *L'Escarmouche* and
 reproduced in the December 3, 1893,
 issue
Inscribed lower left in pencil, *No 89*
Wittrock 34/I; Adriani 49/I; Delteil 44;
 Adhémar 47

The first issue of *L'Escarmouche,* the weekly newspaper that Lautrec was instrumental in creating, appeared on November 12, 1893. During the two months until its demise on January 14, 1894, the artist made twelve lithographs for reproduction in the paper. Among the other artists whose work appeared in *L'Escarmouche* were Pierre Bonnard, Henri Ibels, and Félix Vallotton. Lautrec's original lithographs were printed in editions of one hundred and sold by Kleinmann. This one, which was reproduced in the December 3 issue, presents the rehearsal of a pantomime ballet by Courteline and Marsolleau, *Bal des Quat'z'Arts,* which opened December 16. It shows Mariquita, the director of ballet at the Folies Bergère, instructing Émilienne d'Alençon (Émilie Andrée), usually described as a demimondaine. She had debuted at the Cirque d'Été in 1889 with her white rabbits and appeared somewhat later at the Casino de Paris with her *ânes savants* (an animal act with smart donkeys). In the 1890s she also appeared as a dancer at the Olympia and elsewhere in Paris and London. She was later called one of "the beauty queens of the belle epoque."[1] In 1896, d'Alençon was the probable model for two of the artist's color prints, *Au Concert* (cat. 60) and *La Grande Loge* (cat. 61). Lautrec also included her portrait in a group of thirteen lithographs of 1897 devoted to actors and actresses.

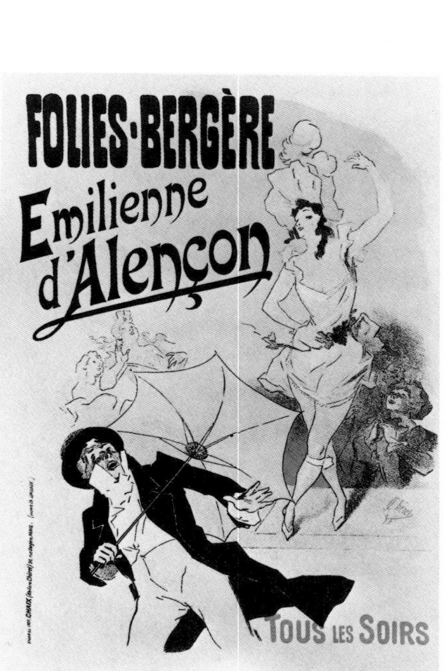

Jules Chéret, *Folies Bergère, Emilienne d'Alençon,* color lithograph. Private collection.

1. André Sallée and Philippe Chauveau, *Music-Hall et café concert.* (Paris: Bordas, 1985), p. 19.

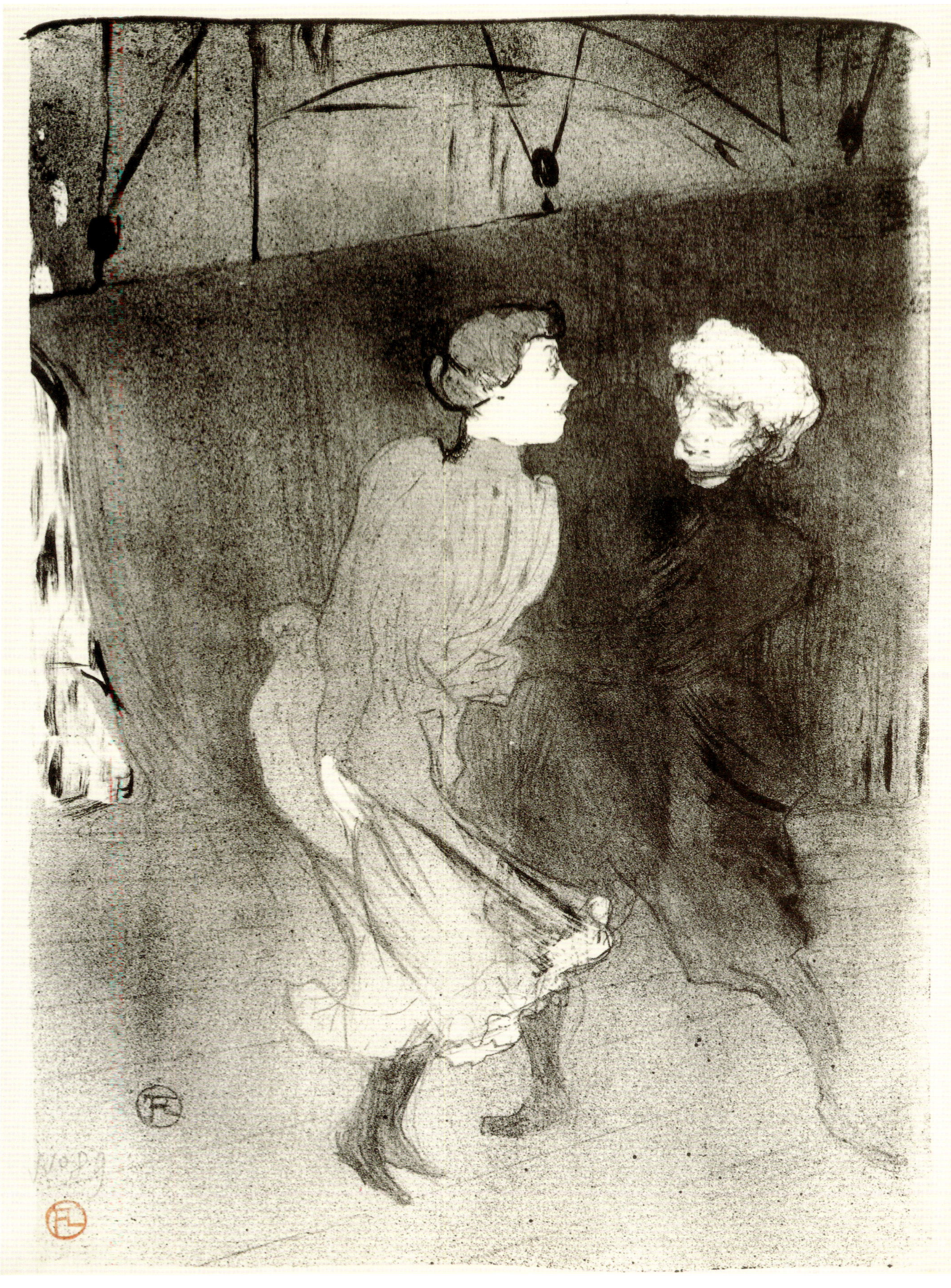

21

A la Renaissance: Sarah Bernhardt dans Phèdre

1893
Crayon, brush, and spatter lithograph
   on wove paper
Image: 13⅛ × 9⅜ in. (33.3 × 23.8 cm)
Sheet: 15 × 11⅛ in. (38.1 × 28.3 cm)
Only state, number 5
Printed by Edw. Ancourt & Cie, Paris
Published by *L'Escarmouche* and
   reproduced in the December 24, 1893,
   issue
Inscribed lower left in pencil, *5*
Wittrock 37; Adriani 52; Delteil 47;
   Adhémar 50

In 1893, after a two-year world tour, the nearly fifty-year-old Sarah Bernhardt decided to open her own theatre, the Renaissance, which began its first season with a play called *Les Rois.* The play's failure to draw a significant audience may have been due to Bernhardt's exaggerated estimation of its author, Jules Lemaitre, who was rumored to be her lover at the time. Some of Bernhardt's romantic liaisons with actors had already resulted in theatrical catastrophies. This time, however, her own enterprise was at stake, so in order to fill the house she had to revive one of her famous roles. Bernhardt had first brought her admirers to tears with her portrayal of Racine's Phèdre nineteen years earlier. In Lautrec's lithograph, based on a photograph, Bernhardt is shown as Theseus's wife being drawn to a tragic fate by her nurse, Oneone. The artist has contrasted the two women by producing the effect of bright light on Phèdre, with only lines defining her, while the nurse is clothed in black and surrounded by darkness. Most notable among those who remembered Bernhardt in this role was Marcel Proust. In *A l'ombre des jeunes filles en fleurs,* the second volume of *A la recherche du temps perdu,* Proust's idealized actress, Berma, was a composite of Bernhardt and Réjane. However, as he described the character's appearance in *Phèdre,* it could only have the divine Sarah who evoked his youthful skepticism of fame. This print, one of the group Lautrec contributed to *L'Escarmouche,* appeared in the issue for December 24, 1893.

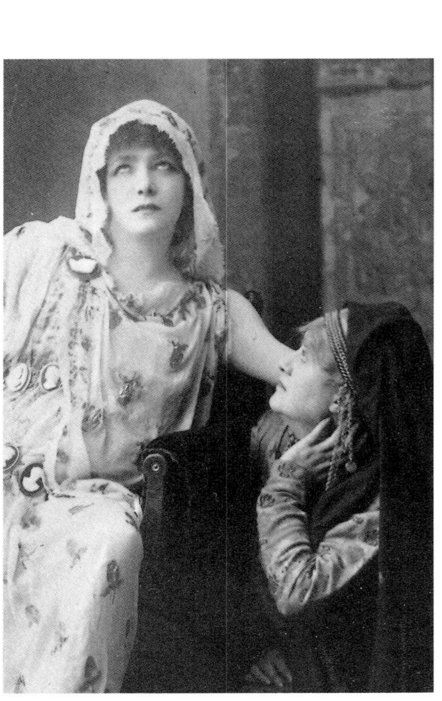

Sarah Bernhardt in Phèdre, photograph.
Bibliothèque Nationale, Paris.

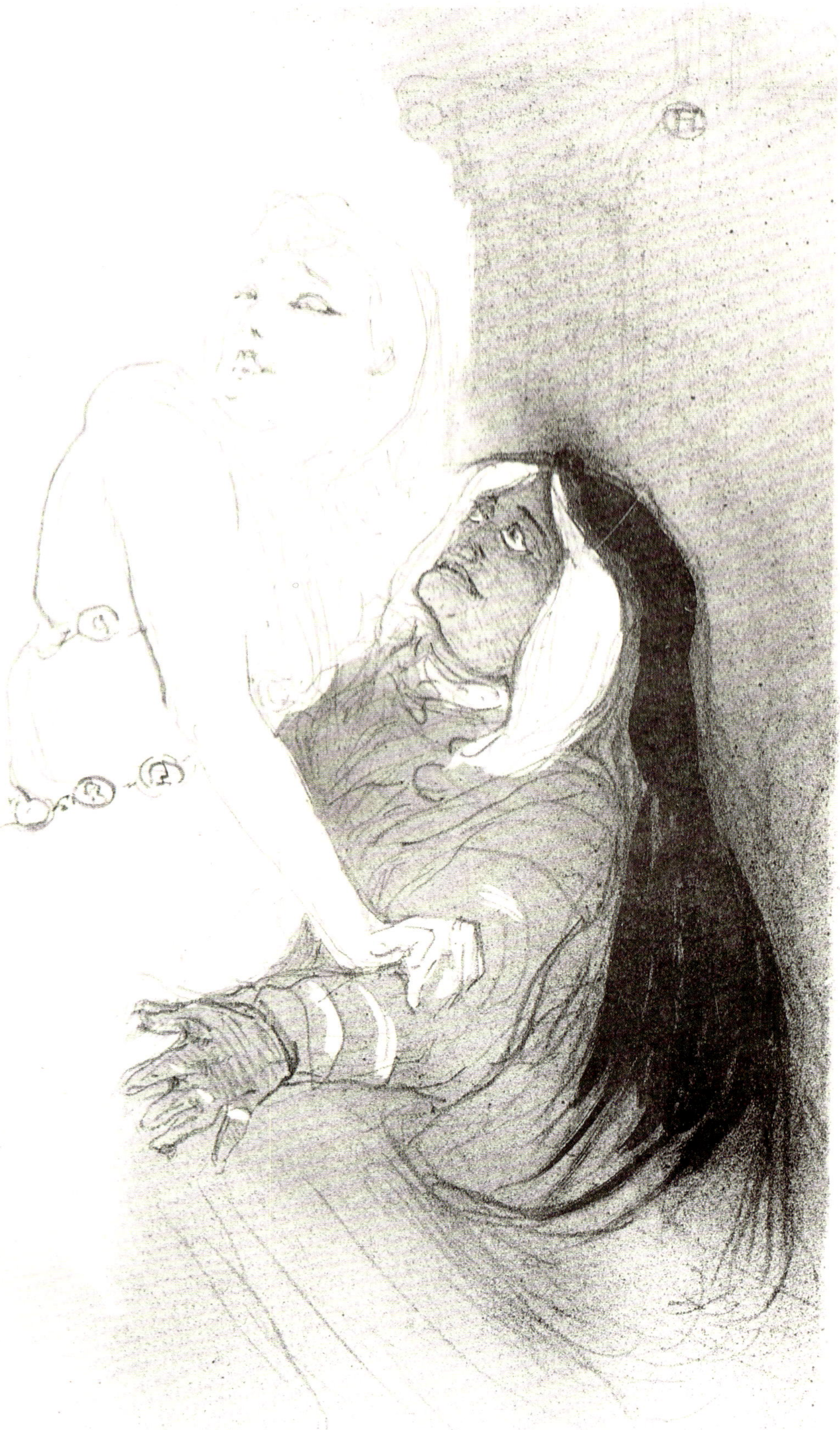

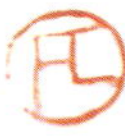

La Loge au mascaron doré

1893
Crayon, brush, and spatter lithograph in
five colors on wove paper
Image and sheet: 12⅛ × 9½ in. (30.8 ×
24.1 cm)
Second state, theater program edition of
1894
Printed by Edw. Ancourt & Cie, Paris
Wittrock 16; Adriani 69/II; Delteil 16/
II; Adhémar 72

In 1893 Lautrec became involved with several people whose lives were centered around the legitimate theatre. He had begun to attend performances frequently in 1890, and by 1893 he agreed to design a program for André Antoine's Théâtre Libre. His first lithograph was for a double program: *La Faillite,* by Bjørnstjerne Bjørnson, and *Le Poète et le financier,* by Maurice Vaucaire, which opened November 8, 1893. It depicts a woman having her hair combed, probably unrelated to any episode in either play, but evocative of both playwrights' Naturalist approach. The second program, shown here, was for *Le Missionnaire* by Marcel Luguet. Kleinmann issued one hundred copies of its edition before letters were added. Other than his *Divan Japonais* poster (cat. 8), this was Lautrec's first color print that focused on the audience. It clearly had no relationship to the subject of the play, and the sketch for it was made well before the play's opening on April 24, 1894. In the balcony, a woman holding opera glasses seems transfixed by the performance, while next to her Lautrec's friend, the British painter Charles Edward Conder, is expressionless. Conder appears in several of Lautrec's scenes of entertainment, having been part of the art-and-bar scene since his arrival in Paris from Australia in 1890. On the front of the balcony is the mask of an open-mouthed satyr illuminated by the stage light, a satirical allusion to the sexual relationship of the box's occupants.

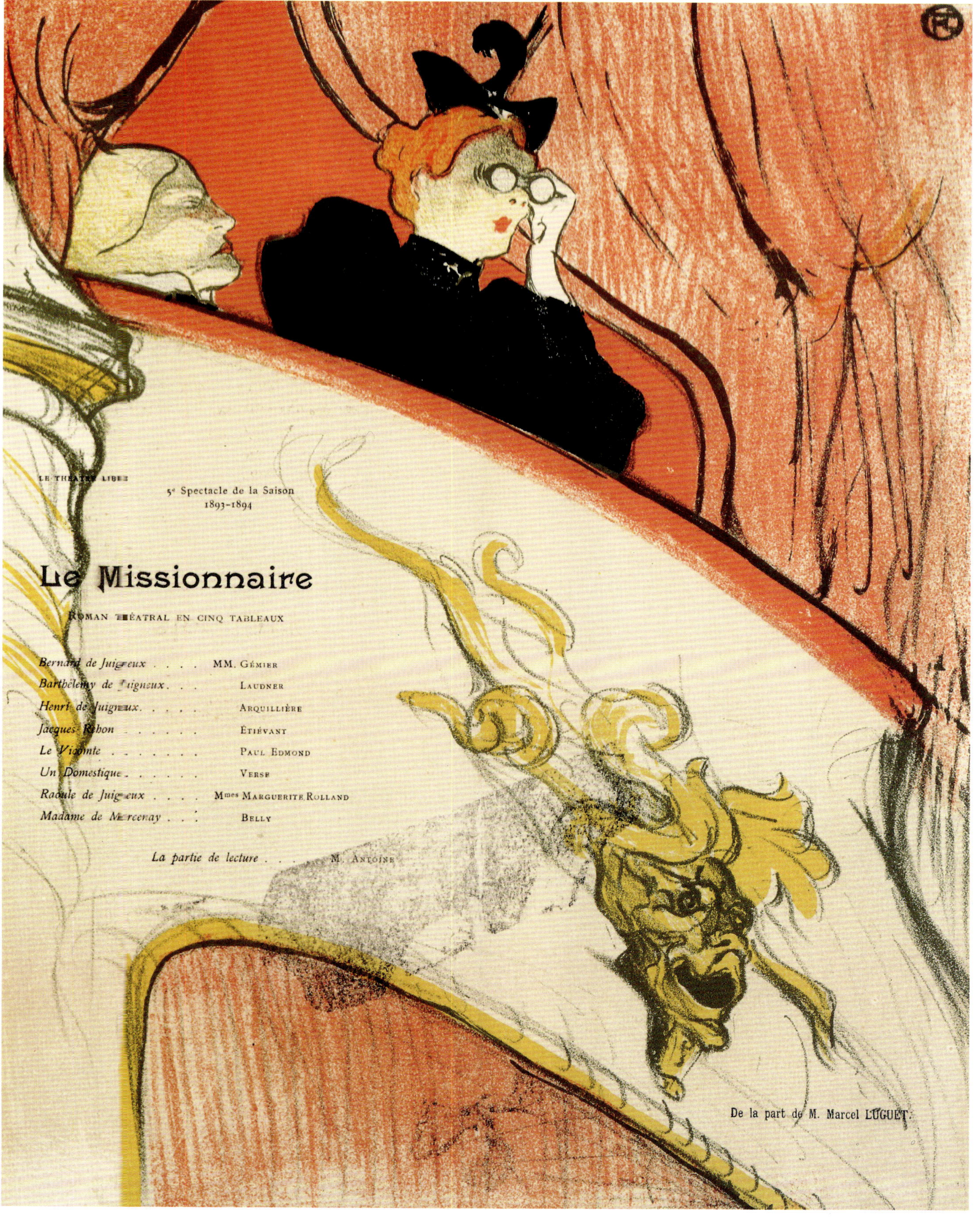

LE THÉÂTRE LIBRE
5e Spectacle de la Saison
1893-1894
Le Missionnaire
ROMAN THÉATRAL EN CINQ TABLEAUX
Bernard de Juigneux . . . . MM. Gémier
Barthélemy de Juigneux . . . Laudner
Henri de Juigneux . . . . Arquillière
Jacques-Rehon . . . . . Étiévant
Le Vicomte . . . . . . Paul Edmond
Un Domestique . . . . . Verse
Raoule de Juigneux . . . . Mmes Marguerite Rolland
Madame de Mercenay . . . Belly
La partie de lecture . . . M. Antoine
De la part de M. Marcel Luguet.

23

Babylone d'Allemagne

1894
Brush and spatter lithograph in five
  colors on wove paper
Image: 47⅛ × 32⅜ in. (119.7 × 82.2 cm)
Sheet: 48½ × 33⅜ in. (123.2 × 84.8 cm)
Printed by Chaix, Paris
Commissioned by Victor Joze
Tax stamp upper center
Wittrock P12/B; Adriani 58/II; Delteil
  351; Adhémar 68

This was the second of Lautrec's posters to advertise a novel by Victor Joze, and it was surrounded with as much controversy as the earlier *Reine de joie* (cat. 3). The book again dwelled upon an easily exploited prejudice of many Frenchmen. Instead of anti-Semitism, Joze examined the bankruptcy of German society, taking as his title a reference to the whore of Babylon. Just over twenty years after Prussia had succeeded in humbling the French by starving Paris into submission, there continued to be an audience for anti-German themes. Lautrec's poster, based on one of the chapters in Joze's satirical examination of immorality, combined several motifs that alluded to the negative character of the entire work. German soldiers on horseback are seen from the rear, a favorite vantage point for Lautrec, but an affront to the Germans. A helmeted guard, standing at attention outside a sentry box in the foreground, has the general appearance of Kaiser Wilhelm II (who in the novel reviews a military parade led by the depraved subjects of this episode). When the poster appeared in January 1894, the Prussians were insulted, touching off a diplomatic crisis and considerable publicity. Lautrec's design was also used for the book's jacket, with the guardhouse stripes appearing on the spine. Spatters are used heavily for the sentry's coat and lightly behind the central horse and rider. Olive-green ink spatters and outlines indicate the disappearing soldiers at the top of the composition as well as a civilian couple walking along the sidewalk. The short, top-hatted gentleman appears to be accompanied by a streetwalker, who is more interested in the officer on horseback than in her companion.

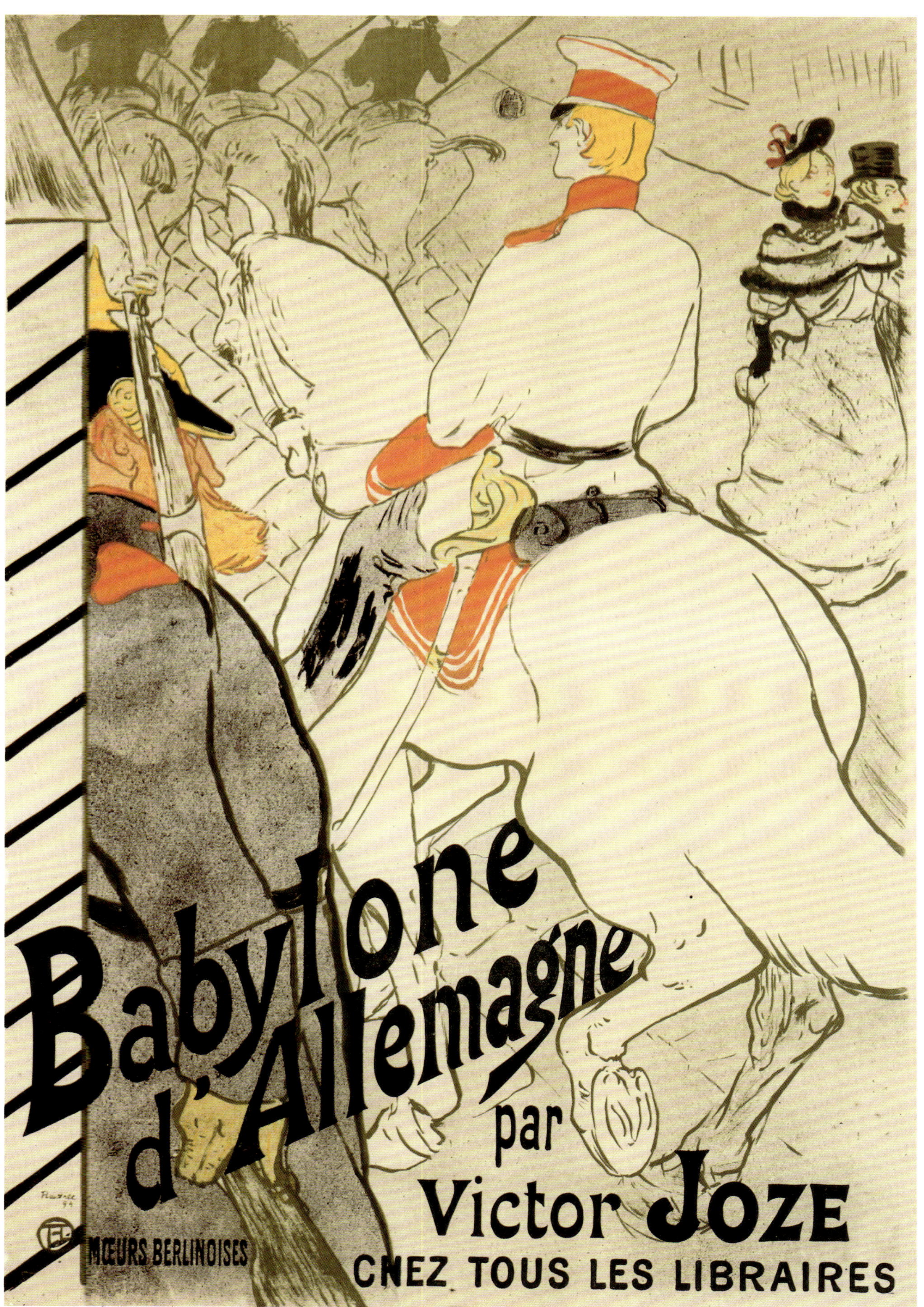

MŒURS BERLINOISES
Babylone
d'Allemagne
par
Victor JOZE
CHEZ TOUS LES LIBRAIRES

24

Au Café-concert: Aux Ambassadeurs

1894
Brush and spatter lithograph in six colors
  on wove paper
Image: 11⅞ × 9⅜ in. (30.2 × 23.8 cm)
Sheet: 24 × 17 in. (61 × 43.2 cm)
Printed by Edw. Ancourt & Cie, Paris
Published by André Marty in *L'Estampe
  originale*
Signed lower left in pencil, *HT Lautrec;*
  stamped in lower right with blindstamp
  of *L'Estampe originale* (Lugt 819)
Wittrock 58; Adriani 70; Delteil 68;
  Adhémar 73

Edgar Degas used the setting of the Ambassadeurs *café concert*—its globes of gaslight illuminating the garden in which the stage stood—for several of his most charming paintings and lithographs of the 1870s. In the midst of the Champs-Élysées since 1775, the Ambassadeurs was one of over 270 cafés in Paris at the time. Unlike Degas in his lithographs, Lautrec used color to depict a singer on stage emoting to an indistinct audience under the trees. The differences in dress, too, reveal the particular character of the singers: Degas shows his as ingenues, with black neckbands, low décolletés, fitted waists, and tight or nearly no sleeves; Lautrec's performer also has a black neckband, but since she is seen from the side, her voluminous dress and leg-of-mutton sleeves give her a mature shape, relieved by the suggestively bare nape of her neck. Lautrec's characteristic spattering provides the softness of the woman's hair and the less important spaces behind and below her. Each area is flat, yet the semblance of deep space opens up behind the chanteuse through the hint of a chandelier and the banks of electric lights around the audience. In the foreground, occupying one-third of the picture, is a lightly traced latticework around the stage. This lithograph appeared in the sixth *L'Estampe originale* album of April–June 1894, printed at Ancourt's, as Lautrec's album cover had been. The unidentified singer bears a remarkable resemblance to Lautrec's portrayal of Misia Natanson on the cover of the final album of *L'Estampe originale,* published in 1895.

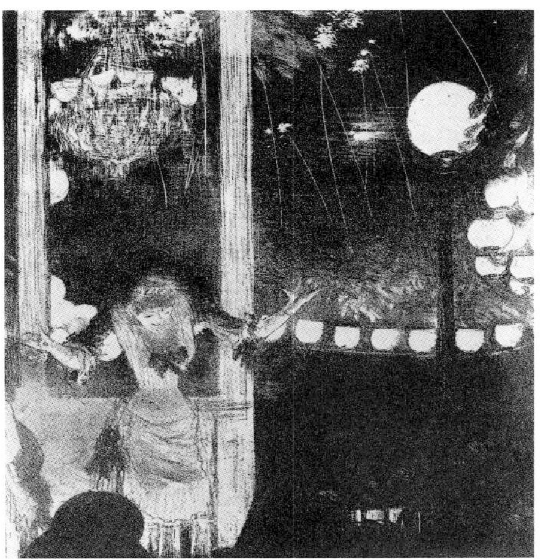

Edgar Degas, *Mademoiselle Becat at the Ambassadeurs*, ca. 1877, lithograph printed in black, 8⅛ × 7⅝ in. The Museum of Modern Art, New York, gift of Abby Aldrich Rockefeller.

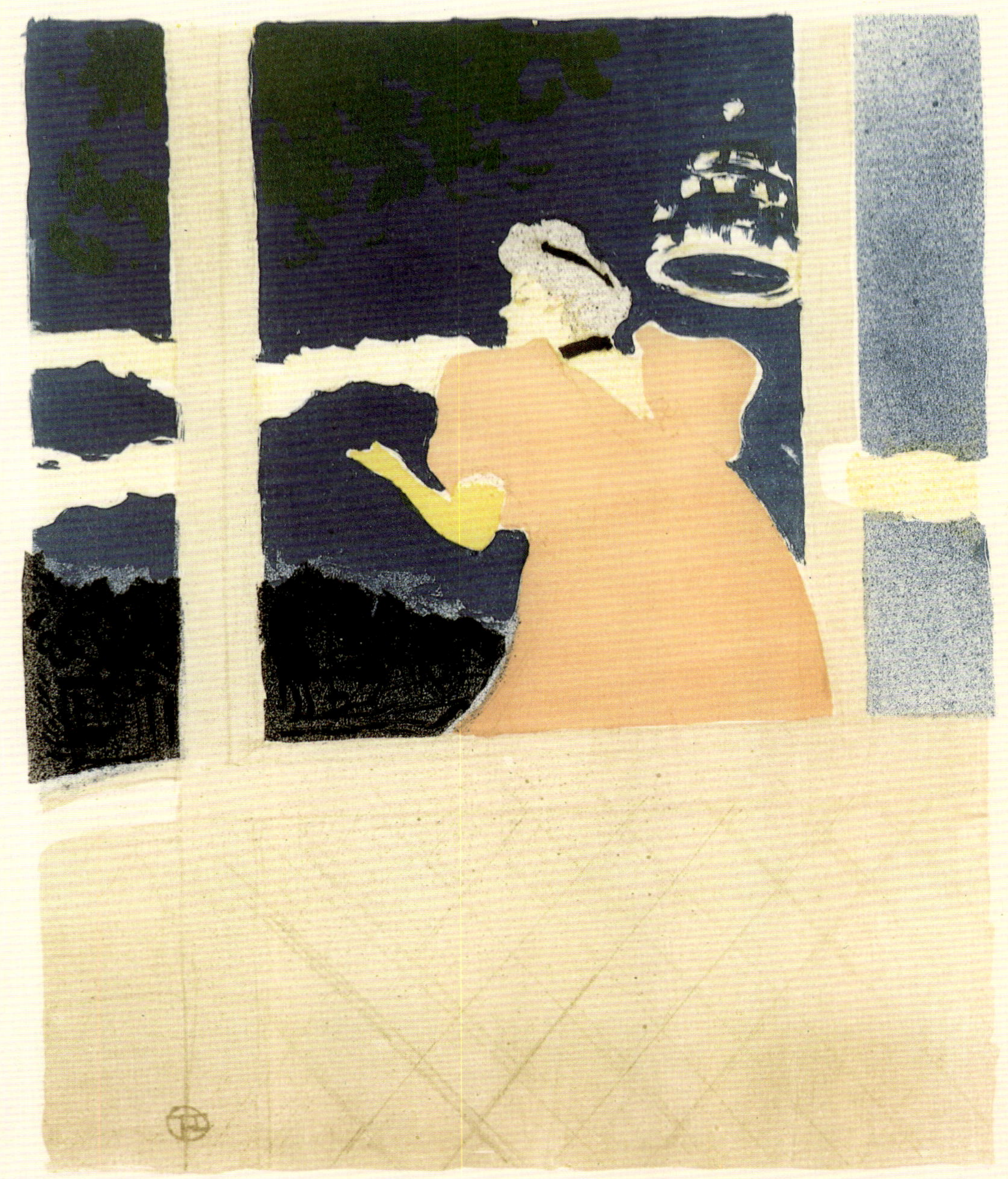

Tlautuc

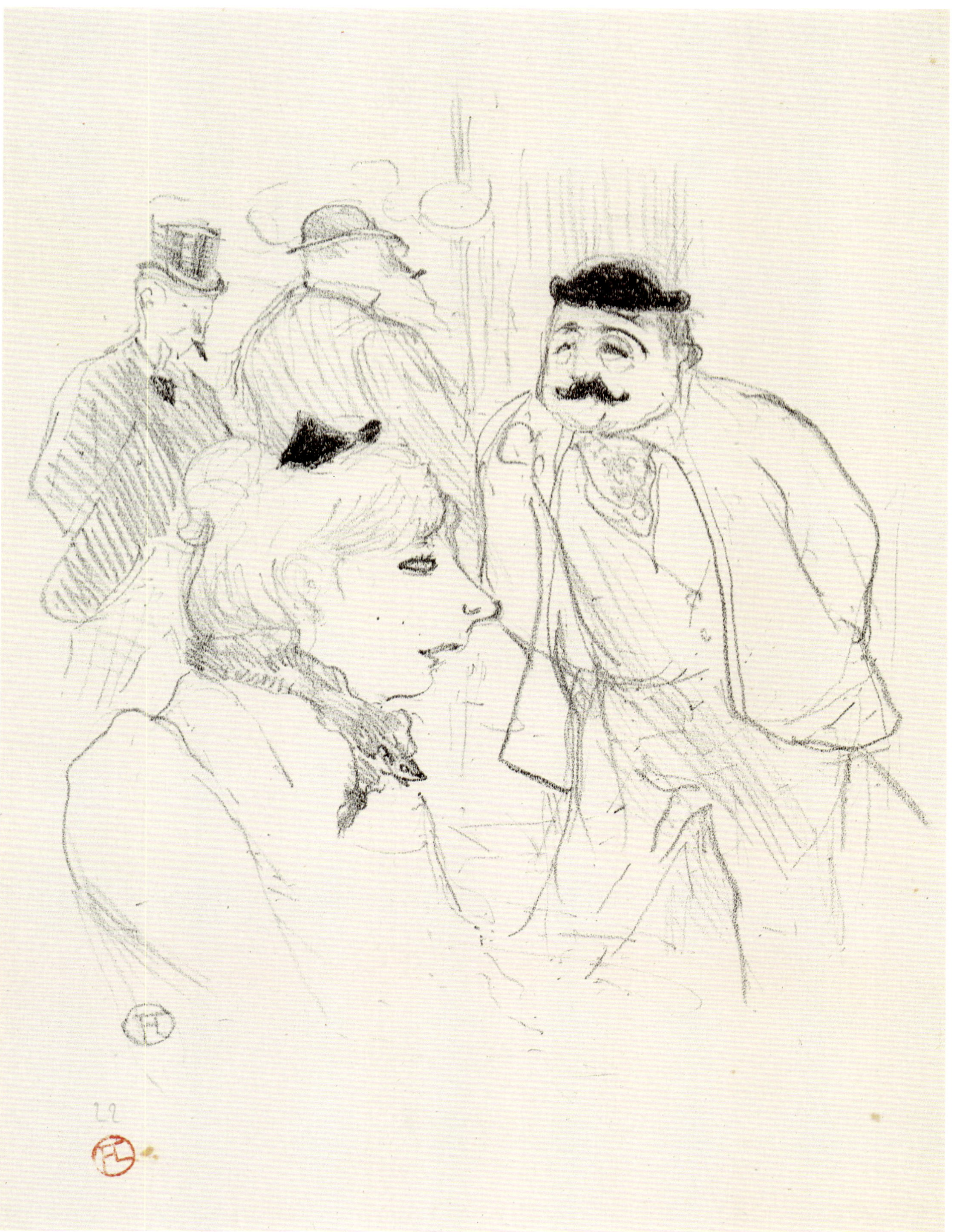

La Tige: Moulin Rouge

1894
Crayon lithograph on wove paper
Image: 11¾ × 9⅞ in. (30 × 25.1 cm)
Sheet: 15¾ × 11 in. (40 × 27.9 cm)
Only state, number 22
Published by Ed. Kleinmann, Paris
Inscribed lower left in pencil, *22*
Wittrock 63; Adriani 97; Delteil 70;
  Adhémar 78

Among the off-color amusements that Lautrec documented during his many nights at the Moulin Rouge was the ritual of picking up women. The title and subject of this print, *La Tige,* has been interpreted in at least three ways. A straight translation from French refers to the stalking procedure during hunting, which Lautrec clearly is using as a metaphor. The slang meaning of the word is also stalk, this time as a noun—that is, a skinny prostitute. Finally, La Tige may actually have been a stage name used by a performer at the Moulin Rouge. The leering man whose pants have been drawn in a suggestive manner is undoubtedly Maurice Guibert, whose eyebrows and black mustache had appeared in Lautrec's works many times before. The two men in the background probably are the artist's cousin Gabriel Tapié de Céleyran, and another friend, Tristan Bernard. The woman has not been identified, but her resemblance to Lautrec's depiction that same year of the highly regarded stage actress Berthe Bady is uncanny, and may have been intended as a joke.

La Goulue

1894

Crayon, brush, and spatter lithograph
  with scraper on wove paper
Image and sheet: 13¼ × 10⅝ in.
  (35 × 27 cm)
Song sheet edition
Printed by Chaimbaud & Cie, Paris
Published by A. Bosc
Wittrock 65/II; Adriani 95/II;
  Delteil 71; Adhémar 77

One of several covers for music and monologues that Lautrec created during 1894, this portrayal of La Goulue and her partner Valentin le Désossé dancing together was made for a waltz written in honor of the star of the Moulin Rouge. Like three monologues that Maurice Donnay wrote for Yvette Guilbert for which Lautrec designed covers the same year, the first state of this lithograph was of a larger dimension than the one published with lettering. Frequently, such monochrome lithographs were transferred to several stones or plates with the added text in order to produce larger and more economical editions. Unlike many others, particularly the large series *Mélodies de Desiré Dihau* of 1895–96, it does not seem that there were later editions made of *La Goulue*. The overall olive green of the composition contributes to the impression of light-stepping dancers who are shown as the artist had already drawn them: Valentin's distinctive, sharp profile in the Moulin Rouge poster of 1891 (cat. 1) and La Goulue's alluring back in the 1892 print *La Goulue et sa soeur* (cat. 6). Next to La Goulue's elbow is the head of a bearded man who was first shown sitting at a table at the Moulin Rouge in Lautrec's famous painting of 1892–95 (see fig., cat. 34). He has usually been identified as Maurice Guibert, who Lautrec more often depicted clean shaven, as in *La Tige: Moulin Rouge* (cat. 25).

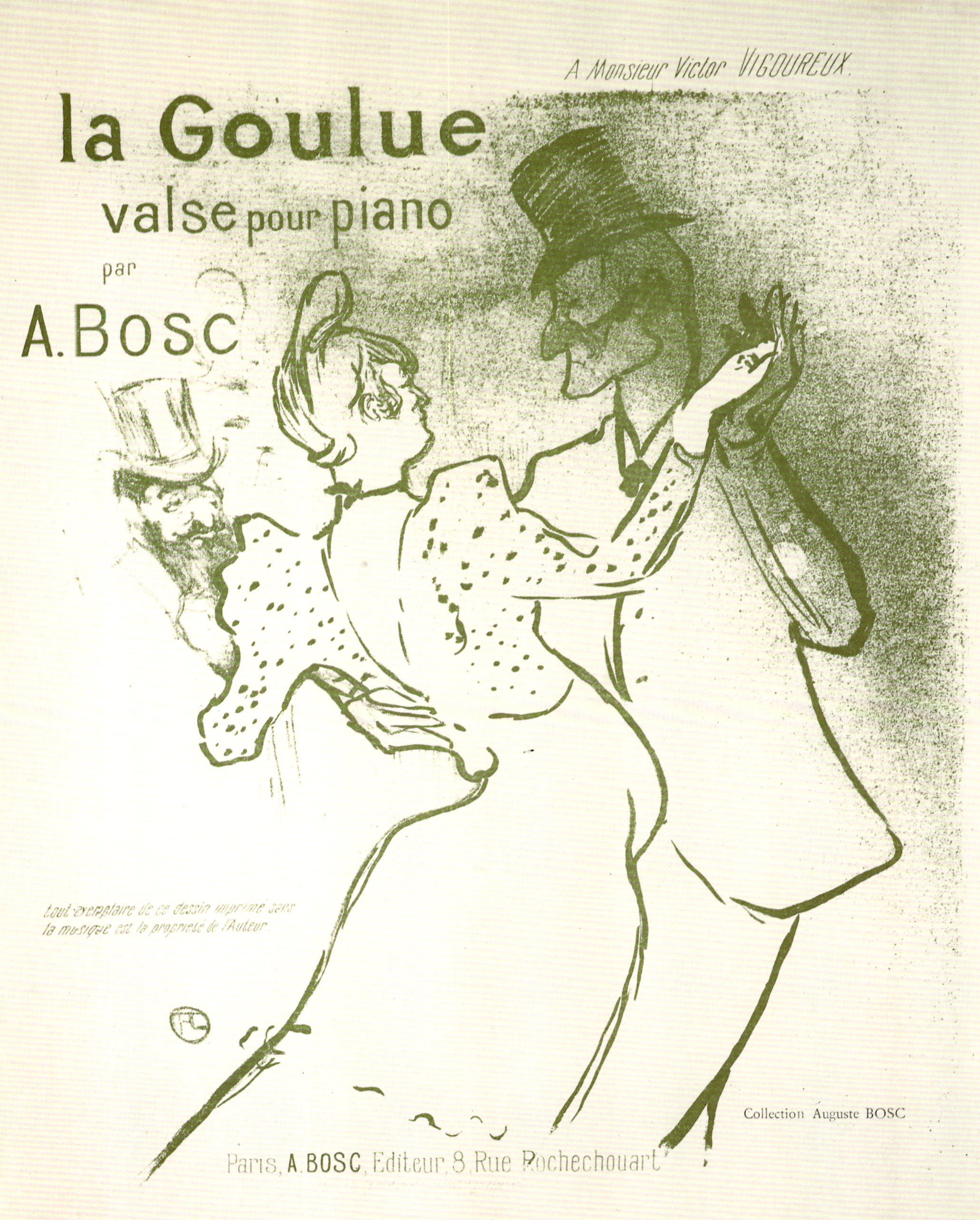
A Monsieur Victor VIGOUREUX.
la Goulue
valse pour piano
par
A. BOSC
tout exemplaire de ce dessin imprimé sans
la musique est la propriété de l'Auteur.
Collection Auguste BOSC
Paris, A. BOSC, Editeur, 8 Rue Rochechouart

27

Cecy Loftus

1895
Crayon and spatter lithograph on
  mounted China paper
Image: 14⅝ × 9¾ in. (37.1 × 24.8 cm)
Sheet: 17⅜ × 11⅜ in. (44.1 × 28.9 cm)
Published by Ed. Kleinmann, Paris
Wittrock 113; Adriani 100; Delteil 116;
  Adhémar 105

Cecy Loftus, known in English-speaking vaudeville theatres as Cissie, was born Marie-Cecilia McCarthy in Scotland to Marie Loftus, the "Sarah Bernhardt of the music halls."[1] Cecy began her stage career when she was fifteen, rising to fame as an impersonator of famous performers such as Yvette Guilbert. Henry Irving made her his leading lady after the turn of the century, and she replaced the aging Ellen Terry as Peter Pan in 1905. Loftus later worked in film. Lautrec was in London in June 1894 and may have seen Loftus on the stage there. The subject of the performance depicted in this print is not known, but the top hat, cane, and oversized gloves must have been the distinguishing features of another popular performer of the time.

1. Raymond Maner and Joe Mitchenson, *British Music Hall* (London: Gentry Books, 1965), entry no. 152.

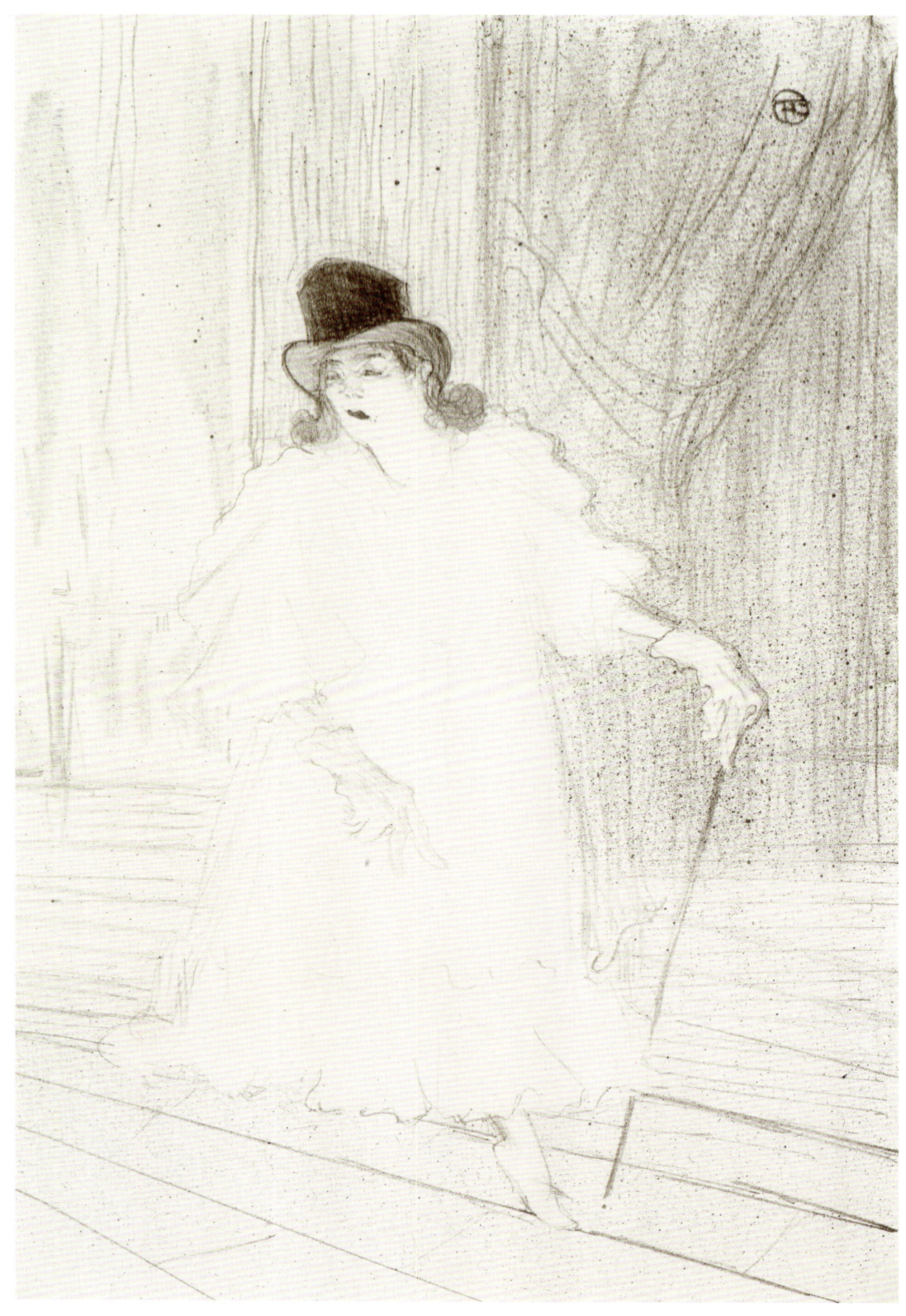

Confetti

1894
Crayon, brush, and spatter lithograph in
  three colors on wove paper
Image: 22⅜ × 15⅜ in. (56.8 × 39.1 cm)
Sheet: 22⅜ × 17⅞ in. (56.8 × 45.4 cm)
Printed by Bella & de Malherbe, London
  & Paris
Commissioned by J. & E. Bella, London
Stamped lower left with Kleinmann
  blindstamp (Lugt 1573)
Wittrock P13; Adriani 101; Delteil 352;
  Adhémar 9

J. & E. Bella was a paper manufacturer in London who sponsored the Royal Aquarium exhibitions of posters there in October 1894 and 1896. Until a disastrous episode in 1892, when over-enthusiastic throwing of plaster bits in Paris caused it to be banned, there had been no such thing as the paper confetti we know today. Lautrec was commissioned to illustrate Bella's new product, which, together with the streamers of paper he had depicted in an 1893 painting, was a less dangerous imitation of plaster confetti. Lautrec conveys the entire story in his poster of a floating, happy woman under a shower of colored pieces thrown by disembodied hands. Her lightness is like that of the new product, and she appears to be holding her hat in the breeze rather than using it as protection. This poster has been compared to Pierre Bonnard's ebullient 1891 poster *France-Champagne,* in which waist-high bubbles surround the figure of a smiling woman. Bonnard, it is said, introduced Lautrec to poster-making that year, so *Confetti* is probably an homage to his friend. As much as Lautrec's *Moulin Rouge* poster was a pioneer step toward a new style of representation, so too was Bonnard's, even though his did not so directly confront Chéret's model. Now, in *Confetti,* Lautrec appropriates Chéret's extravagantly cheerful girl-woman into his own well-organized vocabulary of stylistic idiosyncrasies. The woman's diagonally drifting form is punctuated by her solid black gloves that are in turn echoed by the spattered gray hands reaching out to shower her with confetti.

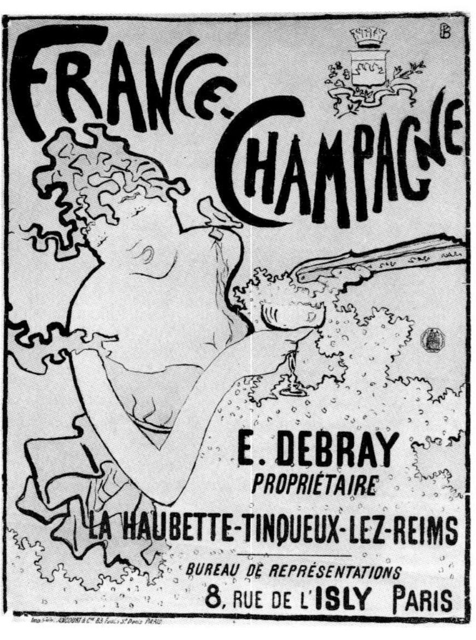

Pierre Bonnard, *France-Champagne,*
1891, color lithograph, 30⅛ × 23 in.
The Museum of Modern Art, New York,
Abby Aldrich Rockefeller Fund.

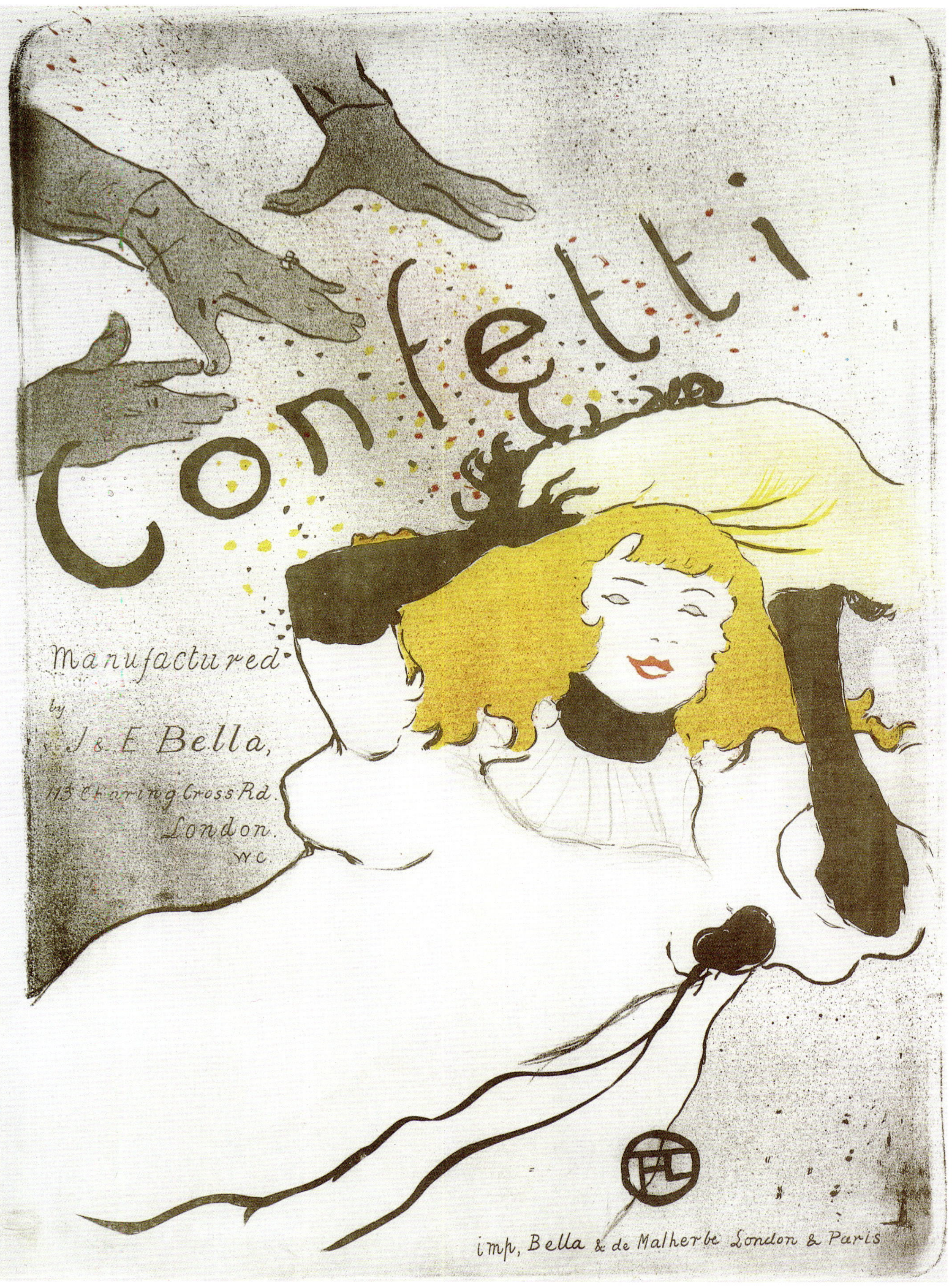
Confetti
Manufactured
by
J & E Bella,
113 Charing Cross Rd.
London.
W.C.
imp, Bella & de Malherbe London & Paris

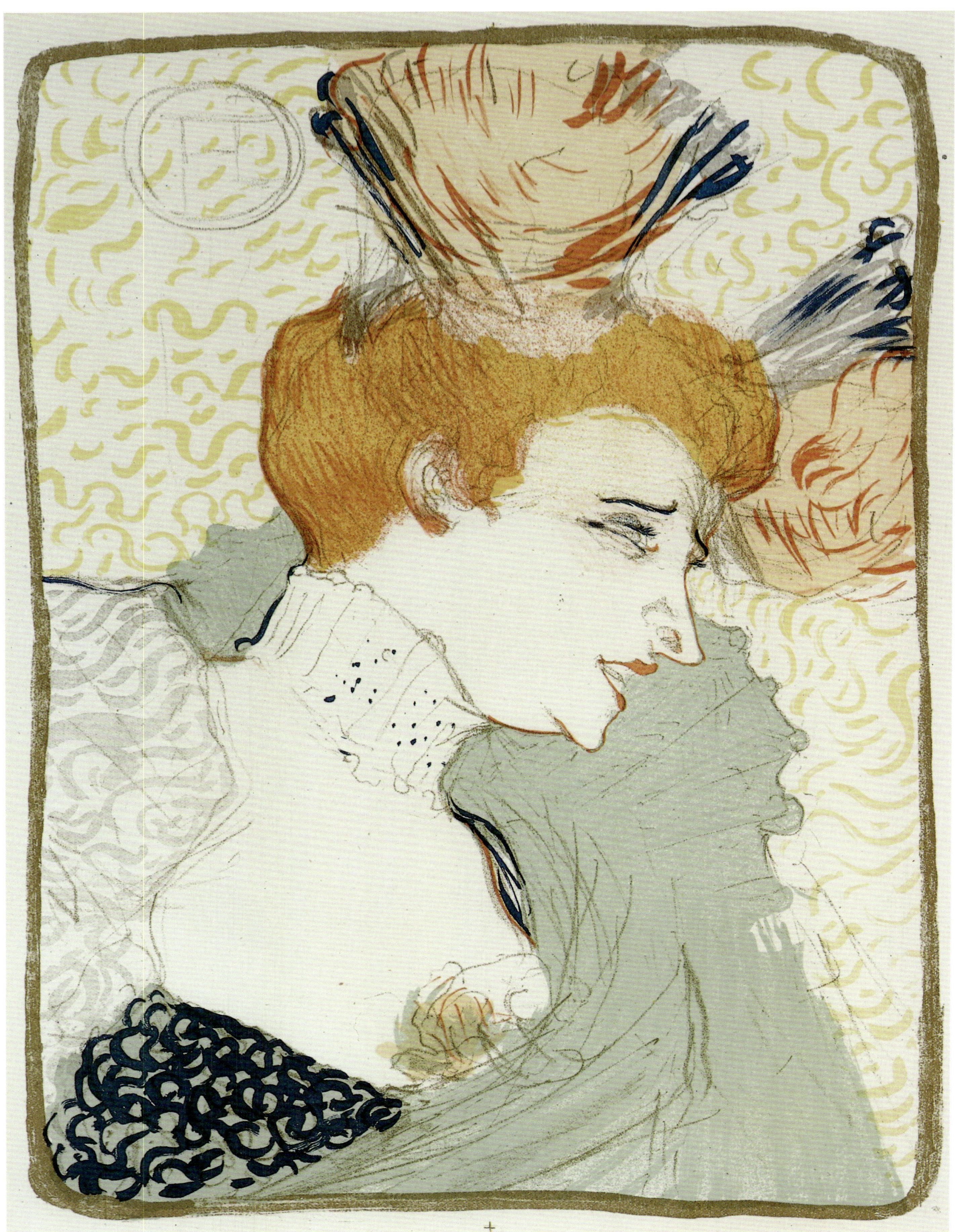

Mademoiselle Marcelle Lender, en buste

1895
Crayon, brush, and spatter lithograph
  in eight colors on Japan paper
Image: 12⅝ × 9⅝ in. (32 × 24.4 cm)
Sheet: 14½ × 14 in. (36.8 × 35.6 cm)
Fourth state, *Pan* edition of 1895
Printed by Edw. Ancourt & Cie
  (H. Stern), Paris
Published by *Pan* magazine in conjunc-
  tion with vol. 1, no. 3; this impression
  was included in the German edition
  of *Pan*
Wittrock 99/IV; Adriani 115/IVb;
  Delteil 102/III; Adhémar 131/III

Lautrec was captivated by the performance of the renowned Marcelle Lender (Anne-Marie Marcelle Bastien) in the role of Queen Galswintha in Florimond Ronger Hervé's operetta *Chilpéric*. Lender, who had acted on the stage since she was sixteen, made an enormous impression on the artist at the Théâtre des Variétés, particularly at the moment in the Merovingian spectacle when she danced for King Chilpéric. Lender's stirring dance, performed in a Spanish dress with large red poppies in her red hair, became the artist's creative focus in a large painting and five lithographs. This lithographic portrait of Lender, her head at nearly the identical angle depicted in the painting, emphasizes her animated face. The gaiety of her performance is vividly conveyed in Lautrec's masterful use of pattern against the brilliant passage from red to orange to green that frames her vivacious countenance. To her costume Lautrec added a pleated wrap at her shoulder and a red rose where, in the painting, her low décolletage had revealed too much. As it was, the print was considered too risqué by the conservative management of *Pan*, the German publication for which it was commissioned. Julius Meier-Graefe, the young editor of *Pan* who had wanted to include the more advanced French artists in the magazine, probably obtained this print from Lautrec at the suggestion of Adolphe Albert's brother Henri, the magazine's French agent. Although he argued successfully for its inclusion in *Pan*, Meier-Graefe lost his job shortly after the print's appearance.

May Belfort

1895
Brush lithograph on wove paper
Image: 31¼ × 24 in. (79.4 × 61 cm)
Sheet: 31⅛ × 23¾ in. (79 × 60.3 cm)
Trial proof
Commissioned by May Belfort
Wittrock P14/trial proof i; Adriani
   126/I; Delteil 354; Adhémar 116

In this and the following example of the fetching poster Lautrec made at the request of May Belfort (May Egan), it is possible to see both the bare bones of the artist's drawn concept and the final result. Underlying most of Lautrec's lithographs is a drawing on the first stone, or keystone. In this and the majority of his other posters, a sketch and/or painted maquette provided the model, sometimes traced onto the stone, but nearly always modified to give the final print the proportions and balances best suited to its use as a poster. First proofs of the keystone were most frequently printed in green and sometimes painted over by the artist in the colors that were to be added. Lautrec's first idea for color was to make Belfort's dress a brushed red. In early proofs, the stone carrying the brushed passage was printed over the image from the keystone. Afterward, Lautrec reworked the red stone so that, when the edition was printed, a solid red covered almost all the brushed areas, as seen in cat. 31.

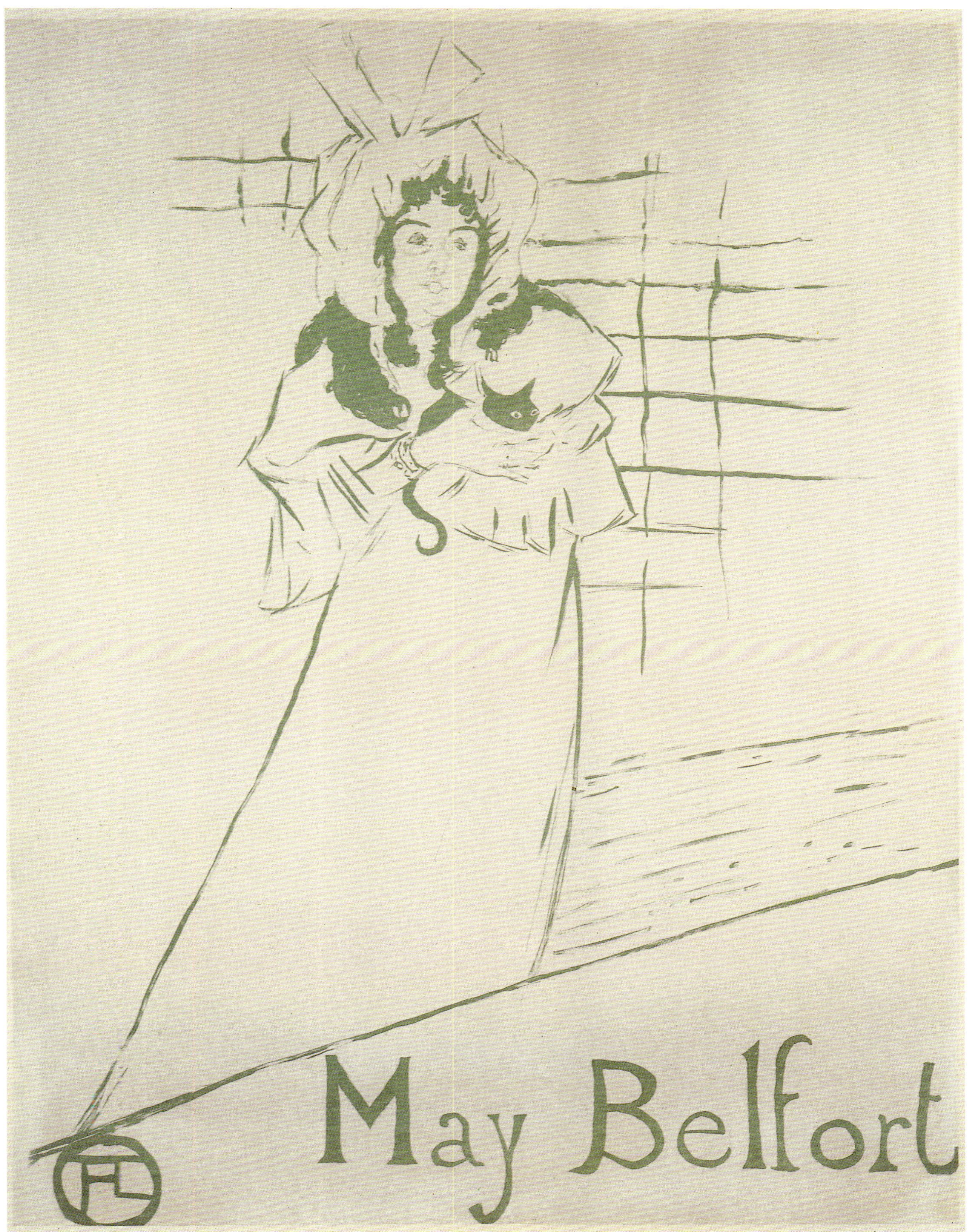
May Belfort

31

May Belfort

1895

Crayon, brush, and spatter lithograph
  in four colors on wove paper
Image: 31¼ × 24 in. (79.4 × 61 cm)
Sheet: 31⅛ × 24⅛ in. (79 × 61.3 cm)
Published by Ed. Kleinmann, Paris
Commissioned by May Belfort
Wittrock P14/Biv; Adriani 126/IV;
  Delteil 354/II; Adhémar 116/II

May Belfort, an Irish singer, asked Lautrec to make this poster for her performance at the Petit Casino. The artist had become enchanted by Belfort's appearance at the Cabaret des Décadents in 1895 and made five lithographs of her in her remarkable costume. The poster portrays her in a frilly baby's bonnet holding a small black kitten, the stage prop for a suggestive song she delivered in a childish voice. Although she had sung in London's music halls and danced at the Jardin de Paris in 1893, her career was made most memorable through Lautrec's pictures of her. She was the lover of another British performer, May Milton, who also commissioned a poster from Lautrec. He obliged Milton with a work of identical size and similar spirit (cat. 34).

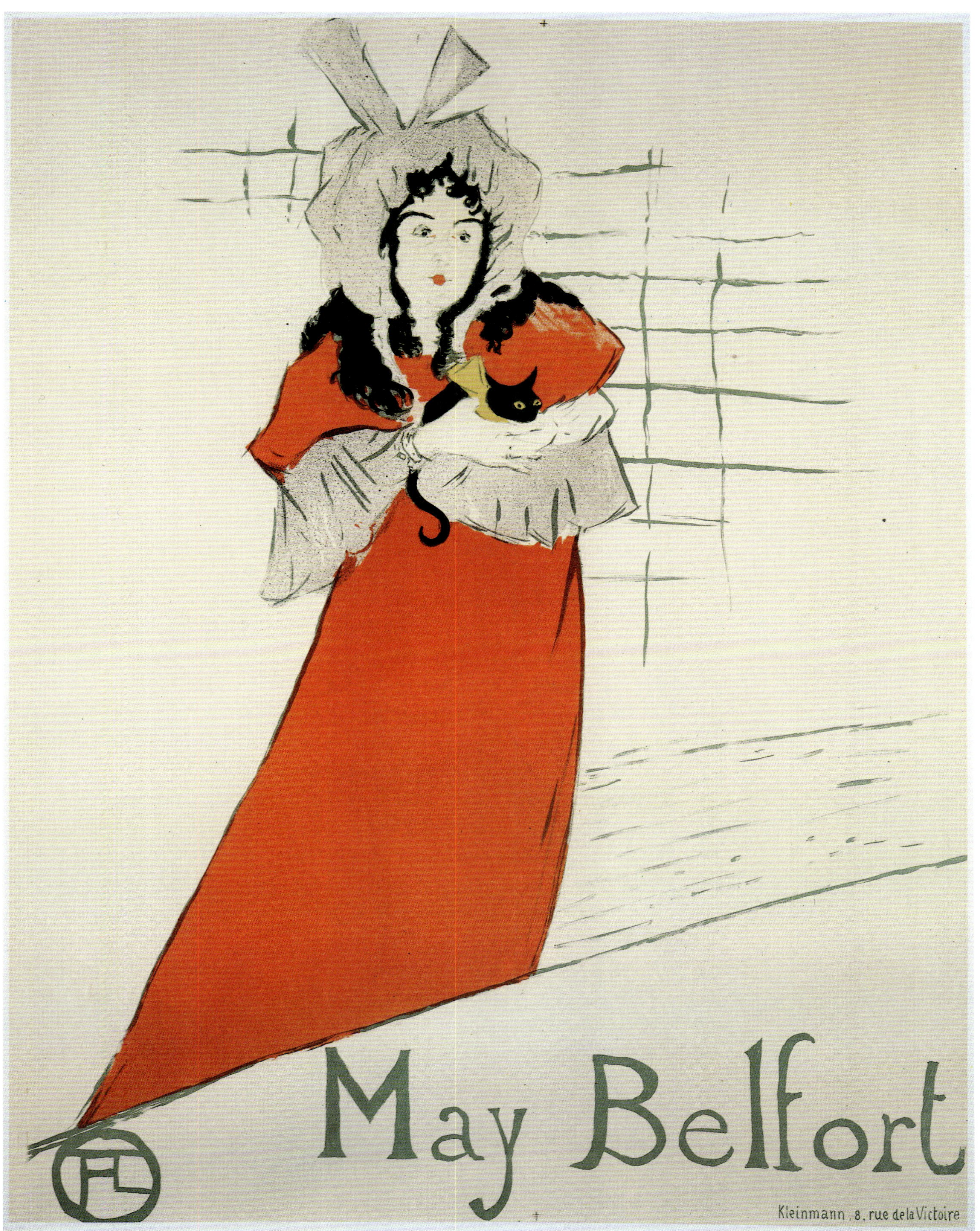

May Belfort
Kleinmann, 8, rue de la Victoire

32

La Revue blanche

1895

Crayon, brush, and spatter lithograph
 in four colors on two sheets of wove
 paper
Image: 48⅞ × 35⅝ in. (124.1 × 90.5 cm)
Sheet: 50 × 36 in. (127 × 91.4 cm)
Printed by Edw. Ancourt & Cie, Paris
Commissioned by *La Revue blanche* as
 their annual poster for 1896
Published by G. Charpentier and
 E. Fasquelle, Paris
Wittrock P16/C; Adriani 130/III;
 Delteil 355; Adhémar 115

Unlike Lautrec's posters of stars, this one advertising the art and literary journal *La Revue blanche* depicts the wife of Thadée Natanson, one of its publishers, a woman of class. Brought up in a convent, Misia Natanson had a charming and free spirit that set her apart. She and her close half-brother, Cipa Godebski, were the children of a successful Polish sculptor who had moved to Paris around 1880. Lautrec chose her image as he had chosen others, for her radiant personality. Misia Natanson was a talented descendant of a musical family on her mother's side and had studied piano with Gabriel Fauré. After her marriage, she welcomed to her home many of France's most outstanding writers and artists, whose work was discussed in her husband's journal. Lautrec was only one of several admirers who spent long hours at the Natanson apartment and at their country homes, even though his hostess had mixed feelings about his appearance, drunkenness, and incorrigible wit. He sketched and painted her, often as she was absorbed in some activity. Lautrec used Misia as a model for his second cover for *L'Estampe originale* in 1895, showing her from the back as a member of an audience. It is clear that Lautrec could not have chosen any other model for this poster, commissioned by *La Revue blanche* for publication in 1896, given his well-documented infatuation with its boss's wife. Here she is performing, so to speak, as she moves toward the left in her skating costume; her feet are not visible and one arm, enveloped in a fur muff, is cut off. The diagonal positioning of Misia's body not only gives an impression of gliding but also allows space for the text of the advertisement. Skating was an activity that Lautrec had observed earlier in 1895 at the Palais de Glace, located at the Rond Point in the Champs-Élysées. He made two prints of a woman skater there, one of which was a sprightly sketch that was appended to the upper right corner of the limited edition without lettering of this poster.

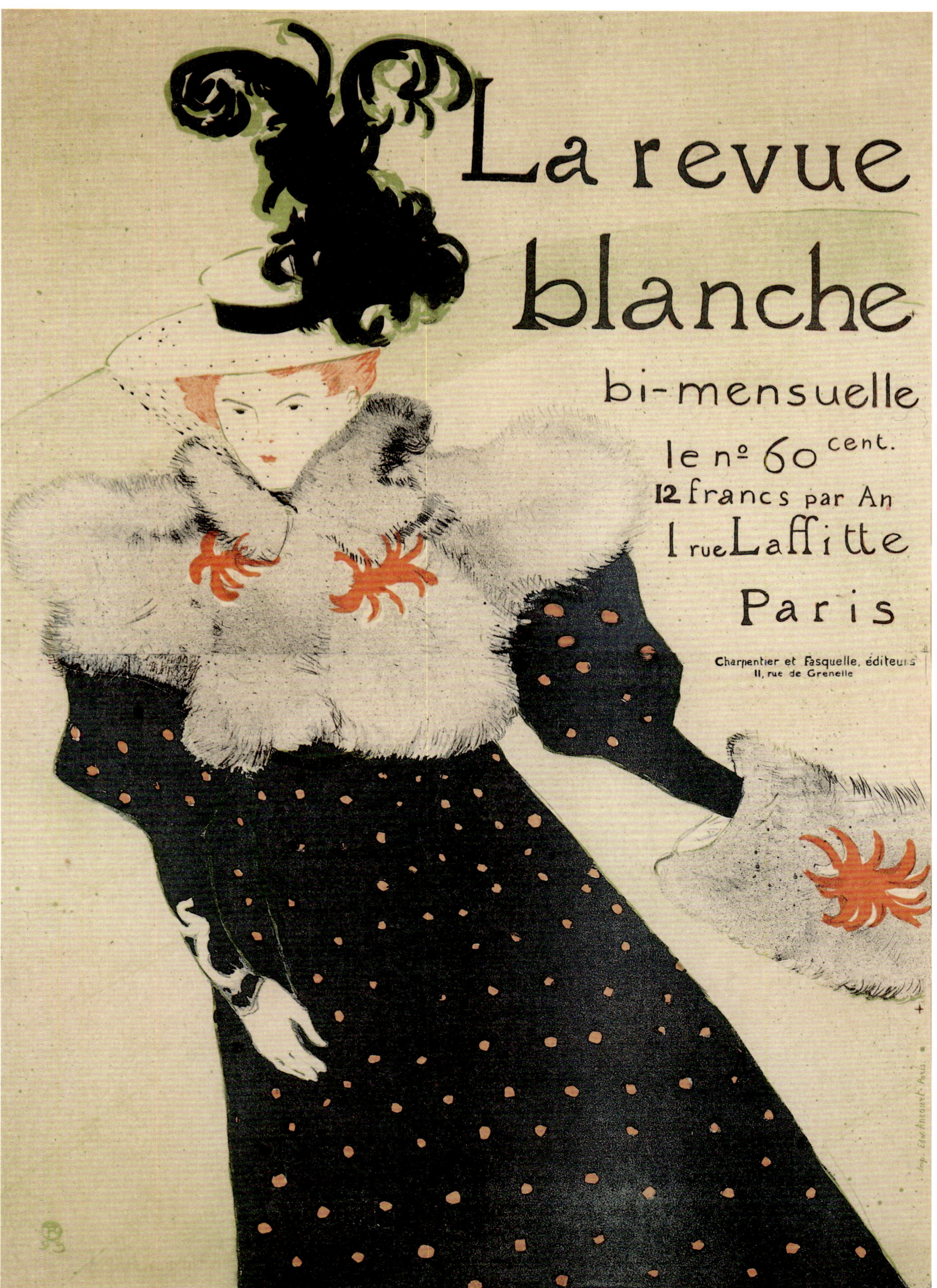

La revue
blanche
bi-mensuelle
le nº 60 cent.
12 francs par An
1 rue Laffitte
Paris
Charpentier et Fasquelle, éditeurs
11, rue de Grenelle

L'Argent

1895
Crayon, brush, and spatter lithograph
  in six colors on wove paper
Image and sheet: 12½ × 9¼ in. (31.8 ×
  23.5 cm)
Second state, theater program edition
  of 1895
Printed by Eugène Verneau, Paris
Published by Théâtre Libre as the
  program for the play *L'Argent*
Wittrock 97; Adriani 133/II; Delteil
  15/II; Adhémar 148

Lautrec made one of his few compositions that embodies the antinaturalist style of Les Nabis as a program for a play at the Théâtre Libre that opened May 5, 1895. The totally flat figures against flat planes indicating an interior show a kinship with the work of his contemporaries Pierre Bonnard, Félix Vallotton, and Édouard Vuillard. Instead of setting the type on the plain area of the woman's dress, someone other than the artist placed it on top of the picture's deserted dinner table, a busy still life upon which the text became nearly illegible. *L'Argent* was a comedy by Émile Fabre, who later managed the Comédie-Française for twenty-three years. The actors depicted are Arquillière and Henriot playing the roles of Mme and M. Reynard. The play concerns Mme Reynard, who is expecting a lifetime inheritance from her husband, a chocolate manufacturer. Lautrec depicts the point at which she reveals that, when he was on the verge of bankruptcy and too spineless to ask for credit, she went to the banker herself. Because he believes she has yielded herself to the banker, M. Reynard turns his back on her, telling her to get out. The rest of the play is about Mme Reynard's revenge. André Antoine played the Reynards' son-in-law in this, his last play as director of the Théâtre Libre.

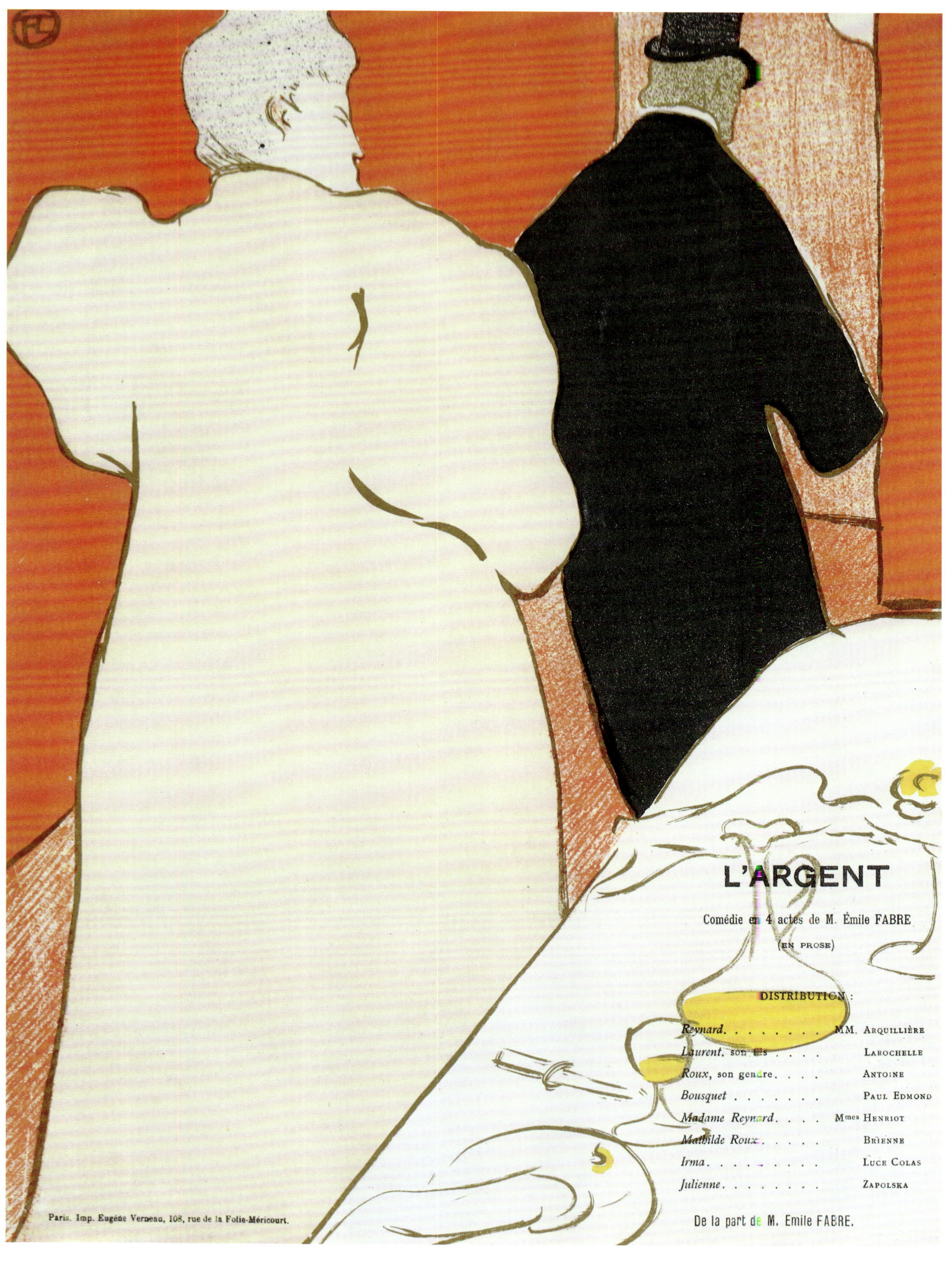
L'ARGENT
Comédie en 4 actes de M. Émile FABRE
(EN PROSE)
DISTRIBUTION :
Reynard. . . . . MM. ARQUILLIÈRE
Laurent, son fils . . . . LAROCHELLE
Roux, son gendre. . . . ANTOINE
Bousquet . . . . PAUL EDMOND
Madame Reynard . . . . Mmes HENRIOT
Mathilde Roux . . . . . BRIENNE
Irma . . . . LUCE COLAS
Julienne . . . . ZAPOLSKA
De la part de M. Emile FABRE.
Paris. Imp. Eugène Verneau, 108, rue de la Folie-Méricourt.

34

May Milton

1895
Crayon, brush, spatter, and transferred
  screen lithograph in five colors on
  wove paper
Image: 31 × 23⅝ in. (78.7 × 60.1 cm)
Sheet: 30⅞ × 23¾ in. (78.4 × 60.3 cm)
Printed by Edw. Ancourt & Cie, Paris
Commissioned by May Milton
Wittrock P17/B; Adriani 134/II; Delteil
  356/II; Adhémar 149/II

Lautrec is thought to have met this English dancer in the same year that she ordered this poster. She was performing, as did her lover, May Belfort, at the Cabaret des Décadents. Her face appears to have been nearly the opposite of Lautrec's: her small upturned nose sunken between small eyes, her mouth and chin jutting forward. Apparently captivated by Milton's looks, Lautrec extended the height and width of his ambitious painting *Au Moulin Rouge* and filled the new space on the right with her eerie stage-lit face. He depicted many of his friends in the painting, and it may have been Jane Avril, one of its main figures, who introduced Milton to Lautrec. Avril, who had commissioned several posters from Lautrec, probably suggested that Milton do the same to publicize her imminent tour of the United States. In the poster Milton is shown like an awkward marionette, one foot kicking out to the back at an impossible angle. Under her simple white dress, a pink-and-black patterned underskirt is revealed, and her yellow hair partly obscures her name. While Belfort continued to figure in Lautrec's work through 1898, Milton disappeared entirely.

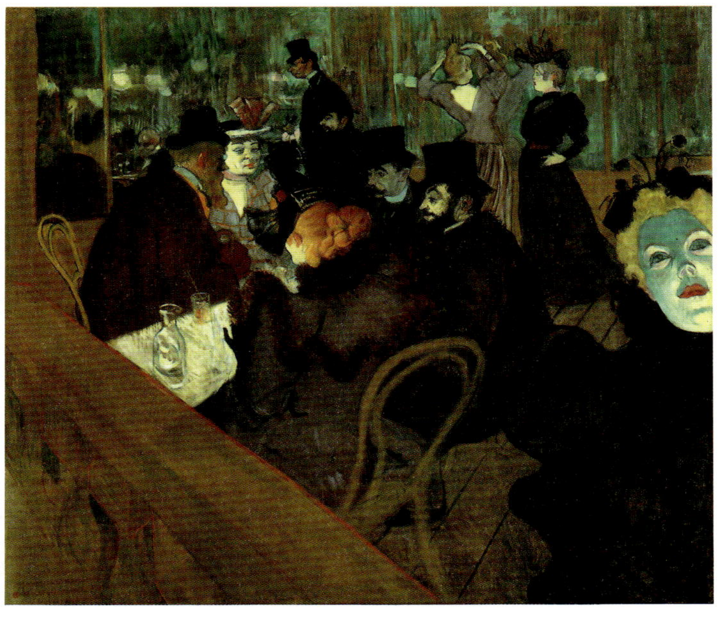

Henri de Toulouse-Lautrec,
Au Moulin Rouge, 1892–95, oil
on canvas, 48⅜ × 55¼ in. The Art
Institute of Chicago, Helen Birch
Bartlett Memorial Collection.

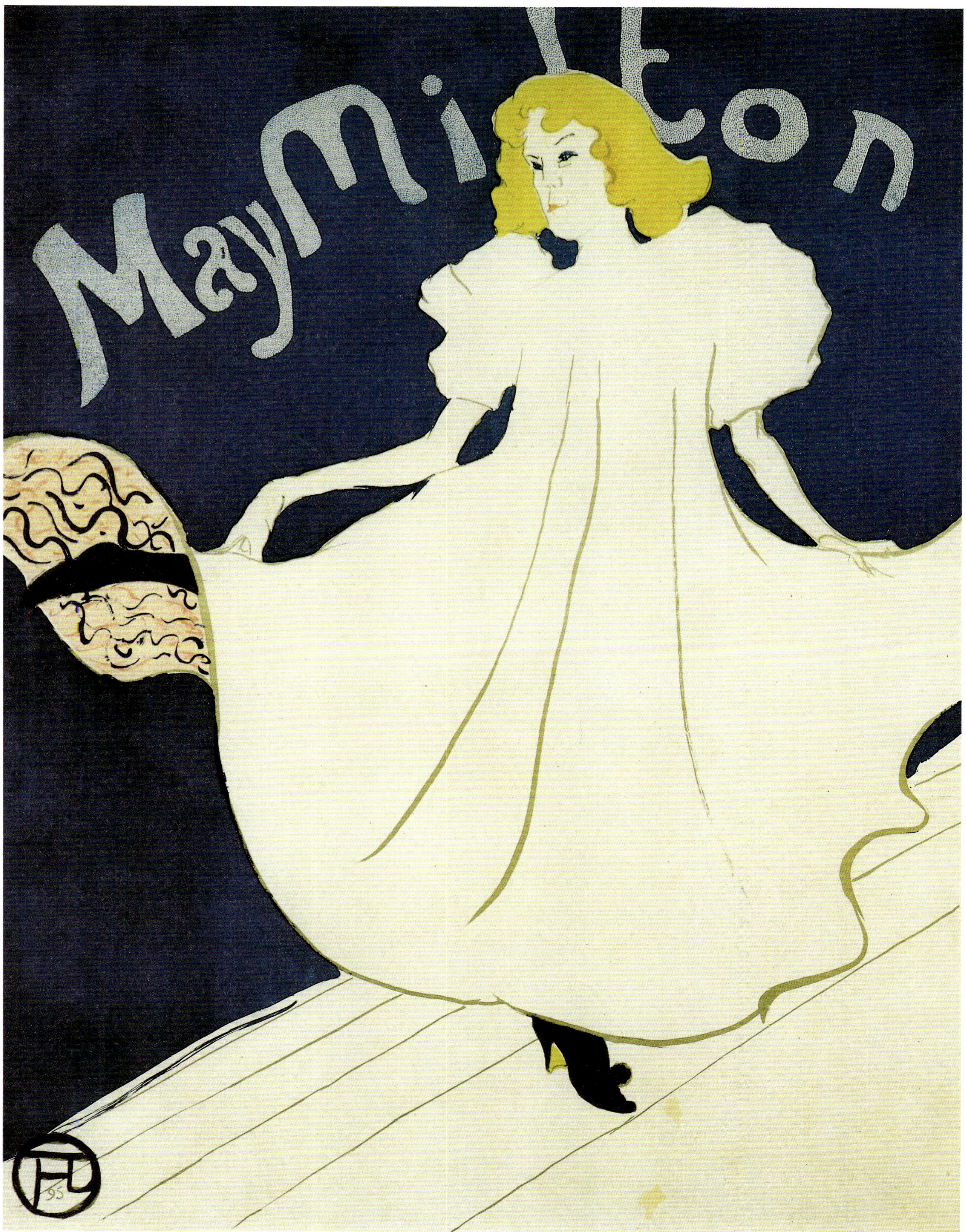
May Milton

35

Napoléon

1895
Crayon, brush, and spatter lithograph
  in six colors on wove paper
Image: 23⅜ × 17⅞ in. (59.4 × 45.4 cm)
Sheet: 24¾ × 19 in. (62.9 × 48.3 cm)
Only state, number 42
Printed by Edw. Ancourt & Cie, Paris
Signed lower left in pencil, *HTLautrec
  No. 42*
Wittrock 140; Adriani 135; Delteil 358;
  Adhémar 150

The serialization of W. Milligan Sloane's *History of Napoleon I* in New York's prominent *Century* magazine was an event that had some publicity value. Maurice Joyant, the director of Boussod, Valadon et Cie and Lautrec's close friend, held a competition to design a poster to advertise the event. A jury consisting of three academic painters and an expert on Napoléon was assembled, and twenty-one artists entered their designs. Lautrec's maquette centered on the figure of Napoléon in a composition he hoped would appeal to the conservative jury. On either side of the emperor ride a mameluke and a marshall, representing his campaigns in Egypt and Europe. Their three horses have been colored blue-black, white, and red-brown, and in their grouping they evoke the French tricolor. Perhaps Lautrec's iconography was too subtle and Napoléon's downcast eyes unheroic; the jury did not choose his poster. Instead, the commission was won by Lucien Métivet, a fellow student of Lautrec at Cormon's studio, whose formal presentation of the emperor held aloft by an eagle was unequivocally the academic vision of the jury. Despite his loss, Lautrec had one hundred copies of his work printed at Ancourt's.

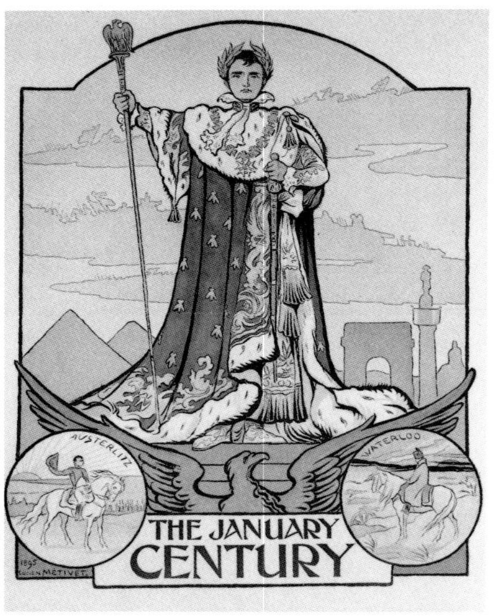

Lucien Métivet, *Napoléon*, 1895, color
lithograph, 22 × 18 in. Private collection.

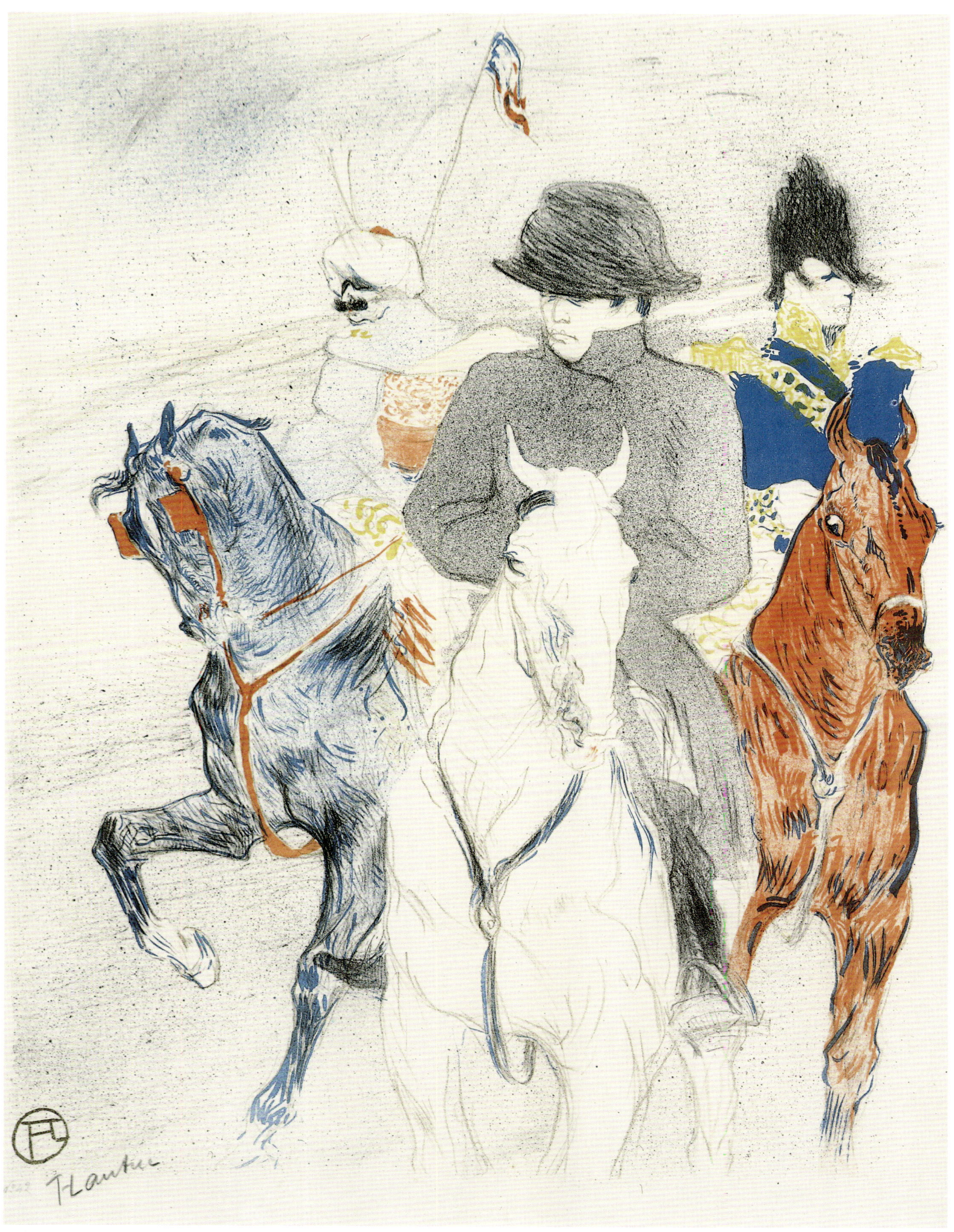

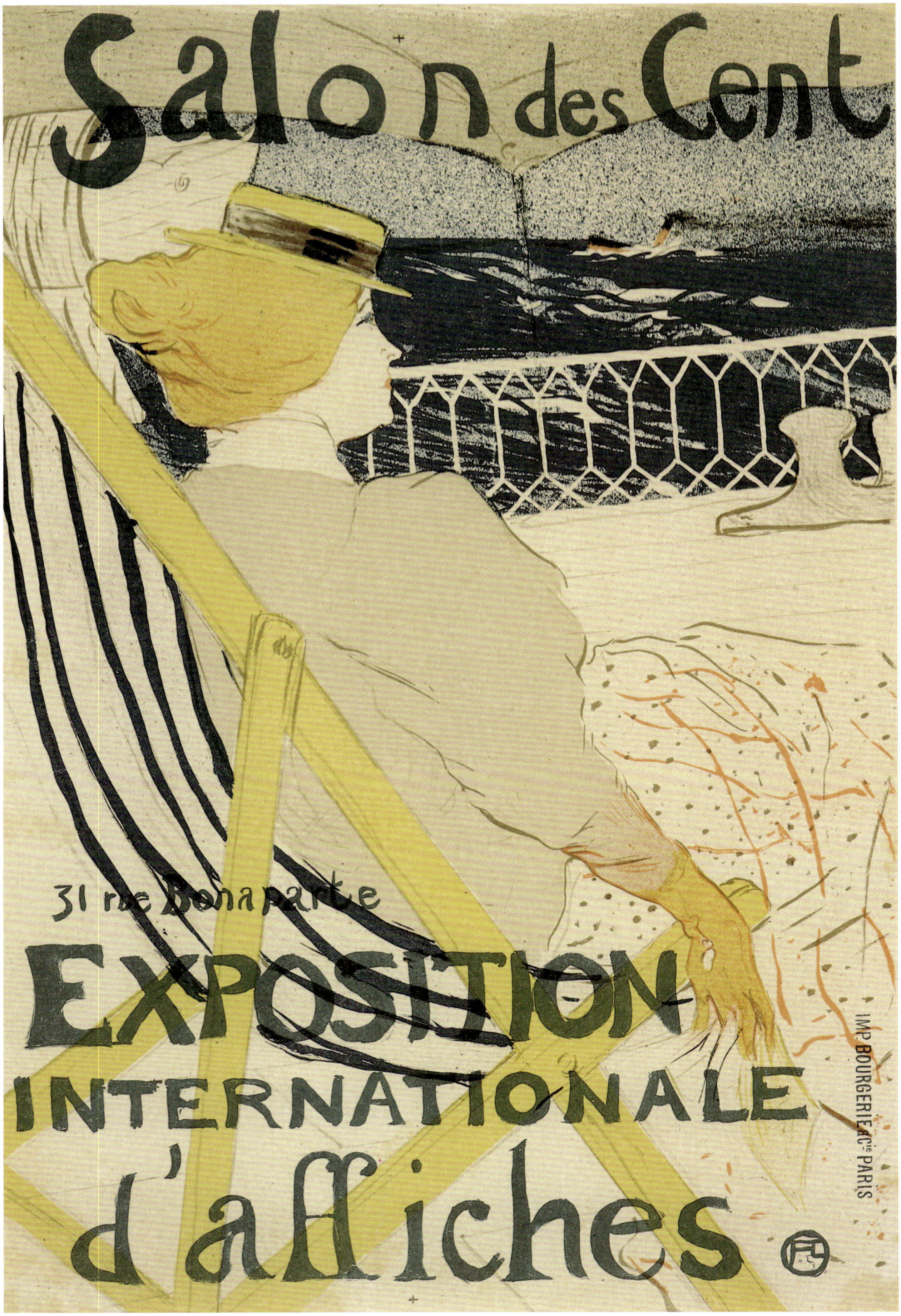

Salon des Cent
31 rue Bonaparte
EXPOSITION
INTERNATIONALE
d'affiches
IMP BOURGERIE&Cie PARIS

36

La Passagère du 54: Promenade en yacht

1895

Brush, crayon, and spatter lithograph
  in seven colors on wove paper
Image: 23⅞ × 15¾ in. (60.6 × 40 cm)
Sheet: 24⅛ × 16 in. (61.3 × 40.6 cm)
Printed by Bourgerie et Cie, Paris
Commissioned by *La Plume* (Léon
  Deschamps) as a poster for an
  international exhibition of posters
  at the Salon des Cent
Wittrock P20/II; Adriani 137/III;
  Delteil 366.II; Adhémar 188/II

In the summer of 1895, Lautrec, Maurice Guibert (his companion on many excursions), and Dr. and Mme Bourges boarded a ship called the *Chili* in Le Havre to begin a voyage to Lisbon. The plan was to leave the ship in Portugal and travel across Spain back to France, ending the trip with a visit to Lautrec's mother near Bordeaux. The ship was to continue south to Africa. On the ship the artist's attention was caught by a beautiful woman who was on her way to meet her husband in Dakar. Guibert took photographs of her, one of which later served as the model for this poster. When he returned to Paris, Lautrec created this lithograph for one of the periodic exhibitions, known as the Salon des Cent, held by the journal *La Plume* at its offices. Beginning in February 1894, nearly every exhibition had a special poster. Lautrec's poster of a beautiful woman followed the pattern of most of the forty-three that were produced before the last show in 1900. The poster without letters was included in the October 1895 special edition of *La Plume*. With letters it may have been used as the generic poster for Salon des Cent exhibitions from October through March or April. The lady from cabin 54, seen from the rear as she calmly views the sea after abandoning her reading, remains an enigma. As he had with his portraits of Bruant and others, Lautrec enhanced the attraction by not letting the viewer see too much. Although Guibert could not have photographed the lovely passenger so many times without having become acquainted, however formally, Lautrec's work provides a sense of detachment and dreaming, the mysterious circumstances of which lure the imagination.

Irish and American Bar, rue Royale: The Chap Book

1895
Crayon, brush, spatter, and transferred
  screen lithograph in five colors on
  wove paper
Image: 15¾ × 22⅞ in. (40 × 58.1 cm)
Sheet: 16⅞ × 23⅞ in. (42.2 × 60.6 cm)
Printed by Chaix, Paris
Commissioned by the magazine *The
  Chap Book*, Chicago
Distributed by *La Plume*, Paris
Wittrock P18/B; Adriani 139/II; Delteil
  362/II; Adhémar 189

Seated at a bar frequented by the British sporting crowd are Baron Rothschild's coachman, Tom, nattily turned out with a flower in his lapel, and a mustached colleague. Behind the bar at 33 rue Royale is Ralph, a bartender of American Indian and Chinese ancestry from San Francisco, mixing a cocktail in a shaker. Both Tom and Ralph were portrayed in other prints by Lautrec around this time. The poster, published by *La Plume*, advertised *The Chap Book*, an American literary periodical distributed by the French publisher. Just a few months before its publication, Lautrec had begun to use a new monogram: an elephant containing his initials. Although the elephant monogram's first appearance was on a page of text by Tristan Bernard in *NIB*, a supplement to *La Revue blanche* issued on January 1, 1895, it did not acquire its tail until its use on this poster much later in the year. The lettering at the top is filled with dots transferred from a screen. This is the first poster Lautrec executed on which he noted that it was printed by Chaix (Atelier Chéret). Small numbers identifying this poster's job record accompany both Chaix's address and its exotic trademark at the lower right.

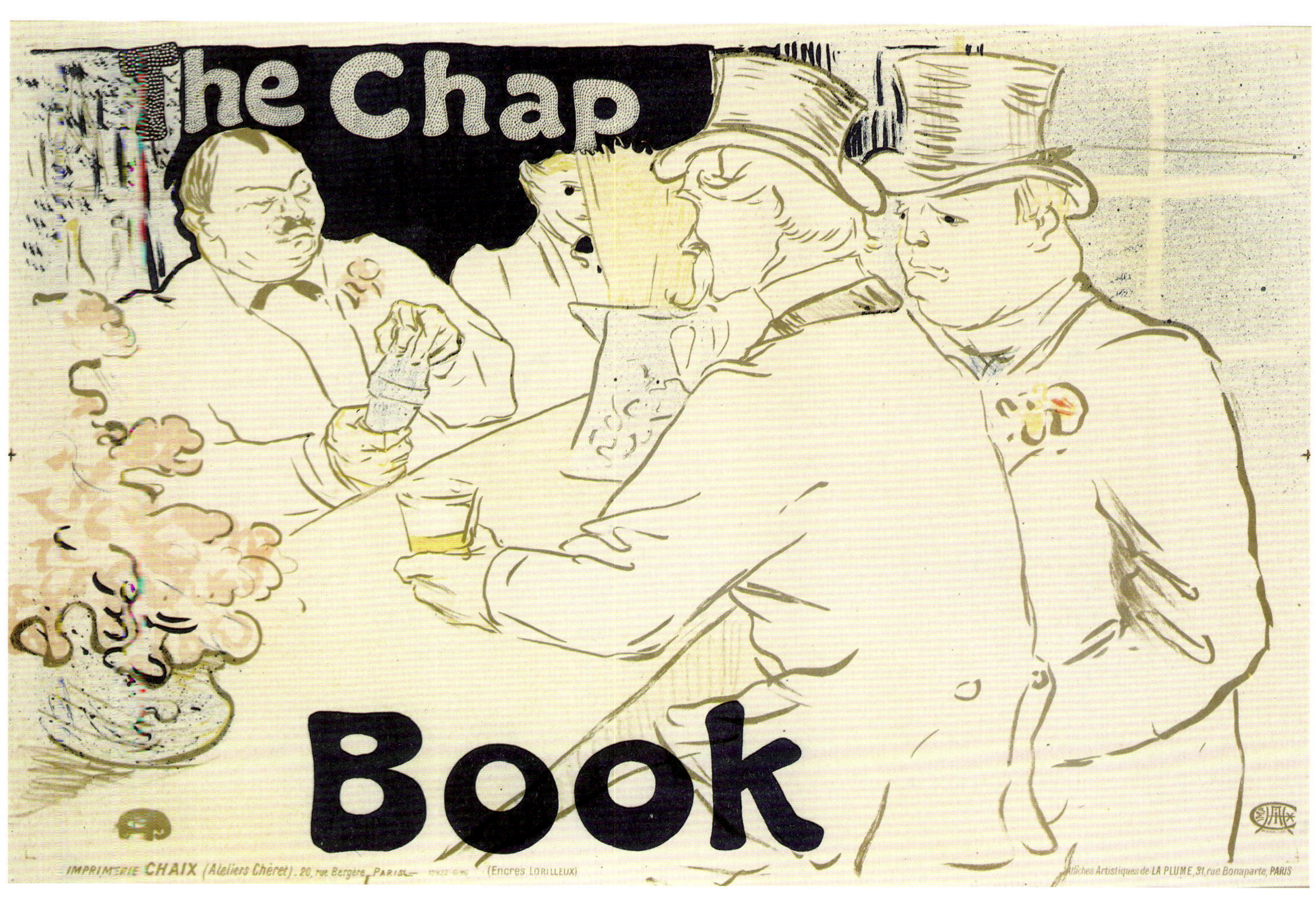

The Chap
Book
IMPRIMERIE CHAIX (Ateliers Chéret), 20, rue Bergère, PARIS — (Encres LORILLEUX)
Affiches Artistiques de LA PLUME, 31, rue Bonaparte, PARIS

38

Mademoiselle Pois Vert

1895
Crayon lithograph on wove paper
Image: 7¼ × 7½ in. (18.4 × 19 cm)
Sheet: 20¼ × 15¾ in. (51.4 × 40 cm)
Published by Ed. Kleinmann, Paris
Wittrock 122; Adriani 141; Delteil 126;
  Adhémar 141

This lithograph was among the last of Lautrec's prints published by Kleinmann. Although a drawing exists, nothing has been found so far to identify Mlle Pois Vert, whose dainty features are realistically rendered with sensitivity. The black band around her neck was part of the customary costume of the women who sang at *café concerts* such as the Ambassadeurs. As she is not shown performing, it is impossible to know why Lautrec chose to make a print of this pretty young woman.

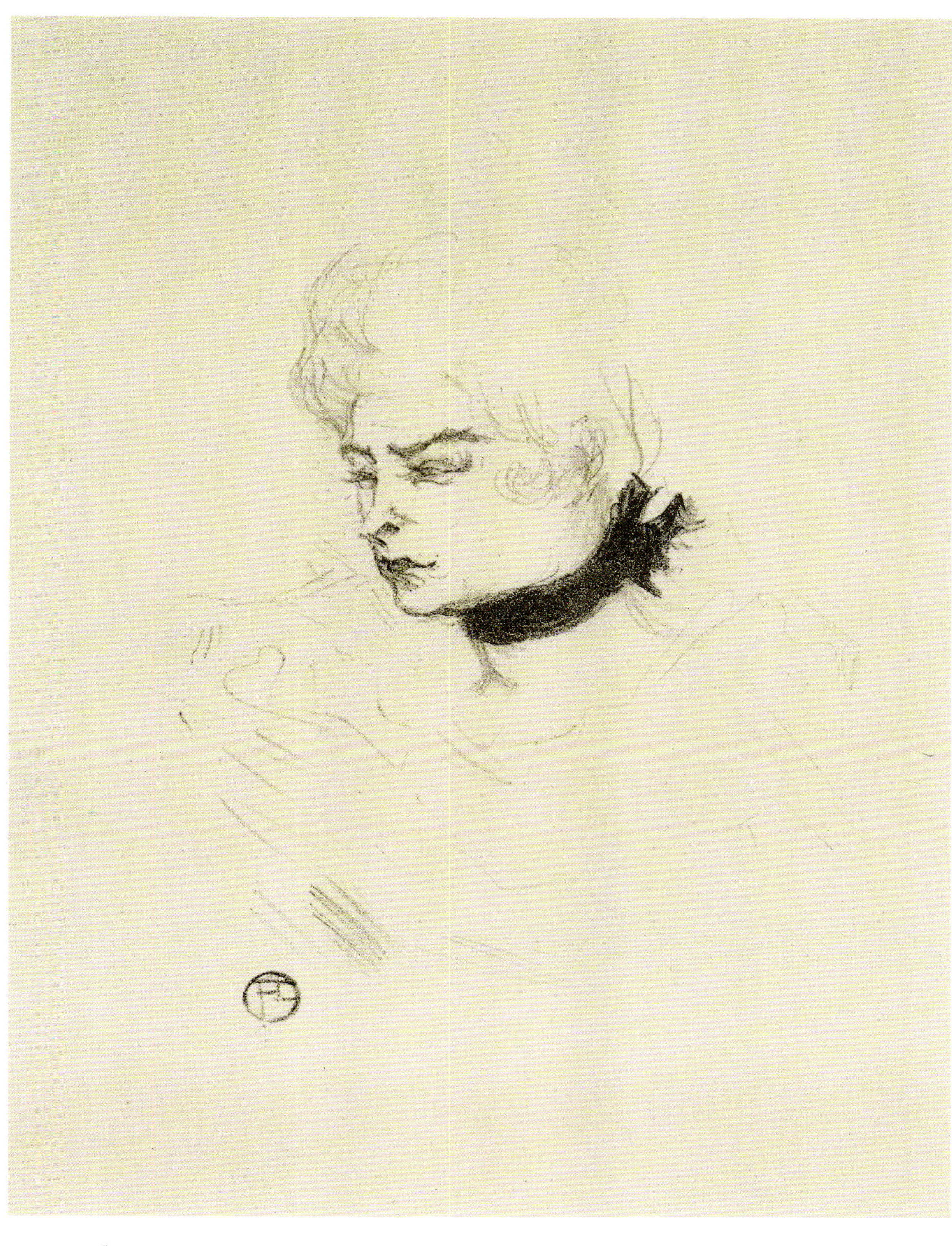

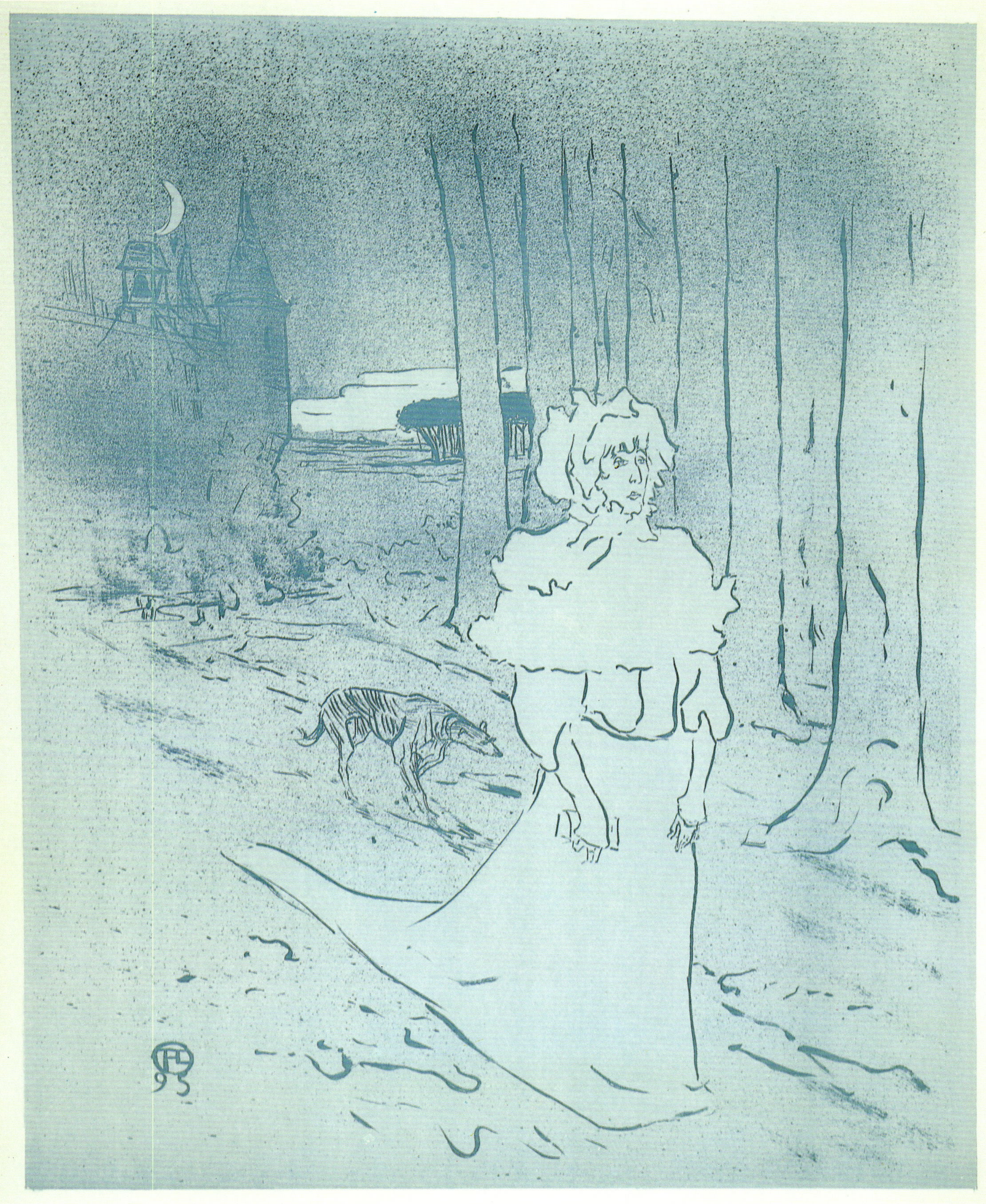

Le Tocsin: La Châtelaine

1895
Brush and spatter lithograph in two
  colors
Image: 22½ × 17¾ in. (57.2 × 45 cm)
Sheet: 23¾ × 19¼ in. (60.3 × 48.9 cm)
First state, before letters
Printed by Cassan fils, Toulouse
Commissioned by the newspaper
  La Dépêche, Toulouse
Wittrock P19/A; Adriani 143/I; Delteil
  357/I; Adhémar 147/I

This poster was the second commissioned by Arthur Huc as an advertisement for the appearance of a serialized book in his Toulouse newspaper, *La Dépêche*. As in the earlier poster, *Le Pendu* (cat. 2), Lautrec used only two closely related colors for his composition. Areas which were to appear prominent, such as the woman and some distant clouds, were masked before the stone was spattered. The spatters and drawing were printed in one color while the second color, printed flat, underlies the entire composition, thus subduing even the masked passages. *Le Tocsin* was one of many lurid novels written by Jules de Gastyne (Jules Benoît). Lautrec has placed *le tocsin*, the alarm bell of the title, in the background, rising from behind the ramparts of a castle, the lines radiating from it perhaps indicating its ringing upon the departure of the ghostly lady from the castle. Unlike his earlier poster for Huc, this one would have had the words of the announcement printed directly on it. This example without letters was produced for collectors. Lautrec designed his posters in a fairly wide range of sizes that were usually determined by where they were to be posted. Another determining factor were the taxes that were levied on most printed matter in France, which were based on the size of paper used.

La Troupe de Mademoiselle Églantine

1896

Crayon, brush, and spatter lithograph
in four colors on wove paper
Image: 24⅜ × 31⅝ in. (62 × 80.3 cm)
Sheet: 24⅝ × 31⅝ in. (62.5 × 80.3 cm)
Commissioned by Jane Avril
Wittrock P21/C; Adriani 162/III;
Delteil 361/III; Adhémar 198/III

Four women dancing the cancan together was called a quadrille (or *quadrille réaliste*), and this spritely one was organized by the dancer Églantine (Wild Rose) Dennay for performances at London's Palace Theatre beginning January 20, 1896. Jane Avril, who ordinarily danced solo, commissioned the poster from Lautrec, writing to him on January 19 about the order in which the names were to be printed. Avril or Églantine also provided him with a photograph of the four dancers, which he followed in general outline but with changes in the costumes and positions of their heads. Unlike the photograph, in which all the women look at the camera, the poster shows only the dancer second from the right glancing outward. The order, too, is different from the way the names are listed, for the first dancer on the left is undoubtedly Avril, while the one second from the right is Églantine. The poster is lively, its bright yellow background surrounding a large area accented by dark-stockinged legs like so many piano keys. Lautrec had the keystone printed in a blue-green, economically combined with only red and yellow, which limited the range of hues but did not diminish the effect that he had attained previously with black. However, the serious expressions on the faces of the dancers may not have projected the excitement that was expected of cancan performances. Having toned down their dancing for the British audience, the four also seem to have bickered on and off stage, which combined to make the Églantine company's visit to London decidedly less successful than Lautrec's poster.

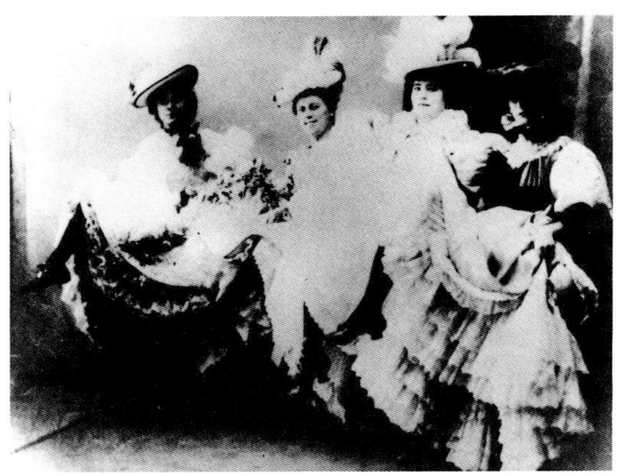

Mademoiselle Églantine's Troupe,
photograph. Private collection.

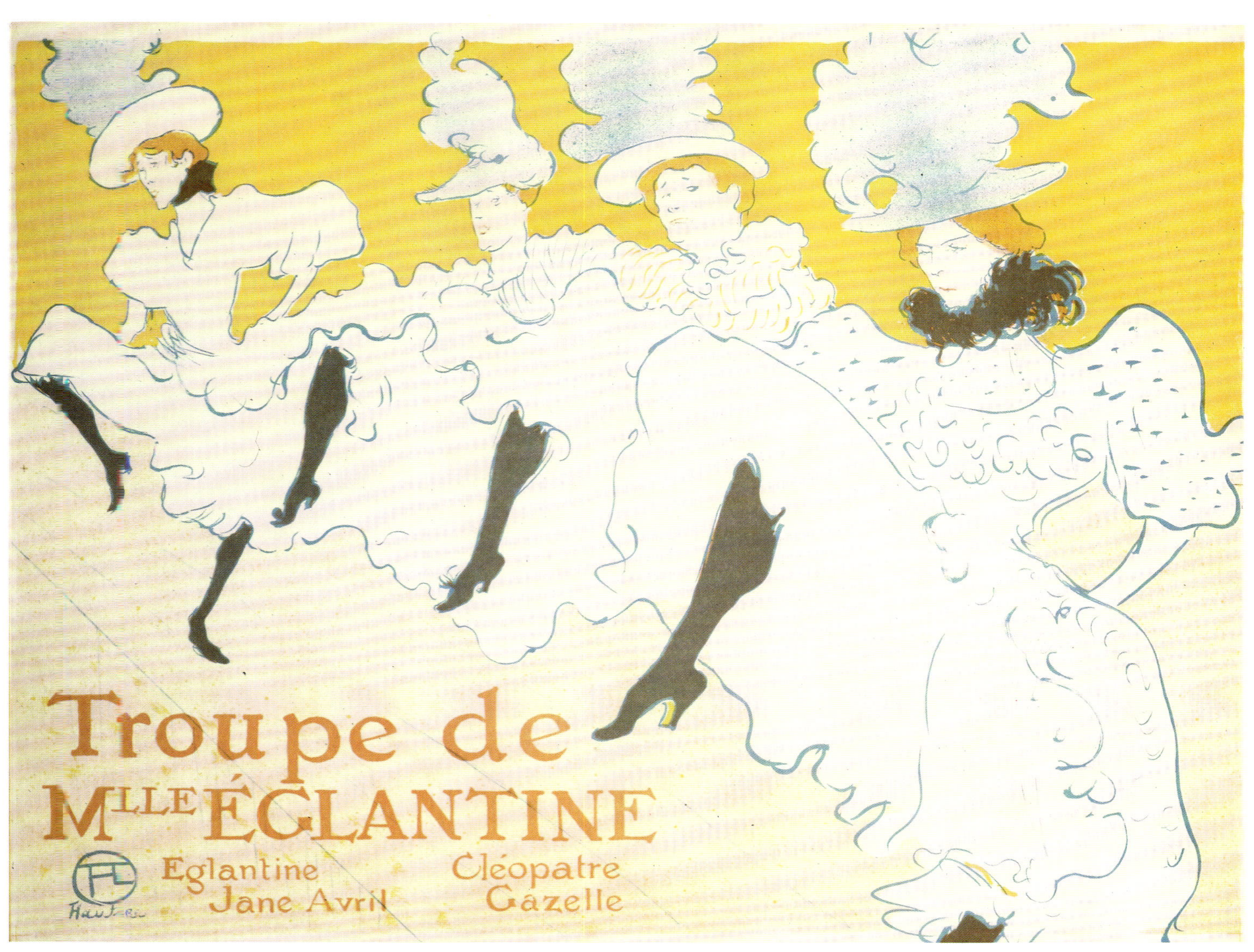

Troupe de
M LLE ÉGLANTINE
Églantine   Cléopatre
Jane Avril   Gazelle

41

Le Photographe Sescau

1896
Brush, crayon, and spatter lithograph
 in four colors on wove paper
Image: 24⅛ × 31½ in. (61.3 × 80 cm)
Sheet: 24¼ × 31½ in. (61.6 × 80 cm)
Second state
Commissioned by Paul Sescau
Wittrock P22/B; Adriani 60/II; Delteil
 353; Adhémar 69

Paul Sescau, a professional photographer Lautrec surely knew at the outset of his career, was one of several of the artist's male friends whom he painted in preparation for his participation in the Salon des Indépendents of 1891. Undoubtedly, Lautrec hoped that his representations of men would bring him some portrait commissions. In contrast to his reputation for fun and sex—alluded to by the artist's addition of a remarque (a marginal sketch) of a naked female wielding a whip over a trained dog in the final state of this poster—Sescau had been shown in his formal portrait with a top hat and walking stick. His long nose, small chin, and swept-up mustache—not visible here—were caricatured by Lautrec in other prints, one of which shows him playing a banjo. The woman upon whom the photographer has focused his camera looks back in a flirting way, but has yet to put her lorgnette to her eyes. The anonymity implied by her mask is echoed in her costume, which is covered with question marks. This pattern also appears in reverse as the wallcovering in another poster of this year, *L'Artisan moderne* (cat. 42). It is impossible to avoid interpreting the subtle devices Lautrec has added to amuse Sescau and those who knew him, for in the 1890s many photographers made their living by taking pictures of naked prostitutes and of sexual acts. Even Lautrec's customary elephant monogram in the lower right has been slightly changed so that its tail is provocatively raised.

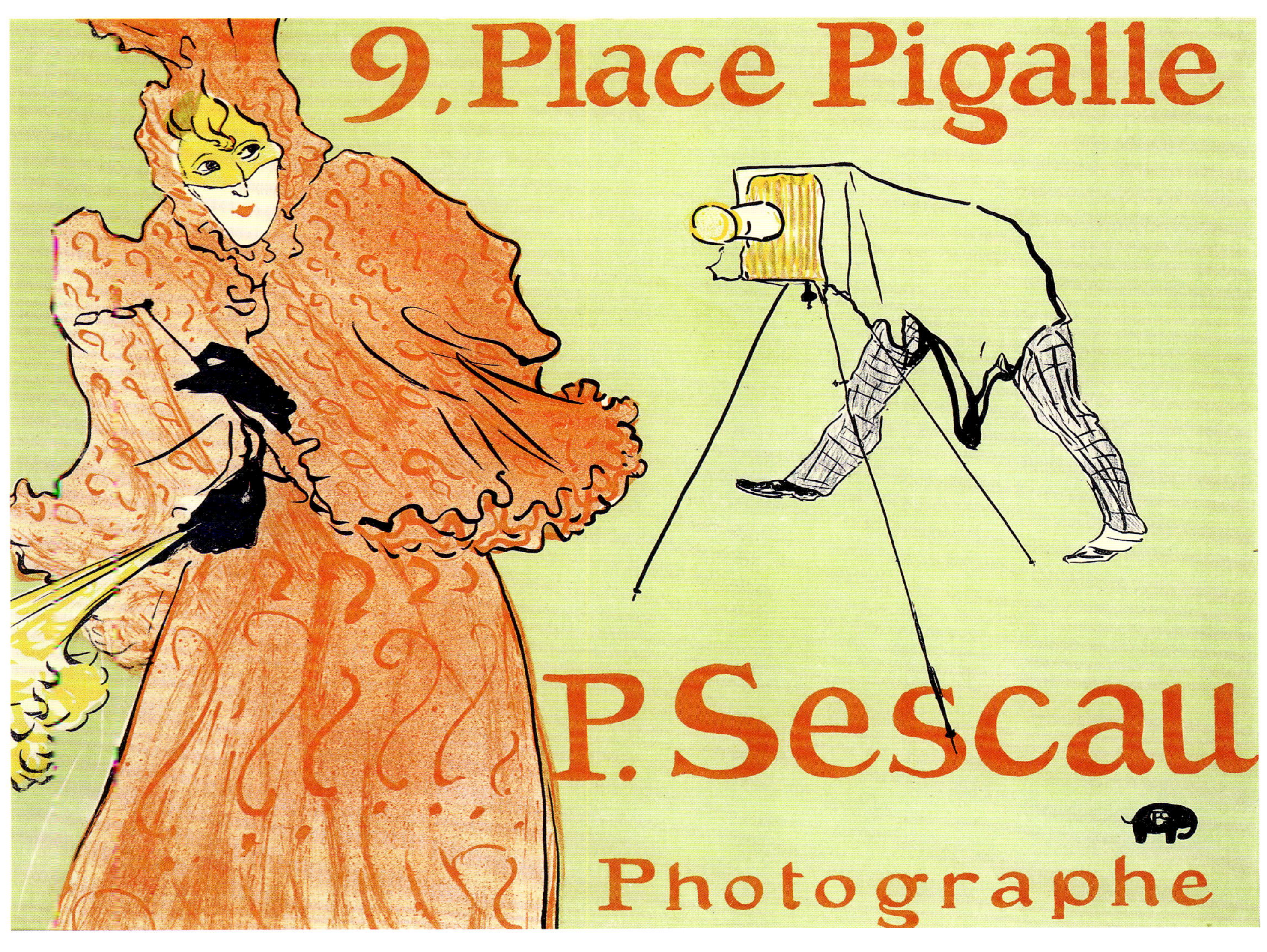

9, Place Pigalle
P. Sescau
Photographe

42

L'Artisan moderne

1896
Crayon, brush, and spatter lithograph
  in four colors on wove paper
Image and sheet: 36⅝ × 24⅝ in. (93 ×
  62.5 cm)
First state, before letters
Printed by Bourgerie & Cie, Paris
Commissioned by André Marty
Wittrock P24/A; Adriani 59/I; Delteil
  350/I; Adhémar 70

André Marty announced his newest project to produce objects of high quality, L'Artisan Moderne, in the November 1896 issue of his journal *Le Livre vert*. Henri Nocq, one of the artisans associated with the project, is shown in this poster, which Lautrec created to advertise the places where works by the craftsmen could be purchased. Nocq was a Belgian jeweler, graphic designer, and medalist whose full-length portrait Lautrec painted in 1897, and who later wrote the catalogue of medals in the Louvre's collection. Marty planned to produce items by Nocq and other jewelers, lampshade makers, binders, and ceramists in editions of one hundred to be sold to subscribers or in shops, three of which were listed on the poster along with the types of work offered: objets d'art, furniture, and decorative ensembles. This example is a proof without letters with a variant printing in orange-red of parts of the dog. This suggestive bedroom encounter between a woman client and Nocq, dressed as a workman, was undoubtedly intended as an inside joke, although a serious purpose may also be read into it. On his toolbox is the name Niederkorn, a furniture designer in the group, and Lautrec's monogram. On the wall is a pattern that includes reversed question marks along with the standard art nouveau motifs. The maid's open mouth and sideways glance, together with Nocq's leer, convey Lautrec's mischievous intent. The long French tradition of settling affairs of state and business at the bedside is presented here as a farce, with the woman's lap dog situated where the workman might put his "tool." An alternate reading, reflecting Marty's vision for his project, presents the visiting artisan curing the woman, the embodiment of France, of her sickness, brought on by shoddy industrial products. The poster was printed by Bourgerie & Cie, the printers of Bruant's problematic *Eldorado* poster (cat. 5).

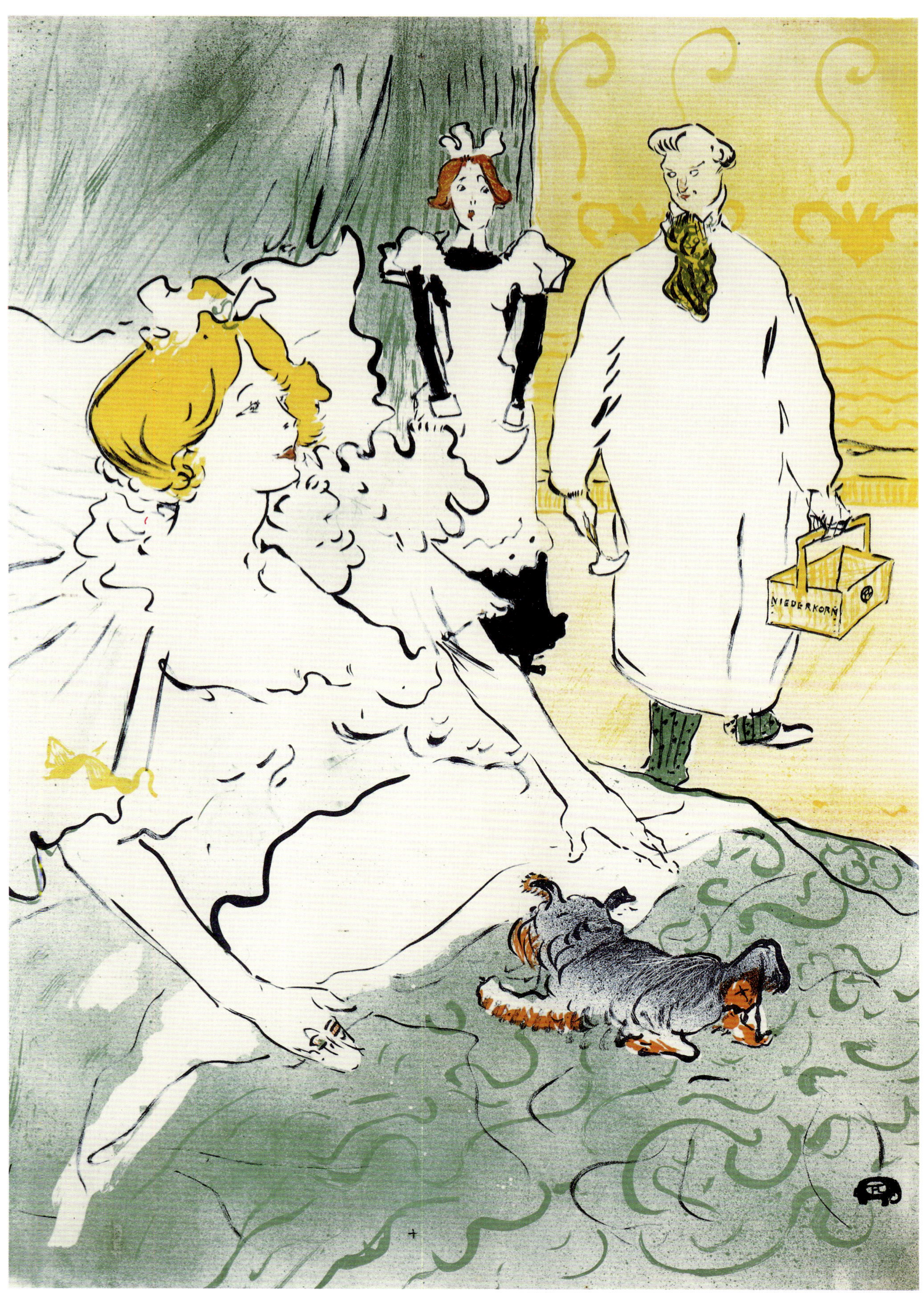
NIEDERKORN

43

La Vache enragée

1896
Crayon, brush, and spatter lithograph
  in four colors on wove paper
Image: 31⅛ × 23 in. (79 × 58.4 cm)
Sheet: 31⅜ × 23¼ in. (79.7 × 59.1 cm)
First state, before letters
Printed by Chaix, Paris
Commissioned by the magazine
  La Vache enragée
Wittrock P27/A; Adriani 165/I; Delteil
  364; Adhémar 197

In March of 1896, the artist Adolphe Willette founded a new arts magazine, *La Vache enragée*. The title, taken from a book by Émile Goudeau about a starving artist that had been published more than ten years earlier, derives from the idiomatic expression for a raging hunger, "manger à la vache enragée," literally to eat like a mad cow. Lautrec created this poster to announce the publication of the first issue. Parisians would have recognized the subject, since it recalled incidents of less than three years earlier when the annual Bal des Quat'z'Arts (founded in 1892 by the students of the École des Beaux-Arts as their own event, but opened to the public in 1893) had included a procession with nearly nude tableaux. The police action, subsequent riot in which a bystander was killed, and trial resulted from the activities of Senator René Beranger, "Père la Pudeur," the self-appointed leader of a morals squad. The wildly running man in Lautrec's poster is a caricature of Père la Pudeur, who is followed by the metaphoric cow-artist. One of the clowns on the bicycle is Willette, whose album *Pauvre Pierrot* of 1884 was well known. The waiter may also refer to Willette's work, since he contributed to the decor of the Chat Noir café and drew illustrations for its publication, *Le Chat noir,* edited by Goudeau. Days after the first appearance of the new magazine, a "Vachalcade" procession was organized to compete with the annual Parisian Boeuf Gras (Fat Bull) parade. In the hands of some of the artists who had organized the Incohérents in the late 1880s, the inspiration to recapture the more outrageous days of Montmartre as the century was ending was not catching. Both the Vachalcade and Willette's magazine appeared only once again, in May 1897.

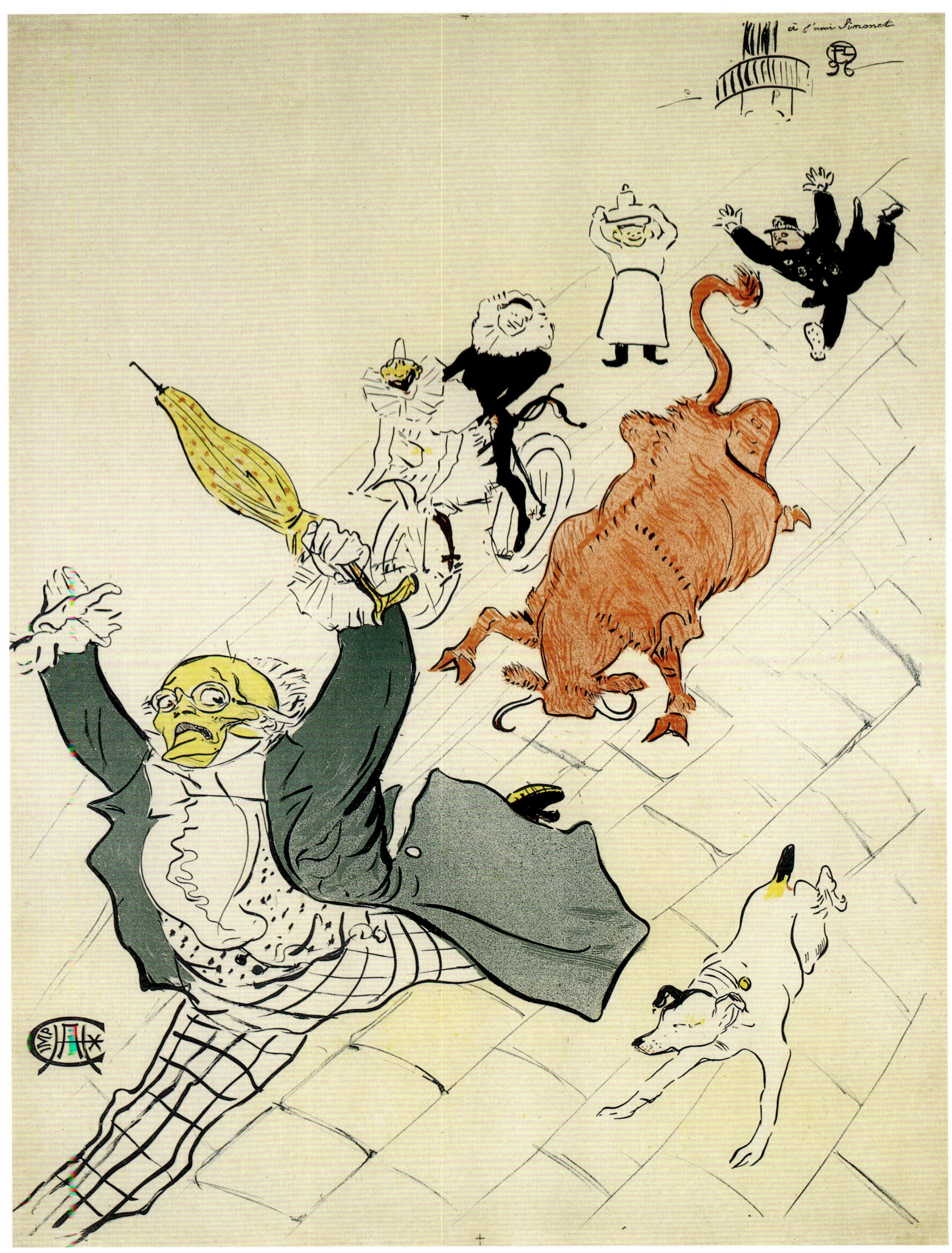
à l'ami Simonet

44

Elles: Couverture

1896
Crayon, brush, and spatter lithograph
  on laid japan paper
Image and sheet (folded around boards
  and closed): 21 × 16¼ in. (53.2 ×
  41.5 cm)
First state, cover edition
Published by Gustave Pellet in the
  Elles series
Inscribed lower right in pen, *série no. 39,*
  with Gustave Pellet's paraph; stamp
  of Gustave Pellet (Lugt 1190)
Wittrock 155/I; Adriani 171/I

Elles was an album of twelve prints commissioned by Gustave Pellet and published in an edition of one hundred in April 1896. It was luxuriously produced, with special paper watermarked with Lautrec's and Pellet's names, and each composition was printed to the edges of the sheet, an unusual and attractive presentation. However, its cover and frontispiece were identical, and five of the plates were only one or two colors and therefore clearly not as valuable as the more colorful ones. The subject of the album—prostitutes—might have drawn a number of male customers, but after they saw the prints it must have been obvious that *Elles* was not going to fulfill their erotic curiosities. It was not surprising then that the sales of *Elles,* priced at 300 francs, were extremely disappointing.

Pellet specialized in prints that showed nudity and suggestive themes, and his publishing plans for 1896 included prints by both Félicien Rops, whose erotic etchings had not been editioned before, and Lautrec. Because Lautrec had spent a considerable amount of time in the Parisian brothels between 1892 and 1895, creating numerous drawings and several paintings, Pellet undoubtedly believed that Lautrec had plenty of material to draw upon for his series. In 1896, Pellet's albums would have been in competition with at least two other sets of prints depicting women, both published by André Marty: a new series titled *Études de femmes,* to which Lautrec contributed a print for the first number, and an album of ten prints by Hermann-Paul (Hermann René Georges Paul) titled *Images pour les demoiselles.* Lautrec had already completed several large print projects with Marty, including an album-book about the *diseuse* Yvette Guilbert, so he may have expected Pellet to publish something other than his brothel scenes. For example, Lautrec had recently made a number of compositions depicting the clowness Cha-u-Kao dressing, sitting, standing, and so on. It is possible that Pellet, who later published another print of the clowness, may have agreed to publish a series devoted to her and changed his mind when he learned of Marty's plans. The first plate in *Elles* is a picture of the clowness, not a prostitute. *Elles* thus became a mixed collection of compositions which mostly documented the night-to-night activities of women who worked where they slept.

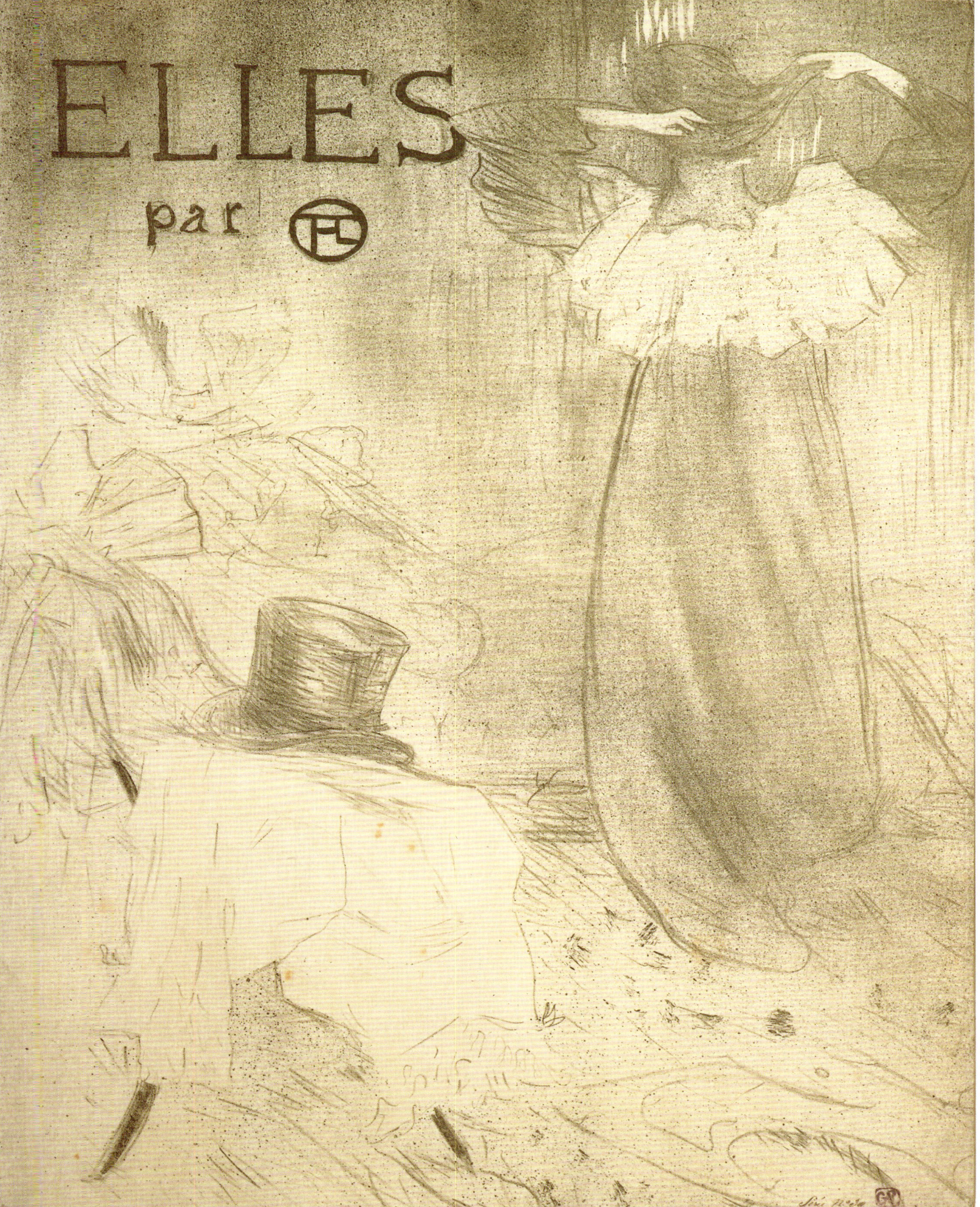

ELLES
par

45

Elles: Frontispiece

1896
Crayon, brush, and spatter lithograph
  in three colors on wove paper
Image and sheet: 20⅞ × 16 in.
  (53 × 40.8 cm)
Second state, frontispiece version,
  number 39
Published by Gustave Pellet in the
  Elles series
Inscribed lower right in pen, *série no. 39,*
  with Pellet's paraph; stamp of Gustave
  Pellet (Lugt 1190)
Wittrock 155/II; Adriani 171/II; Delteil
  179; Adhémar 200/I

This composition was used in three ways: as the monochromatic wrapper-cover of the album (cat. 44), as its frontispiece (slightly reduced on the right side), and as a poster announcing its publication. The poster version advertised the album as being exhibited at La Plume (Salon des Cent), for which Lautrec's *La Passagère du 54* (cat. 36) had been the most recent poster. In this print, Lautrec shows a woman undoing her hair, an indication of the theme of *Elles*, since it was understood that adult women took their hair down only when they were preparing to go to bed. The presence of a man's top hat, an object never brought into a proper woman's bedroom, clarifies the setting as a room taken for the purpose of having sex, a *maison close*. Lautrec collected Japanese prints and owned a series of them devoted to "green houses" or brothels. The motifs and compositional traditions from those prints became so embedded in his vision of the world that a picture such as this one is merely a faint echo of a similar Japanese setting.

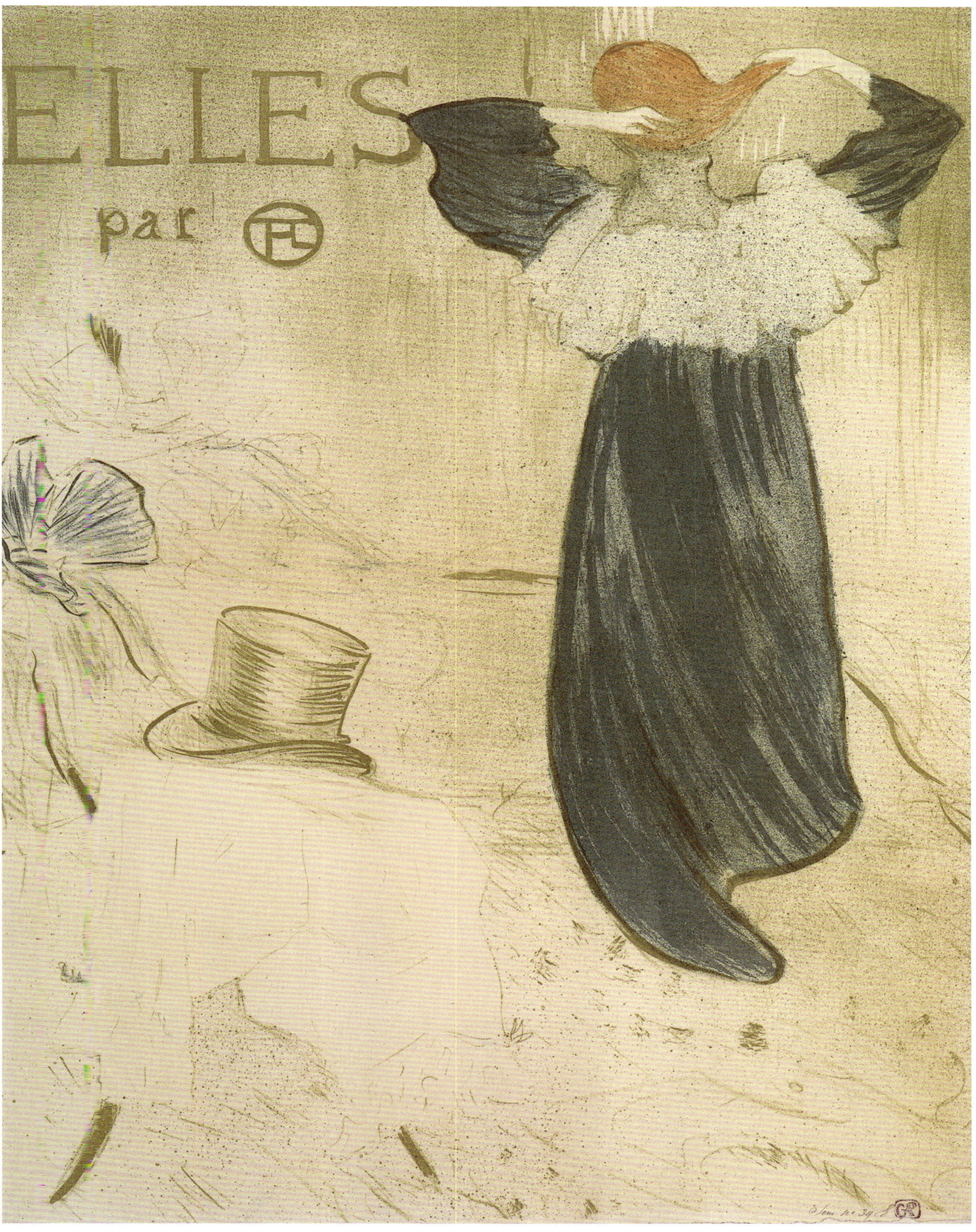

ELLES
par

Elles: La Clownesse assise; Mademoiselle Cha-u-Kao

1896
Crayon, brush, and spatter lithograph
with scraper in four colors on wove
paper
Image and sheet: 20⅞ × 15⅞ in.
(53 × 40.4 cm)
Published by Gustave Pellet in the
Elles series
Inscribed lower right in pen, *série no. 39*,
with Pellet's paraph; stamp of Gustave
Pellet (Lugt 1190)
Wittrock 156; Adriani 172; Delteil 180;
Adhémar 201

The stage name of the colorful contortionist who dressed like a clown, Cha-u-Kao, is a phonetic rendering of *chahut-chaos*, or the chaotic cancan. While Lautrec made several studies of the clowness, he never showed her performing. The lithograph included in *Elles*, the first after the frontispiece, shows her in a seated position, her black-stockinged legs spread apart in a sign of welcome appropriate to the theme of women who made their living "between their legs." The clowness was a lesbian whose appearance captivated Lautrec. In this print, her white-haired head emerges from the yellow ruffled collar of her stage costume as from a sunny flower. In a print not in *Elles*, *La Danse au Moulin Rouge*, she is shown offstage in a somber suit emulating male attire, dancing with another woman. An argument has been made, based upon the clowness's presence in the album, that *Elles* is about lesbian life.[1] In 1897 Pellet published two larger single-figure lithographs, one of Cha-u-Kao (*La Clownesse au Moulin Rouge*, cat. 62) and another of Elsa, la Viennoise, who was a prostitute at the house on rue des Moulins, where it is believed that Lautrec observed his models for *Elles*. Such a conjunction might indicate that the clowness was also associated with such a place.

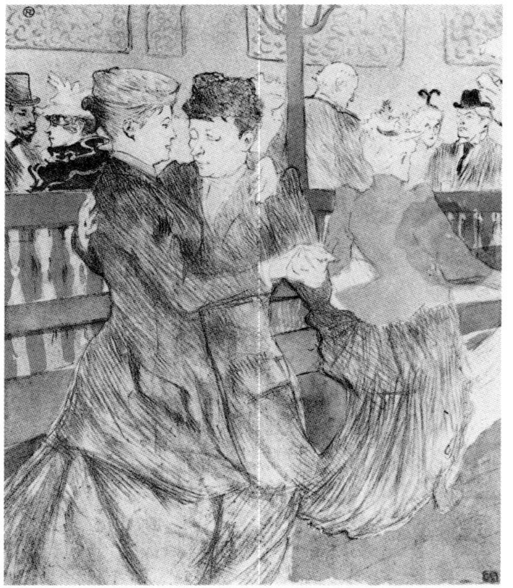

Henri de Toulouse-Lautrec, *La Danse au Moulin Rouge*, 1897, color lithograph, 16⅜ × 13½ in. The Art Institute of Chicago.

1. Naomi E. Maurer, in *Toulouse-Lautrec Paintings* (Chicago: Art Institute of Chicago, 1979), pp. 155–59, asserts that lesbians could be the theme of the entire set of *Elles*, with the clowness appearing in other plates, on the basis of Lautrec's remark quoted in Thadée Natanson's memoirs of him, *Un Henri de Toulouse-Lautrec* (Geneva, 1951), that his idea for *Elles* came from observing "the two bodies of a lesbian couple."

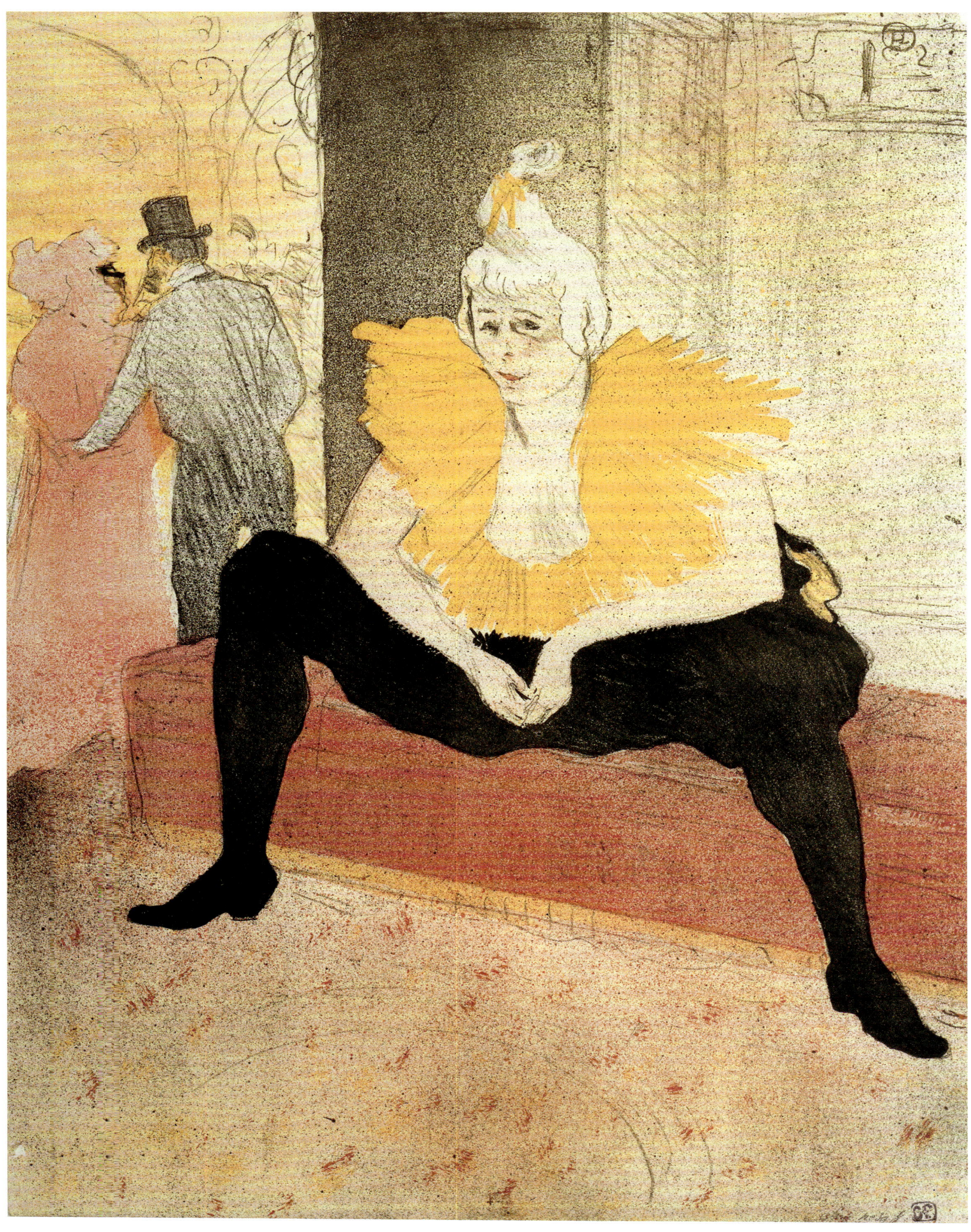

 **47**

Elles: Femme au plateau, petit déjeuner; Madame Baron et Mademoiselle Popo

1896
Crayon lithograph with scraper on wove
  paper
Image and sheet: 15⅞ × 21 in. (40.4 ×
  53.3 cm)
Published by Gustave Pellet in the
  Elles series
Inscribed lower right in pen, *série no. 39,*
  with Pellet's paraph; stamp of Gustave
  Pellet (Lugt 1190)
Wittrock 156; Adriani 173; Delteil 181;
  Adhémar 202

After the frontispiece, this is the first print in the album to depict life in a brothel. It shows a heavy woman, Madame Juliette Baron, and a young prostitute, her daughter Mademoiselle Popo (Paulette Baron). Typical of most daughters raised in *maisons close*, Mlle Popo followed her mother into the same trade. Mme Baron appears to have just ended a conversation at her daughter's bedside, and is carrying away her coffee cup and milk pitcher. Although it is not possible to state with certainty the identity of each of the figures in *Elles,* Mlle Popo appears to be the subject of at least three other prints in the series.

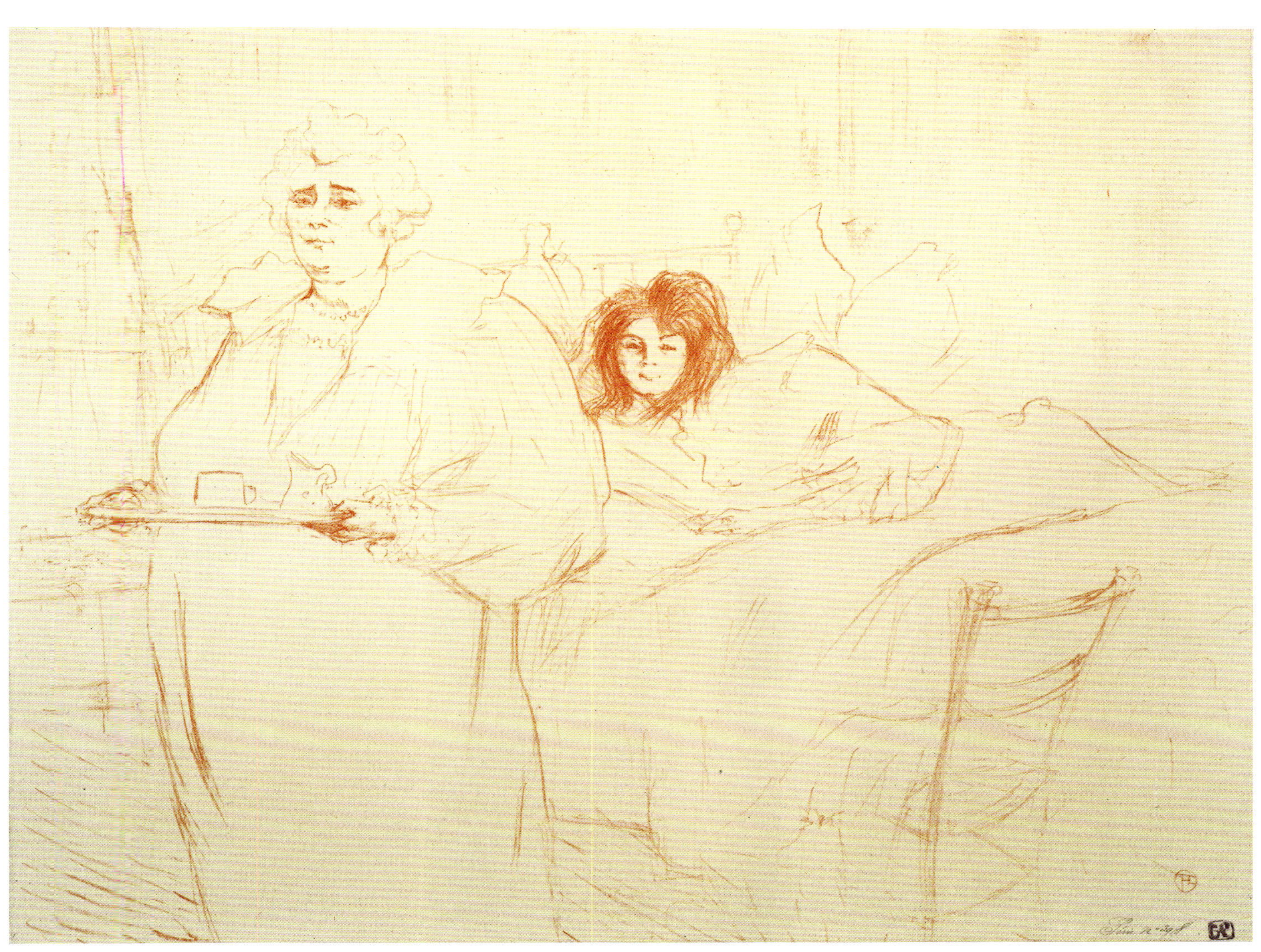

48

Elles: Femme couchée; Réveil

1896
Crayon lithograph with scraper on
  wove paper
Image and sheet: 16 × 20¾ in. (40.5 ×
  52.9 cm)
Published by Gustave Pellet in the
  Elles series
Inscribed lower right in pen, *série no. 39,*
  with Pellet's paraph; stamp of Gustave
  Pellet (Lugt 1190)
Wittrock 158; Adriani 174; Delteil 182;
  Adhémar 203

Among the *Elles* prints are several that are quite close to freehand drawings, with concentrations of lines in one area and a preponderance of nearly empty spaces. Opening her eyes to another day is Mlle Popo, who in the previous composition had just finished her coffee. The bleary-eyed face is no longer a partial caricature but a real, dead-tired one. Lautrec chose, particularly in this album, to reveal rather than to comment upon the personalities he pictured. Appropriate to the theme, this composition is horizontal, and its abbreviated but convincing intimacy is perhaps closest to the final print in the album (cat. 55).

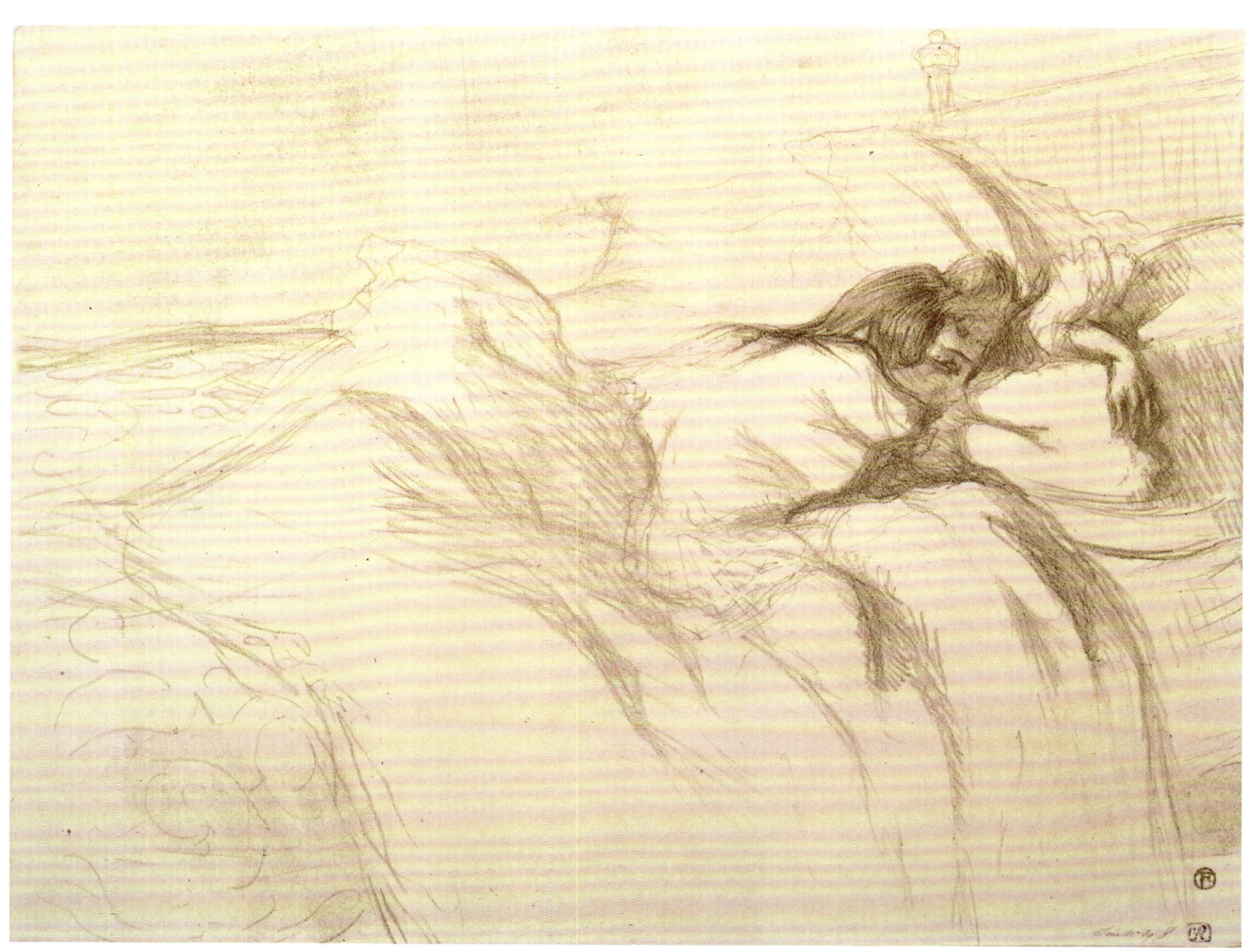

49

Elles: Femme au tub; Le Tub

1896
Crayon, brush, and spatter lithograph
  in six colors on wove paper
Image and sheet: 16 × 20⅞ in. (40.5 ×
  53 cm)
Published by Gustave Pellet in the
  Elles series
Inscribed lower right in pen, *série no. 39,*
  with Pellet's paraph; stamp of Gustave
  Pellet (Lugt 1190)
Wittrock 159; Adriani 175; Delteil 183;
  Adhémar 204

This quiet print of a woman pouring water for her bath is sprinkled with barely visible symbols of her trade. The picture behind her is of either Leda and the Swan or Eve and the Serpent, both fabled sexual encounters. The large standing mirror is well positioned for anyone in bed wanting to observe his or her activity, though in the picture the bed is merely rumpled from its last use. In contrast to the way she was represented awaking in *Femme couchée* (cat. 48), here the woman is flattened and placed between two objects, a water pitcher and a tub, that are drawn in contradicting perspectives.

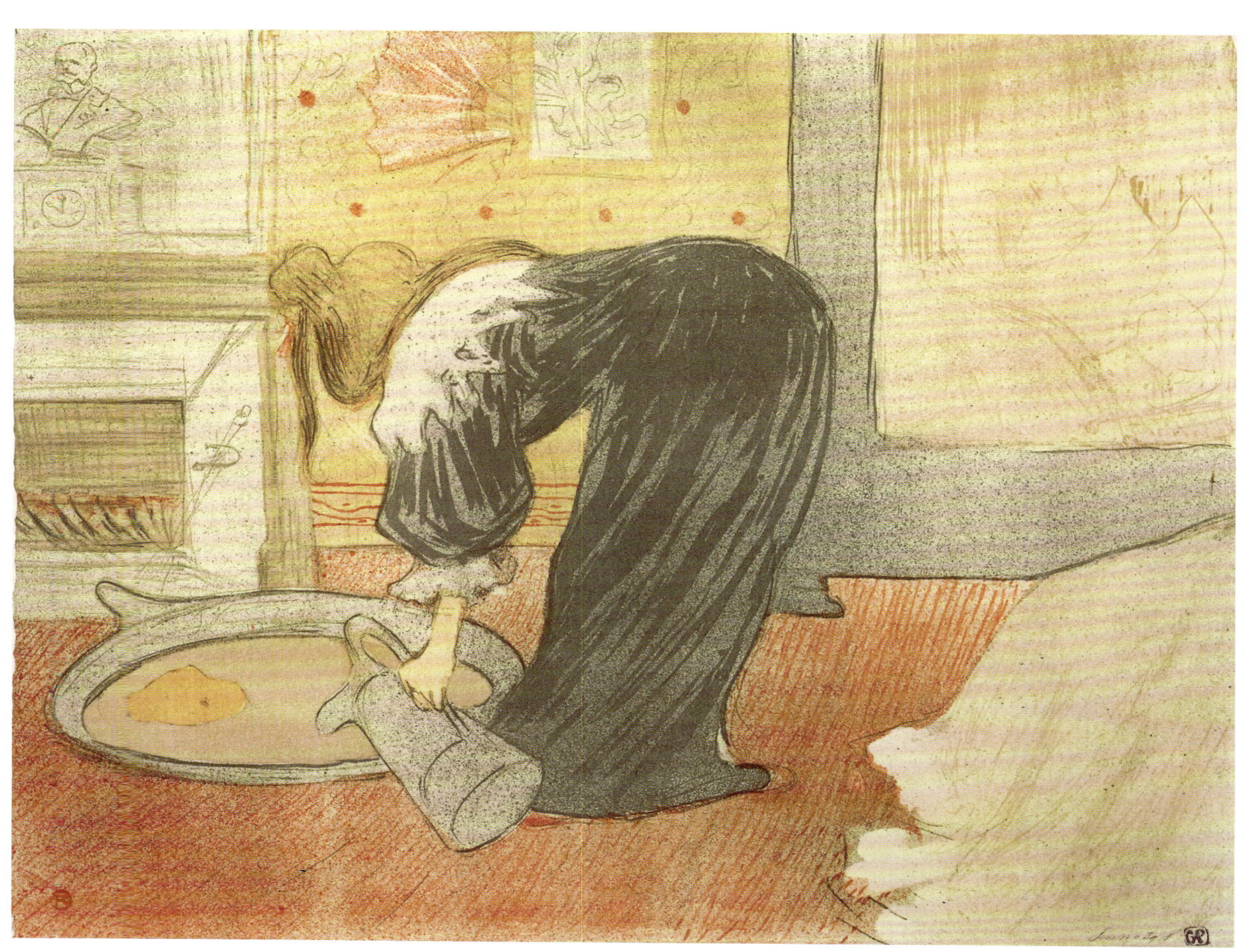

50

Elles: Femme qui se lave; La Toilette

1896

Crayon lithograph on wove paper
Image and sheet: 20⅞ × 16 in.
    (53 × 40.8 cm)
Published by Gustave Pellet in the
    Elles series
Inscribed lower right in pen, *série no. 39,*
    with Pellet's paraph; stamp of Gustave
    Pellet (Lugt 1190)
Wittrock 160; Adriani 176; Delteil 184;
    Adhémar 205

Finally, we meet a partially naked, somewhat fleshy prostitute. As she washes herself at a basin, her breasts are reflected in the mirror above it. Over the mirror hangs a suggestive picture of a male figure approaching a less well-defined human, providing yet another ambiguous hint of the subject of *Elles.* Here again is a familiar motif taken from Japanese prints, but now filtered through the vision of Mary Cassatt, whose charming color drypoint and etching of a half-nude woman washing (*Woman Bathing,* 1891) Lautrec might have seen. Unlike Cassatt's subject, Lautrec's is not at all elegant, but rather a voyeuristic representation that emphasizes the homely reality of brothel life.

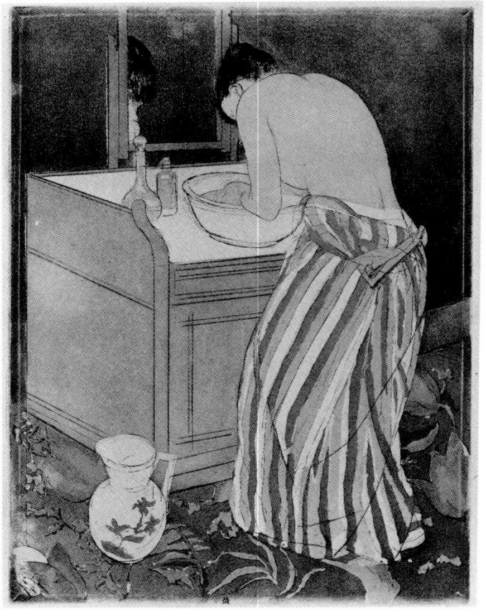

Mary Cassatt, *Woman Bathing*, 1891, color print, with drypoint and aquatint, sheet 17 × 11¾ in. Metropolitan Museum of Art, gift of Paul J. Sachs.

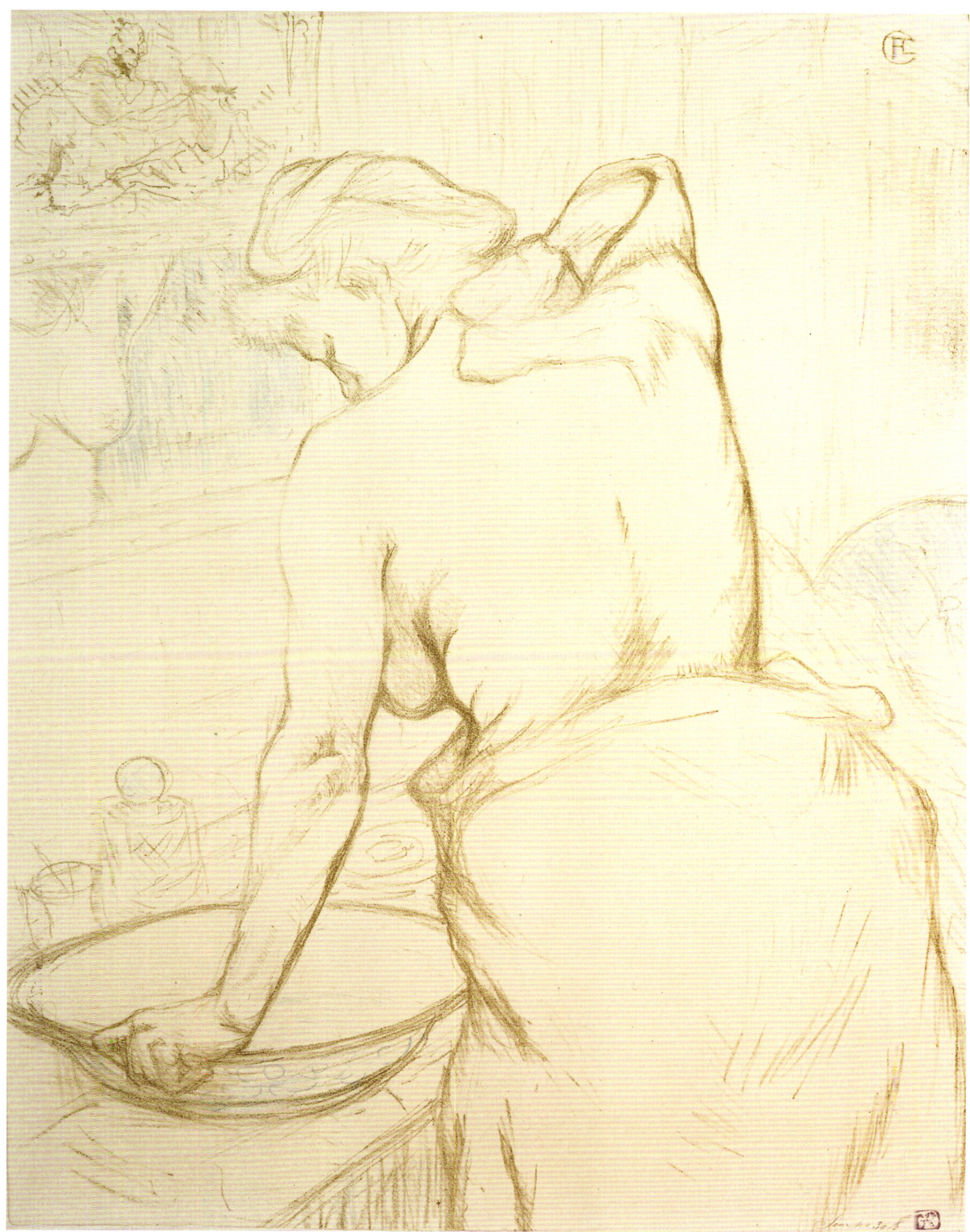

51

Elles: Femme à la glace; La Glace à main

1896
Crayon, brush, and spatter lithograph
  on wove paper
Image and sheet: 20¾ × 15¾ in. (52.8 ×
  40.1 cm)
Published by Gustave Pellet in the
  Elles series
Inscribed lower right in pen, *série no. 39,*
  with Pellet's paraph; stamp of Gustave
  Pellet (Lugt 1190)
Wittrock 161; Adriani 177; Delteil 185;
  Adhémar 206

The subject of this print is checking her recently combed hair in a hand mirror while she stands in front of a clock decorated with a reclining woman, another symbol of the business of sexual accommodation. Domestic touches, such as the slippers next to the bed (strangely, still facing toward it), and the woman's concentration on her reflection, combine to produce a composition of casual simplicity and serious determination. Shown in the ubiquitous clothing of Lautrec's numerous representations of prostitutes lounging around the brothel, this woman in her formless slip has the appearance of a Greek goddess.

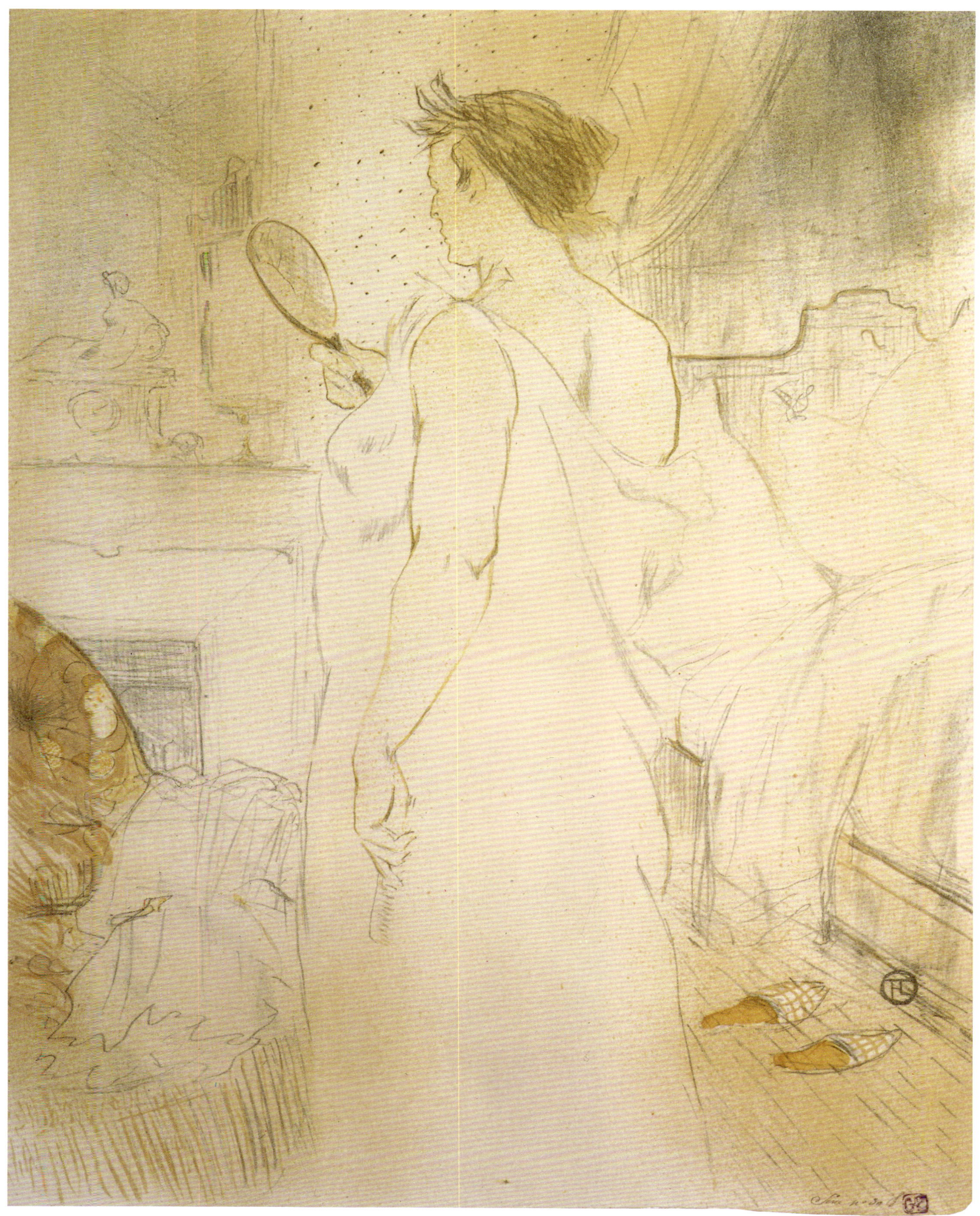

52

Elles: Femme qui se peigne; La Coiffure

1896
Crayon, brush, and spatter lithograph
  printed in two colors on wove paper
Image and sheet: 20⅞ × 16 in. (53 ×
  40.5 cm)
Published by Gustave Pellet in the
  Elles series
Inscribed lower right in pen, *série no. 39*,
  with Pellet's paraph; stamp of Gustave
  Pellet (Lugt 1190)
Wittrock 162; Adriani 178; Delteil 186;
  Adhémar 207

Following any traditional sequence, this woman who is combing her hair might seem out of place and might have appropriately preceded *Femme à la glace* (cat. 51), except that she has already put on her corset. *Elles* does not appear to have an absolute chronological order, following the ordinary routine of the ladies of the night, possibly because Lautrec's drawings were made of several women at different times. The unusual angle at which Lautrec has chosen to show this buxom figure allows the viewer to share with the artist what was for him a special experience of looking down on his subject. He has stressed this aspect by accentuating the woman's fair bosom through its sharp contrast with her very dark hair and dark corset.

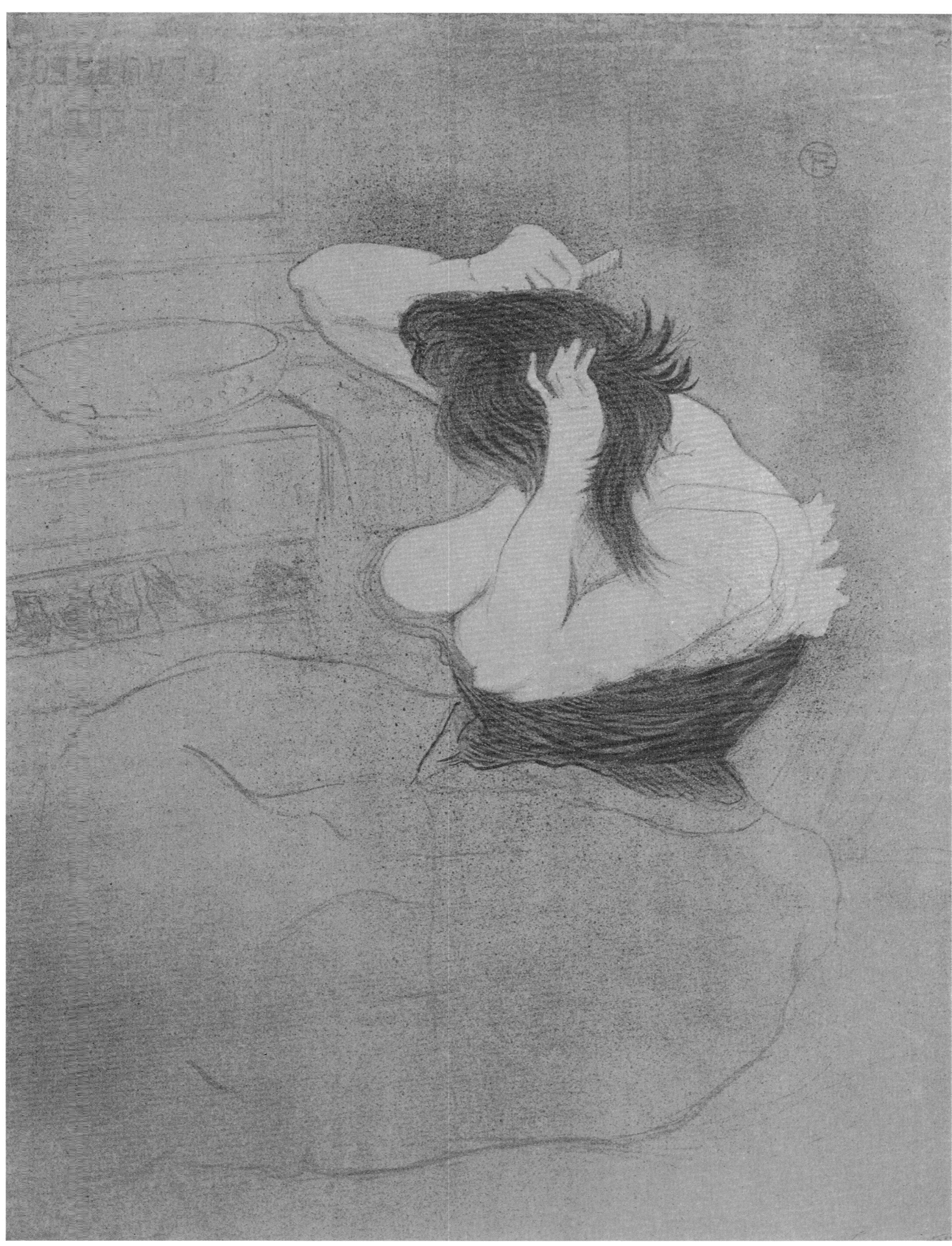

Elles: Femme au lit, profil; Au Petit Lever

1896
Crayon, brush, and spatter lithograph
  with scraper in four colors on wove
  paper
Image and sheet: 16 × 20⅞ in. (40.5 ×
  53 cm)
Published by Gustave Pellet in the
  Elles series
Inscribed lower right in pen, *série no. 39*,
  with Pellet's paraph; stamp of Gustave
  Pellet (Lugt 1190)
Wittrock 163; Adriani 179; Delteil 187;
  Adhémar 208

A stout woman, often identified as Madame Baron, is visiting a young prostitute, probably her daughter Paulette, for a bedside conversation. Since *Elles* covers most of the normal daily events in the lives of prostitutes, with the exception of their actual work, it may be that this is not just a casual conversation but the madam's announcement of the periodic testing for communicable diseases. Lautrec depicted this routine more explicitly in paintings in which the women of the house are shown lined up for inspection. Linking the bulky, older red-haired woman to the younger, colorless one are two large passages of recurring patterns on the bedcovering and the wall.

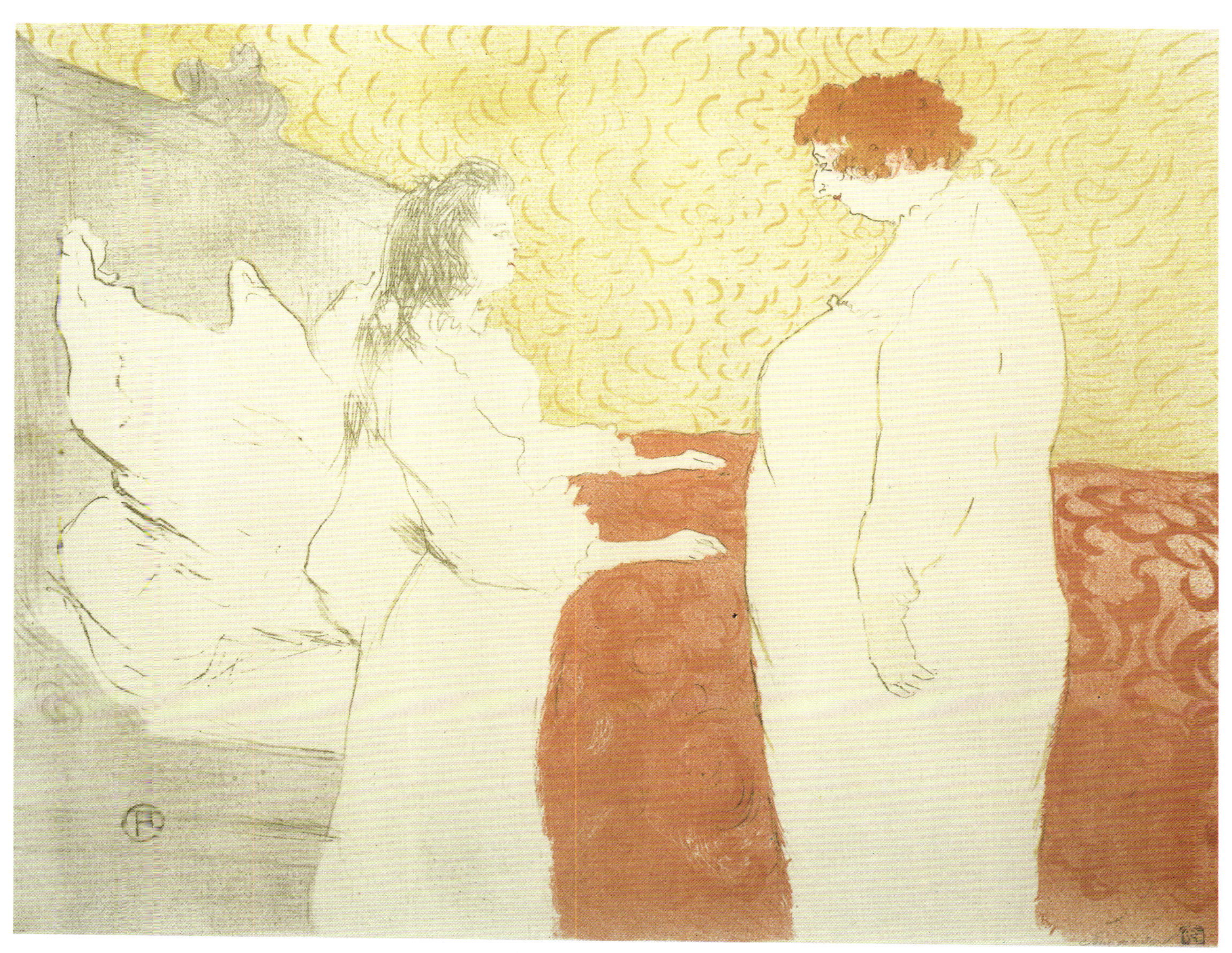

54

Elles: Femme en corset; Conquête de passage

1896
Crayon, brush, and spatter lithograph
  with scraper in four colors on wove
  paper
Image and sheet: 20⅞ × 16 in. (53 ×
  40.7 cm)
Published by Gustave Pellet in the
  Elles series
Inscribed lower right in pen, *série no. 39*,
  with Pellet's paraph; stamp of Gustave
  Pellet (Lugt 1190)
Wittrock 164; Adriani 180; Delteil 188;
  Adhémar 209

A satyr and a nude confront each other in a picture hanging on the wall of this scene, the only one in the *Elles* series in which a man appears. The woman has one foot on the couch as she loosens her corset in front of her visitor, who has not yet removed his hat. In a preparatory sketch, the man portrayed is clearly the painter Charles Edward Conder, but in the print his distinctive face (see *La Loge au mascaron doré*, cat. 22) has been remodeled into an anonymous caricature. The design of stylized flying birds on the upholstered couch may be a clever allusion to the "passing conquest" of the title.

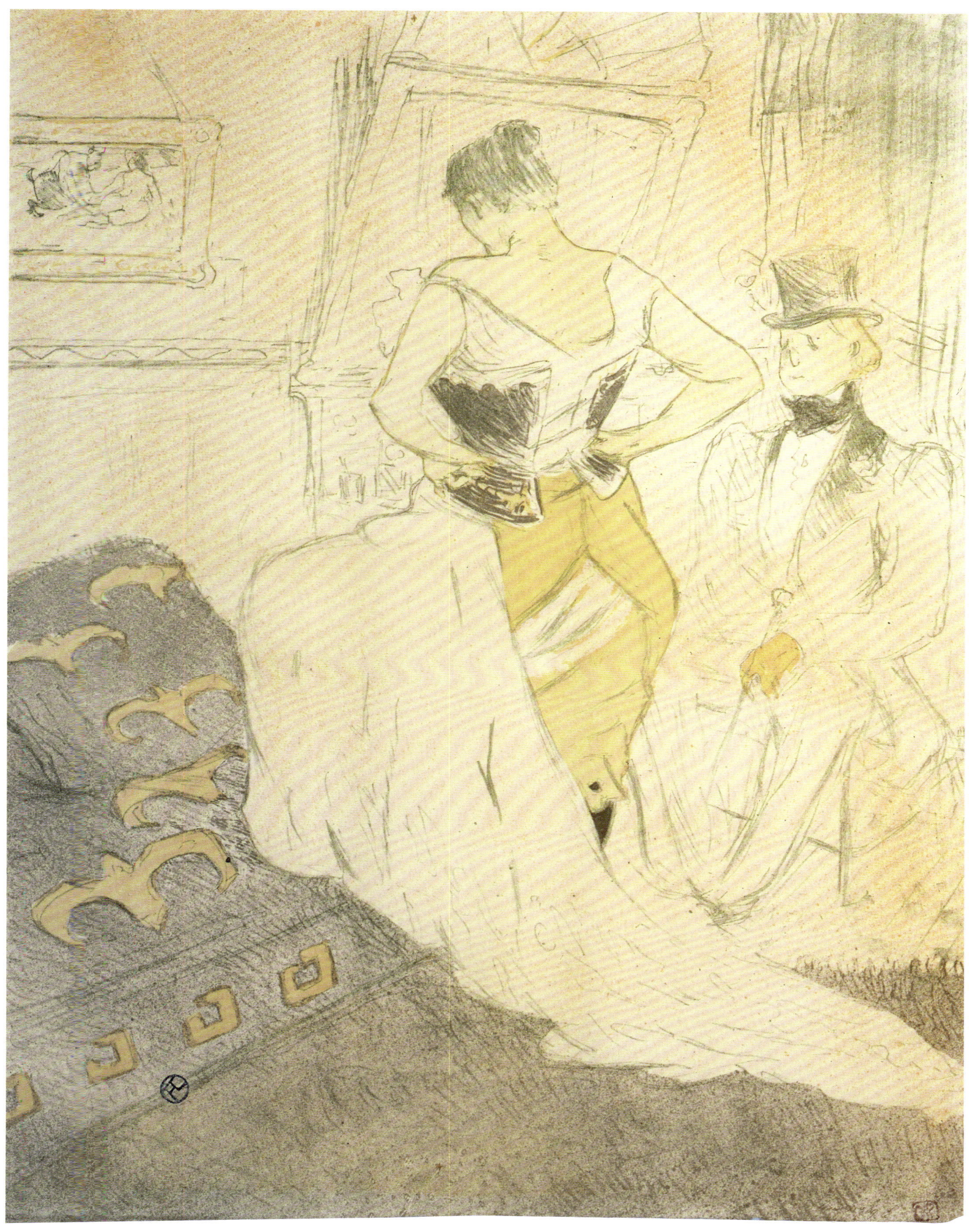

55

Elles: Femme sur le dos; Lassitude

1896
Crayon lithograph printed in two colors
  on wove paper
Image and sheet: 16 × 20¾ in. (40.6 ×
  52.9 cm)
Published by Gustave Pellet in the
  Elles series
Inscribed lower right in pen, *série no. 39*,
  with Pellet's paraph; stamp of Gustave
  Pellet (Lugt 1190)
Wittrock 165; Adriani 181; Delteil 189;
  Adhémar 210

While the first two brothel compositions in *Elles* show "morning after" activities (cats. 44, 45, and 47), this final print appears to be about the end of the working night. The sketchily drawn hat and cast-off street clothing at the left suggest that this prostitute may be a streetwalker, weary after a long night. However, based upon the tradition that an oil sketch similar to this print is of Mlle Popo, another possibility is that she has just returned from an evening with her lover Paul Guibert. As for its relationship to the entire album, this print seems to be the complete antithesis of the composition on the cover and frontispiece, in which a man's hat rests upon the woman's cloak, while she stands preparing for an evening's work.

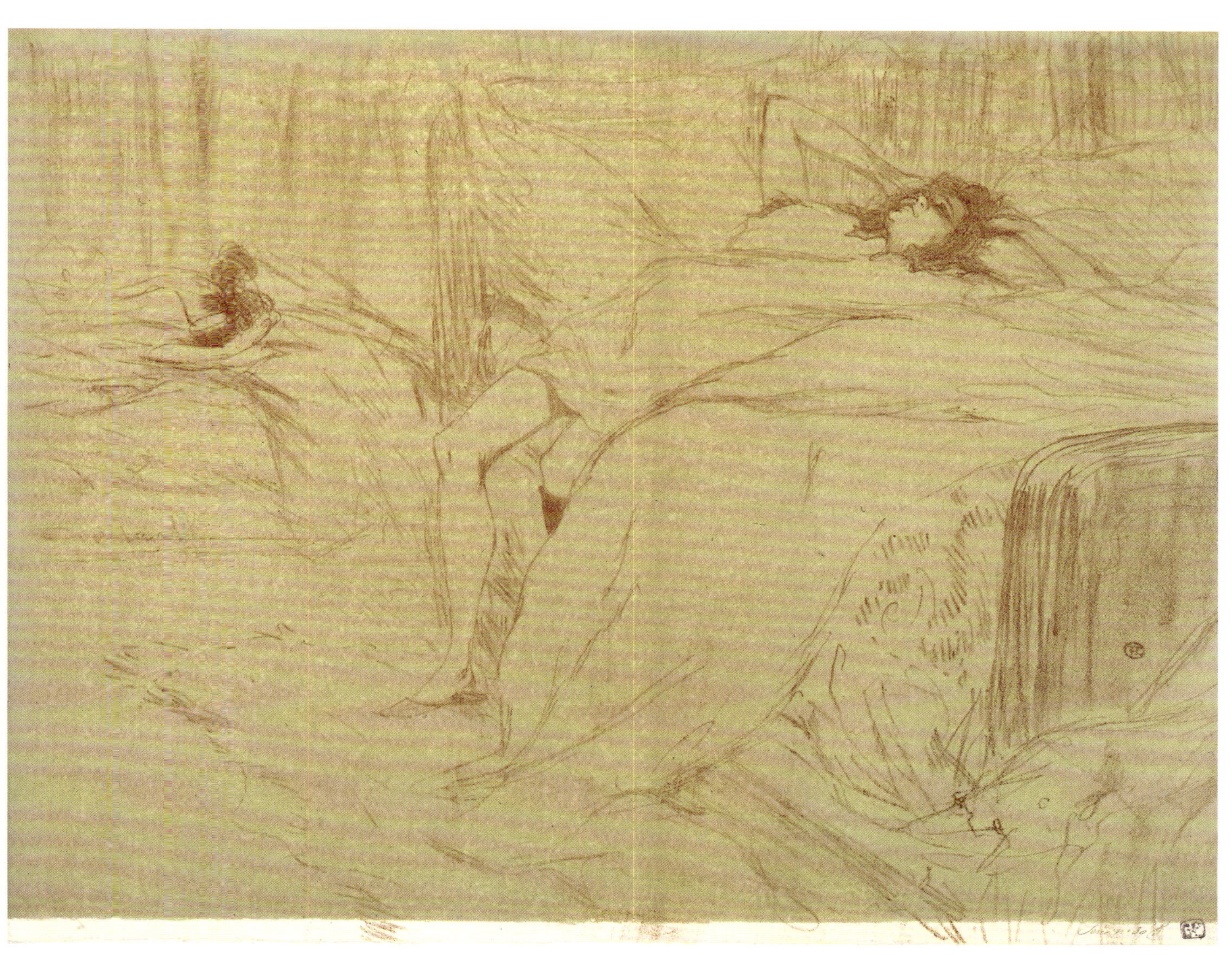

56

L'Aube

1896
Crayon, spatter, and brush lithograph in
   two colors on wove paper
Image and sheet: 24¼ × 31⅛ in. (61.6 ×
   79 cm)
Printed by Edw. Ancourt & Cie, Paris
Commissioned by the magazine *L'Aube*
Wittrock P23; Adriani 184; Delteil 363;
   Adhémar 220

Lautrec made this poster for the illustrated literary magazine *L'Aube* during its first month of existence in the spring of 1896. In its first issue, *L'Aube* planned to include a gathering of the writings of Jules de Goncourt. The famous journals of the Goncourt brothers, carried on by Edmond after Jules died in 1870, ended with Edmond's death in the summer of 1896. The streetlight-lit scene of two women following a horse-drawn cart loaded with bundles, its driver enveloped in his shawl and darkness, evokes the dawn of the magazine's title. The scene may represent poor people evicted from their home in the middle of the night (which may also have given the impression that the magazine had leftist tendencies). However, a more plausible explanation may be that the cart is carrying laundry, a typical early morning activity and one that also evokes the magazine's title. Lautrec often reserved areas by covering parts of the lithographic stone from spatters in order to create uninked spaces representing, for example, a shining moon or a luminous compass against a darkly inked background. In this poster, the rays of light emanating from the street lamp and illuminating only the trudging horse were achieved in this manner. A year later, in his lithographs for Georges Clemenceau's book *Au Pied de Sinai*, Lautrec not only reserved uninked space for the sun over the Sinai desert shown on the cover, but also provided a similarly rendered streetlight in the illustration *The Begging Baron Moses*.

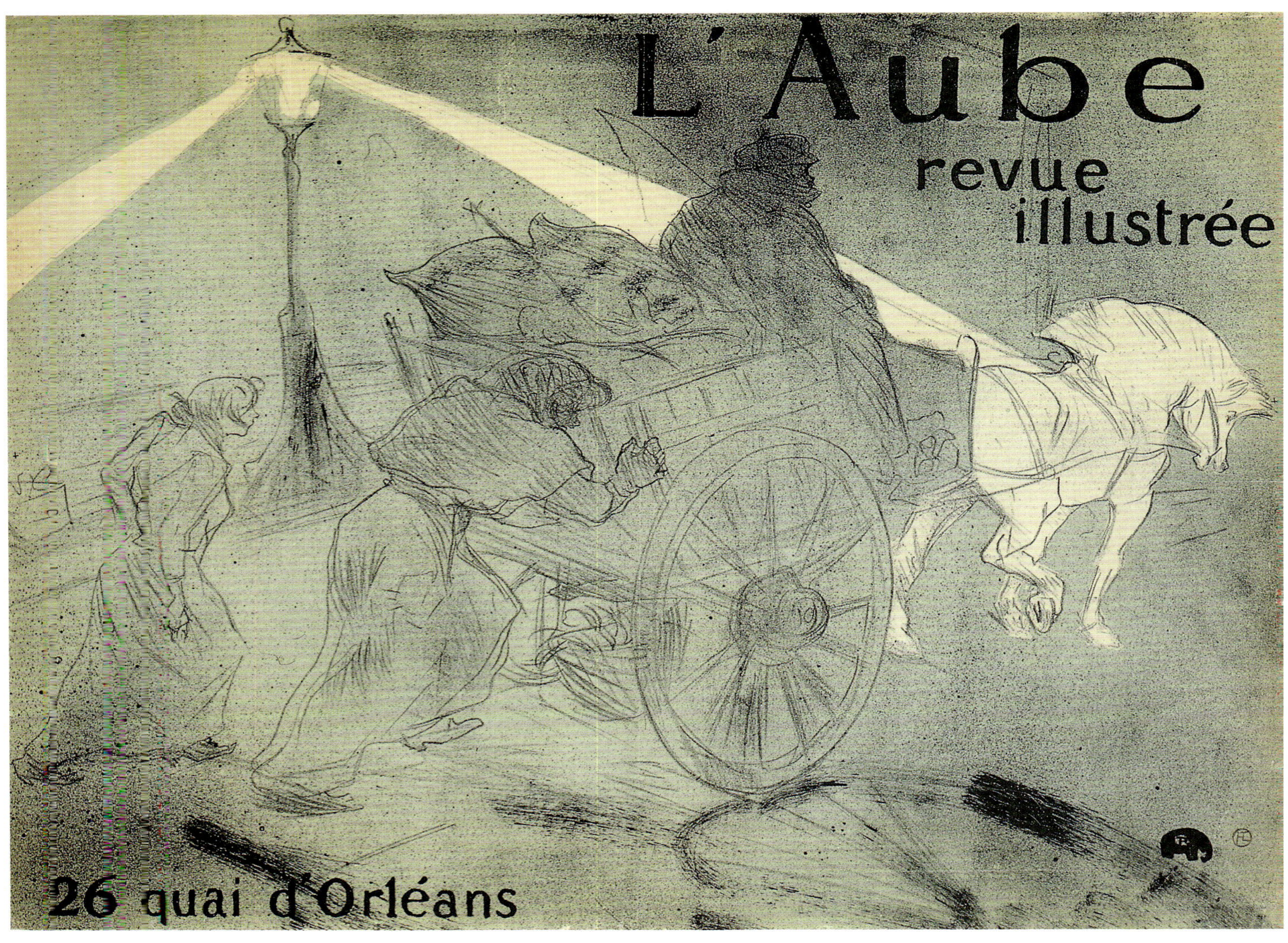

L'Aube
revue
illustrée
26 quai d'Orléans

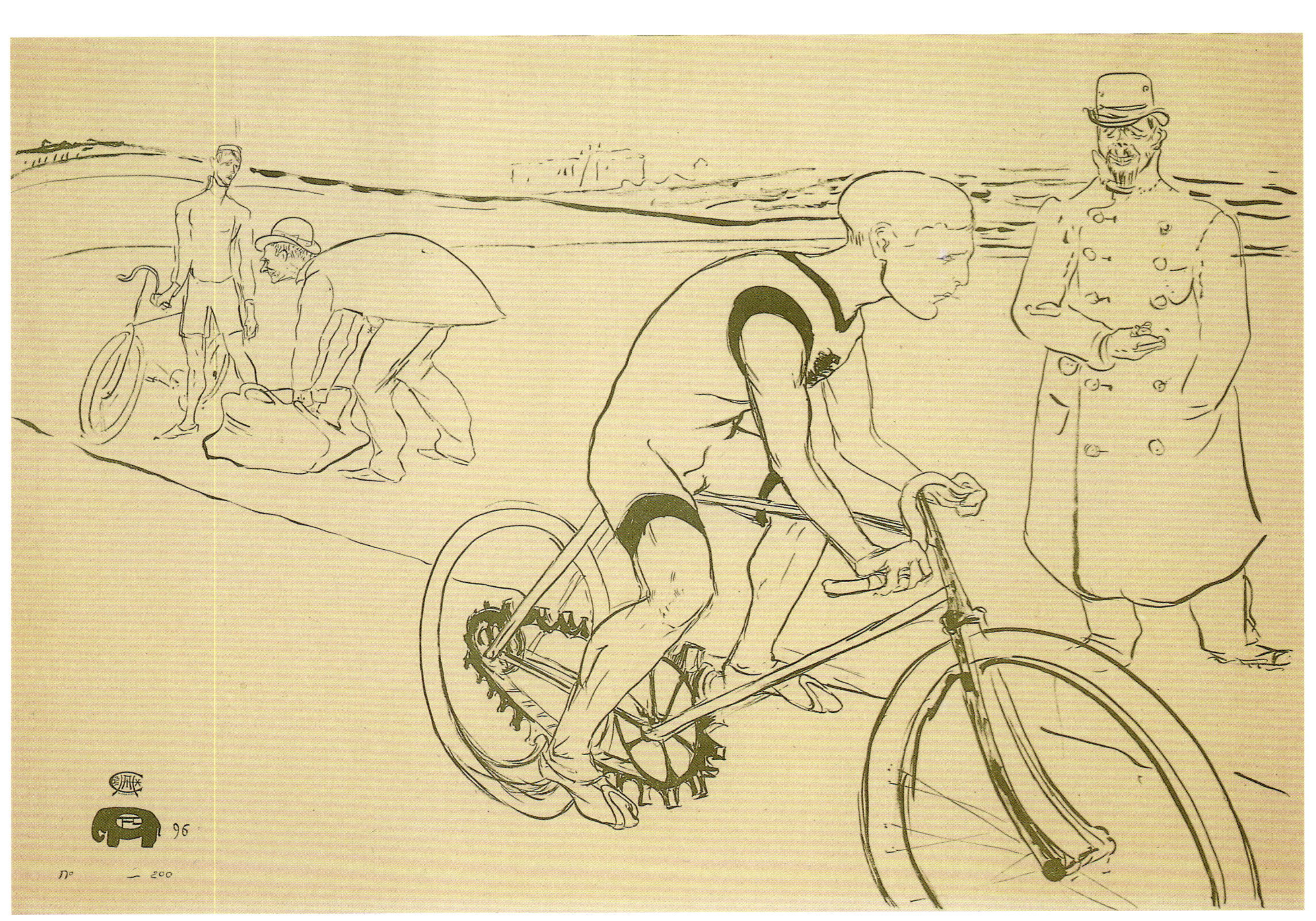

Cycle Michaël

1896
Brush lithograph on wove paper
Image: 32¼ × 48½ in. (82 × 123.2 cm)
Sheet: 34⅞ × 50 in. (88.6 × 127 cm)
Printed by Chaix, Paris
Wittrock P25; Adriani 188; Delteil 359;
  Adhémar 84

This was Lautrec's first attempt at fulfilling a commission from the French representative of the Simpson bicycle company, Louis Bouglé (Spoke), for a poster advertising the English manufacturer's new bicycle chain. The poster, for which Lautrec completed only the drawn keystone, shows the champion Welsh cyclist Jimmy Michaël being timed by sportswriter Frantz Reichel. Inside the track behind him is the trainer "Choppy" Warburton. Spoke was Michaël's manager and an expert on bicycling, a popular sport in the 1890s. At the two racetracks in Paris, the Vélodrome Buffalo and the Vélodrome de la Seine, cyclists who were the equivalent in fame of today's basketball stars rode in races of endurance and cunning skill. Bicycle races began in 1869 in France, but it was not until changes in the bicycle that made racing faster, such as equal-sized wheels and the invention of air-filled tires in 1889, that the craze took off. Simpson's was a major manufacturer of items that contributed to the racing bicycle's reliability, and representing their products correctly was important. Lautrec frequented the races in Paris (his friend Tristan Bernard managed the Vélodrome Buffalo and also edited *Le Journal des vélocipèdistes*), and had probably observed Michaël at an English track with his friend Spoke before beginning this poster. Spoke rejected the poster, however, most likely because Lautrec had neglected to connect the pedal to the bicycle. The artist apparently was indifferent to the inaccuracy and had an edition of two hundred printed, possibly speculating that Michaël's fans would collect his picture anyway.

La Chaîne Simpson

1896
Brush, crayon, and spatter lithograph in
  three colors on wove paper
Image: 32¼ × 47½ in. (82 × 120.7 cm)
Sheet: 32⅝ × 47¾ in. (82.9 × 121.3 cm)
Printed by Chaix, Paris
Commissioned by Louis Bouglé
  (L. B. Spoke)
Wittrock P26; Adriani 189; Delteil 360;
  Adhémar 187

Following the rejection of his first poster for the Simpson Chain, Lautrec produced this more detailed and complex lithograph, which he completed in June.
Undoubtedly, the addition of other racers in competition gave added importance
to the value of Simpson's product. In his *Cycle Michaël* (cat. 57) there was no
sensation of a race nor of speed. In this more successful composition, Lautrec
shows a properly hunched-over cyclist, Constant Huret, racing behind a tandem
bicycle, with two other five-rider tandems on the back track. On the lawn inside
the oval track is a small band, along with W. S. Simpson and Louis Bouglé
(Spoke). Since Spoke and Lautrec had visited London together to see bike races,
Simpson's presence in this scene may place it at a London velodrome. As with
five of his other posters of 1896, Lautrec had the keystone printed in a deep blue
rather than his customary olive-green. He achieved this image of popular appeal
that could vie successfully with other sports posters by filling large areas with
solid blue and yellow punctuated by bright red lettering. The fully saturated
colors and smaller-than-usual areas of spatter may be due in part to the printer's
method, since this and Lautrec's similarly colored but unfinished Bessie
Wentworth print (cat. 59) were both printed by Chaix.

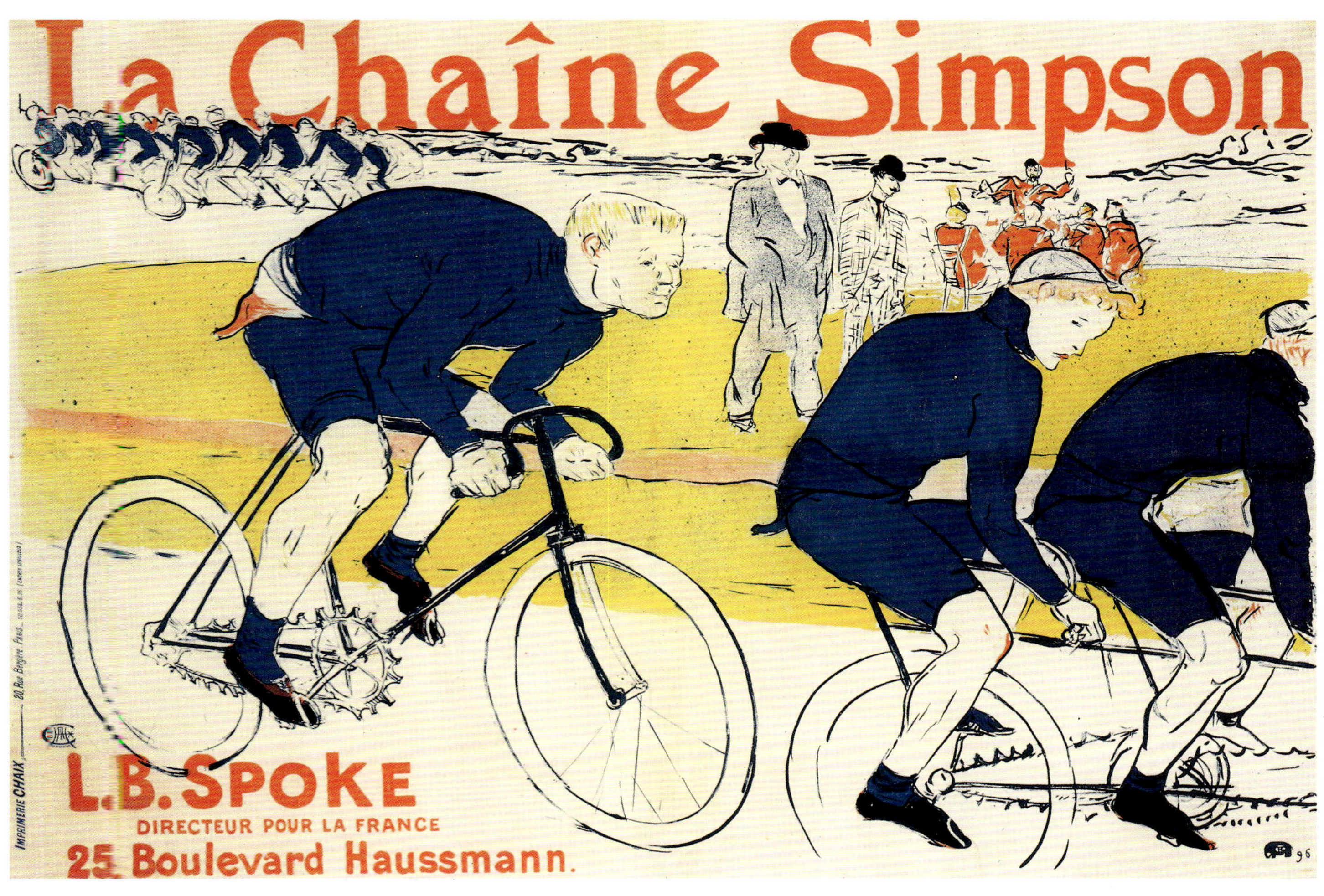

La Chaîne Simpson
L.B. SPOKE
DIRECTEUR POUR LA FRANCE
25 Boulevard Haussmann.
IMPRIMERIE CHAIX

59

Bessie Wentworth Singing "Little Alabama Coon," formerly La Chanson du matelot au Star, Le Havre

1899
Crayon and brush lithograph in four
  colors on wove paper
Image: 13½ × 10¾ in. (34.3 × 27.3 cm)
Sheet: 15¾ × 11⅜ in. (40 × 28.9 cm)
Only state, trial proof
Printed by Chaix, Paris
Wittrock 326; Adriani 352; Delteil 276;
  Adhémar 360

Only recently has the subject of this extremely rare print been positively identi-fied as the English singer Bessie Wentworth (Elizabeth Andrews).[1] The former title, *La Chanson du matelot au Star, Le Havre,* associated it with other works Lautrec produced during and after a visit to Le Havre in 1899, and the per-former's costume was thought to have been that of a sailor, thus "The Sailor's Song." Actually, Wentworth wears the striped costume that was traditionally part of the American minstrel wardrobe. Many American products were popular in Europe in the nineteenth century (cocktails were a Lautrec speciality), so it was not unusual for an English music-hall singer to imitate American minstrels (white men in blackface). Wentworth wears the proper costume but not black-face, since it was not the customary makeup for women. Among her songs were "Looking for a Coon Like Me" and "Little Alabama Coon," which she per-formed in London in April and May of 1896. Minstrel shows, which began much earlier in the nineteenth century, were sometimes called coon shows (from "racoon," a once common reference to African Americans). The subject of this print was suggested by a notation on one copy, "Miss X in the alabamah Coons," found in the archives of the printer Chaix. Lautrec had been in London for a long weekend, most likely between April 30 and May 4, 1896, observing bicycle races with his friend Louis Bouglé. He evidently also saw Wentworth perform during this trip, since a sketch he made of her was reproduced on a Parisian theatre program on May 7. It is probable that he started, but did not finish, this print of her at Chaix, at the same time that he made his poster advertising the new Simpson bicycle chain (cat. 57).

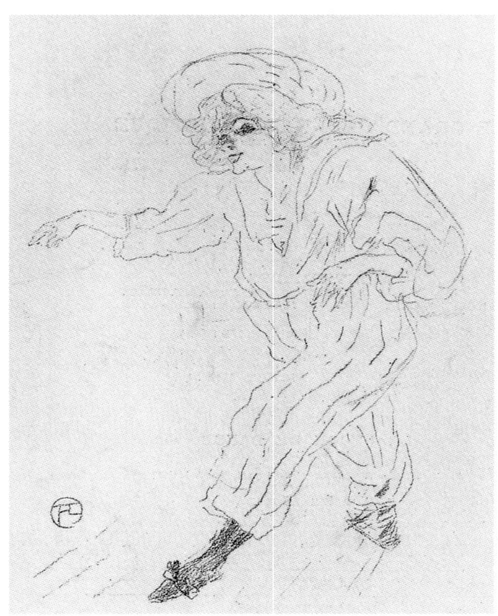

Henri de Toulouse-Lautrec, *Bessie Wentworth*, 1896, pencil on paper. Private collection.

1. Herbert D. Schimmel, "Bessie Wentworth Singing 'Little Alabama Coon,'" *Print Quarterly* 7, no. 3 (1990): 286–91.

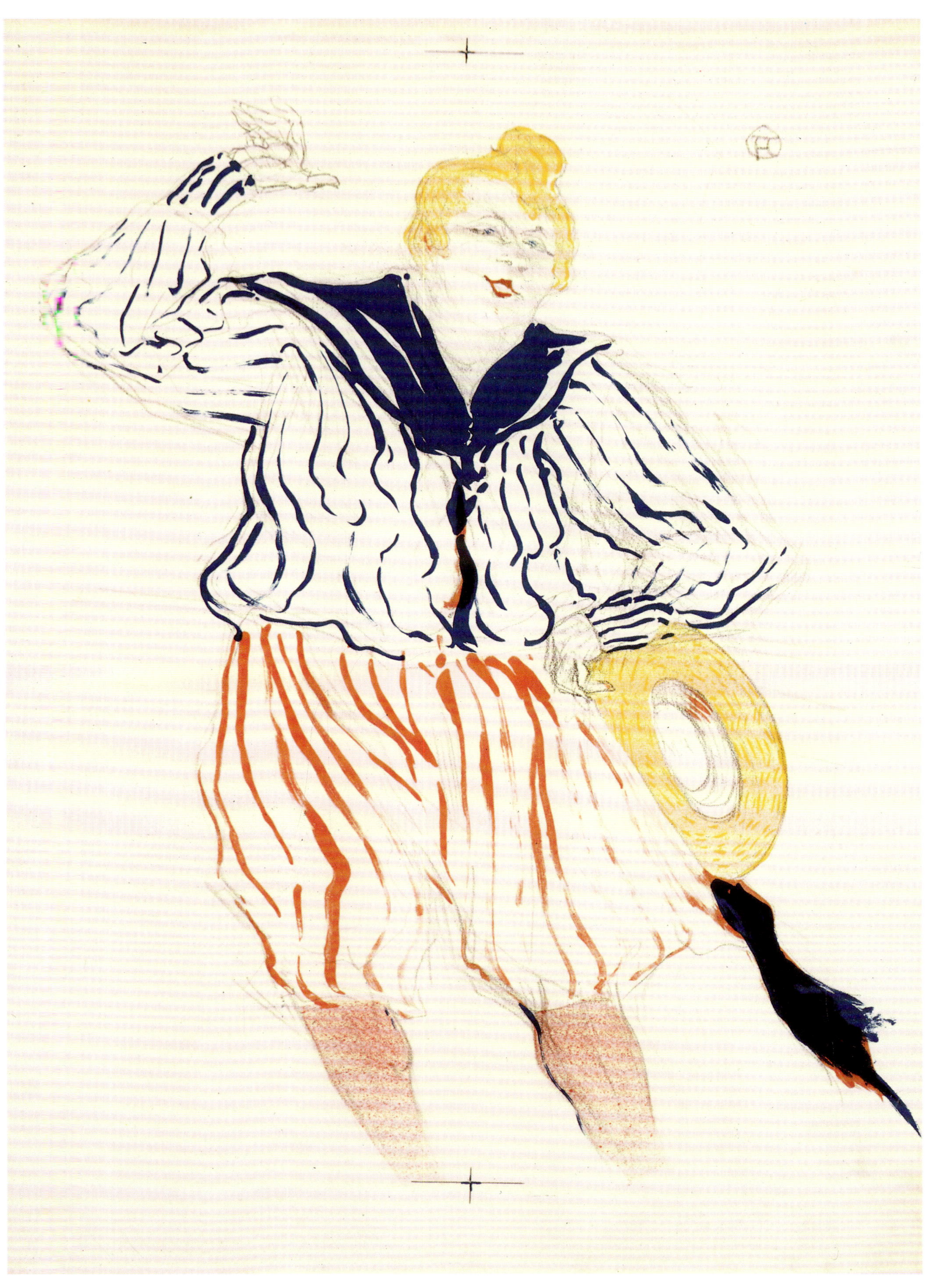

60

Au Concert

1896
Brush and spatter zincograph with
  scraper in four colors on wove paper
Image: 12½ × 10 in. (31.8 × 25.4 cm)
Sheet: 18⅞ × 14 in. (48 × 35.6 cm)
Trial proof
Commissioned by the Ault & Wiborg
  Co., Cincinnati
Wittrock P28/A; Adriani 196/I; Delteil
  365/I; Adhémar 199/I

This poster, pale in color and quite small in scale, may have been modest because it was printed in America from four zinc plates prepared by the artist in Paris. The company that commissioned it, Ault & Wiborg, was a lithographic ink manufacturer in Cincinnati, New York, and Chicago. This proof was most likely printed in Paris before the plates were sent to Charles H. Ault, who printed this edition in Cleveland. One plate carried the outline drawing and the other three carried red, black, and yellow. In this example, the drawing is printed in green (the same lines were printed in brown in the actual edition), and the man's hat is printed in blue-black. Other inconsistencies with the finished edition, such as black spots on the face of the woman and uneven inking, are typical of a proof from plates that have not yet been cleaned up for the final printing. For his subject Lautrec chose two listeners in a loge. The couple seems respectable enough for an American advertisement. There has been some disagreement about who the figures are. The man most often has been identified as Lautrec's cousin Gabriel Tapié de Céleyran, but it has also been suggested that he is Henri Fourcade, Lautrec's banker, whose upturned mustache, fashionable during the Second Republic, is visible in the preparatory sketch. There is also little agreement about who the woman is. One candidate is Émilienne d'Alençon, shown rehearsing in *Répétition générale aux Folies Bergère* of 1893 (cat. 20) and possibly in *La Grande Loge* (cat. 61), dated the same year as this print. Another suggestion is Misia Natanson, whose acquaintance with Hoytie Wiborg decades later may indicate an earlier association with the Wiborg family.

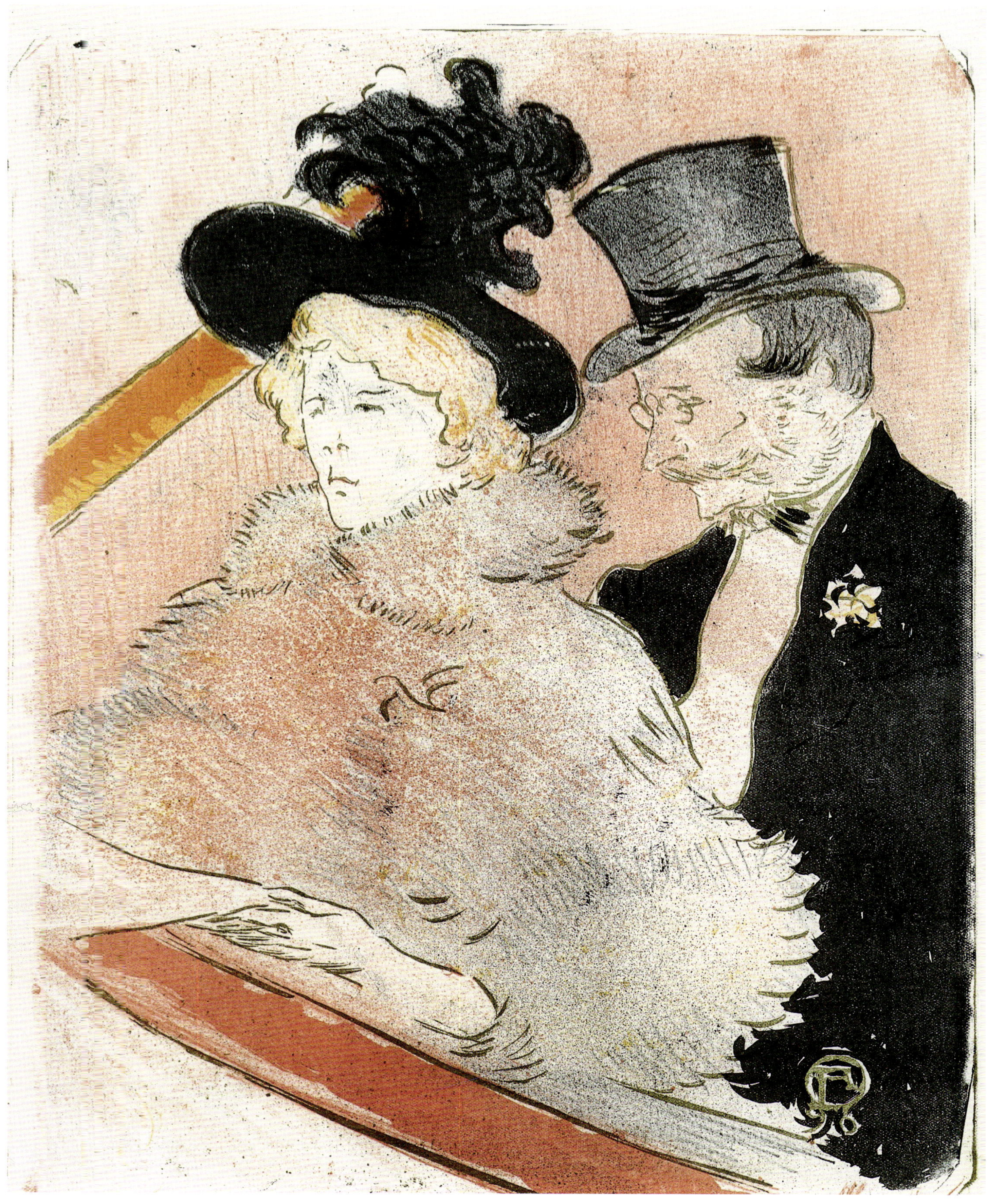

61

La Grande Loge

1897
Crayon, brush, and spatter lithograph in
  five colors on wove paper
Image and sheet: 20⅛ × 15⅝ in. (51.1 ×
  39.7 cm)
Undescribed early state, trial proof
Published by Gustave Pellet, Paris
Inscribed in pencil, *passé*
Wittrock 177; Adriani 202; Delteil 204;
  Adhémar 229

Pellet published this print in an edition of twelve after several stages of color changes. This trial proof is the third of ten made before the edition. It contains the first passages of red on the balustrades, carpet, and chairs. In addition, there are details in ocher on the front of the box and around the peephole at its rear that were effaced in the final edition. As Lautrec worked on a print, after having painted a maquette, he added and subtracted details and altered colors so that the final version inevitably was a more condensed and more arresting image. Among his pictures of people listening to and watching performances in the cafés and theaters, this is his most compelling. In the foreground is Madame Armande Brazier, the proprietor of a lesbian bar in Montmartre called Le Hanneton. She is shown in profile as she watches the performance, while next to her is a pretty woman sometimes identified as Émilienne d'Alençon. Not only is she not paying attention to the stage, but she is facing the viewer while giving a sideways glance to her companion. Brazier wears light-colored tailored clothes while her friend appears in a dark cape and frilly hat. The contrast accentuates the difference between Brazier's manly bulk and d'Alençon's petite femininity. Dozing behind them, oblivious to the charmed liaison two boxes away, is Tom, the coachman of Baron Rothschild, whom Lautrec had observed in a livelier mood in his poster for *The Chap Book* of 1895 (cat. 37).

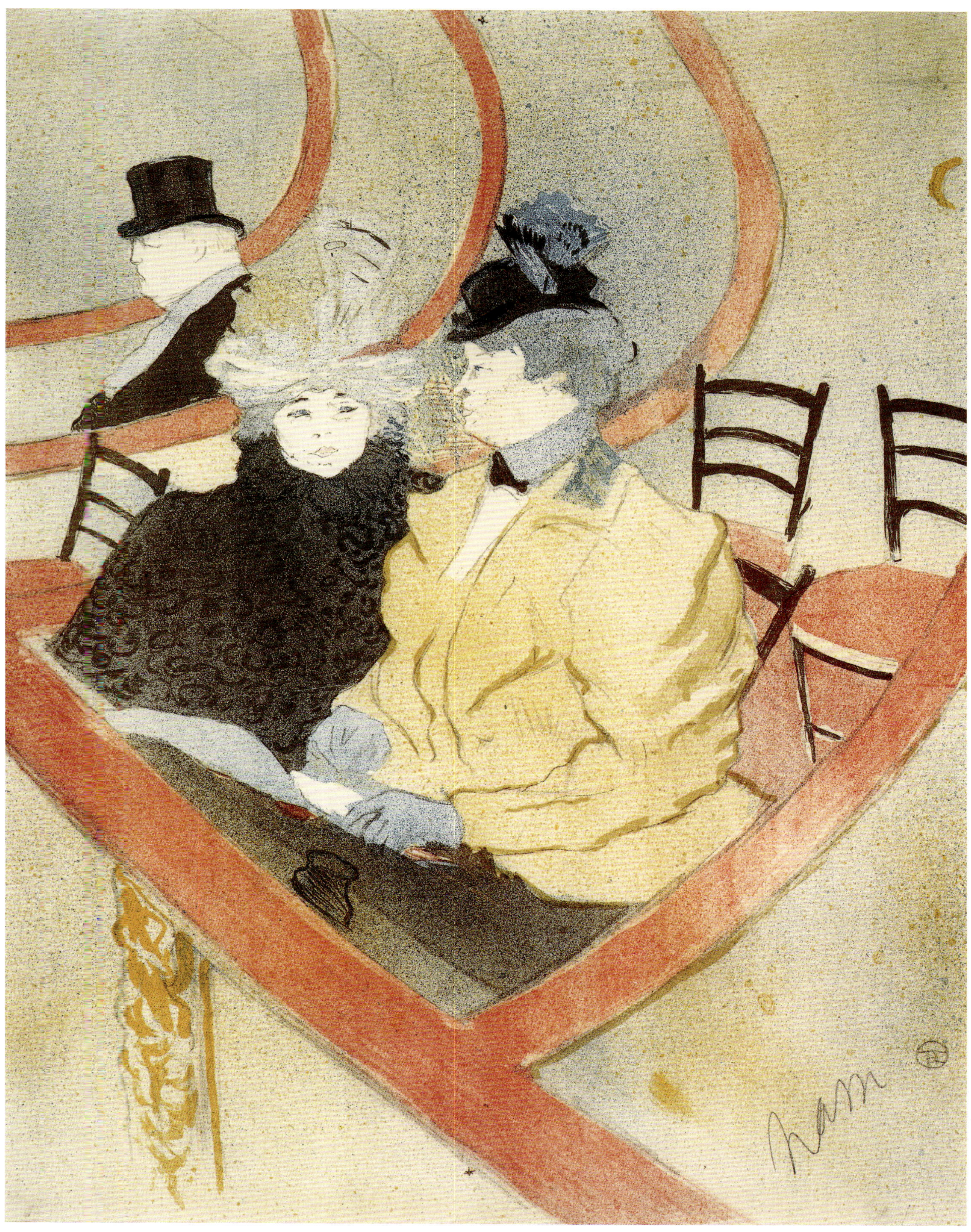

62

La Clownesse au Moulin Rouge

1897
Crayon, brush, and spatter lithograph
  in six colors on wove paper
Image and sheet: 16 × 12½ in. (40.6 ×
  31.8 cm)
Only state, number 7
Printed by Edw. Ancourt & Cie
  (H. Stern), Paris
Published by Gustave Pellet, Paris
Signed lower right in pencil, *HTLautrec
  7;* stamp of Gustave Pellet (Lugt 1190)
Wittrock 178; Adriani 203; Delteil 205;
  Adhémar 231

The clowness Cha-u-Kao, on whom Lautrec concentrated as a model for sketches and paintings in 1895, had a power to inspire him that was evidently as strong as La Goulue's had been four years earlier. In 1895 he produced an important painting of her, *La Clownesse au Moulin Rouge,* purchased by the King of Serbia in 1896. After including the seated clowness in his *Elles* album (cat. 46), Lautrec fulfilled Pellet's request for more prints a year later with two more images of her based on earlier paintings: *La Danse au Moulin Rouge* (after *Au Moulin Rouge: Les Deux valseuses,* 1892) and this print, based on the king's painting. In this effective composition, the dazzling Cha-u-Kao moves across the floor, momentarily hesitating and looking back, as impudent in her glance as she was in the *Elles* print. On her arm is Gabrielle la Danseuse, and behind them is the writer Tristan Bernard. A comparison with Lautrec's 1893 lithograph *La Goulue et sa soeur* (cat. 6) reveals a development in his technique and compositional skill. In the 1893 print, La Goulue was shown as a pale uninflected form, confined by the dense black figures of her companion and the men behind them. Cha-u-Kao, displayed in her characteristic black stockings and pants and yellow ruffle, is framed by lightly sprayed areas which are unified by the blue of the mirrored walls. This setting creates a radiating aura of enchantment around her.

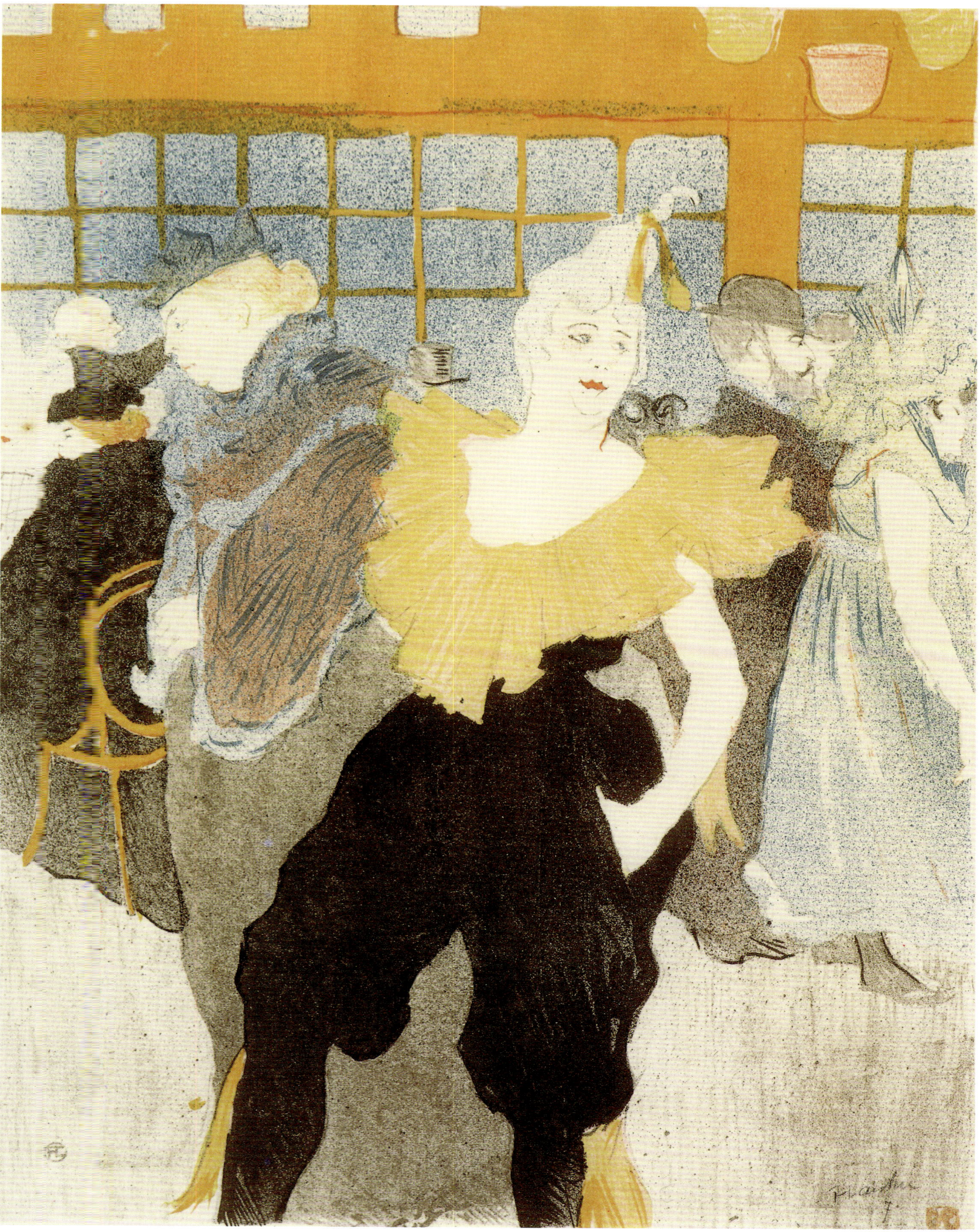

63

Le Marchand de marrons

1897
Crayon lithograph with scraper on gray
  China paper
Image: 10¼ × 6⅞ in. (26 × 17.5 cm)
Sheet: 11¾ × 9 in. (29.8 × 22.9 cm)
Only state, first edition
Printed by Edw. Ancourt & Cie
  (H. Stern), Paris
Distributed by Edmond Sagot, 1901
Signed lower left in pencil, *HTLautrec*
Wittrock 232; Adriani 211; Delteil 335;
  Adhémar 254

This typical Parisian winter scene of a street vendor roasting chestnuts is an unexpected subject for Lautrec. Several illustrations he made for Georges Clemenceau's book *Au Pied de Sinai*, completed in 1897, also depict various aspects of street life he observed in Paris, but they were meant to be set in Poland. With the exception of imaginary scenes created for song sheets and the poster for *L'Aube* (cat. 56), Lautrec did not scrutinize those daily activities on local streets that were the primary subjects for some of his more socially concerned contemporaries, such as Théophile Steinlen. This print may have been an illustration for an unknown work, but it is nevertheless stylistically related to Lautrec's illustrations for the Clemenceau book. Using the side of his crayon, Lautrec produced an impression of the atmosphere and wet pavement of the local scene. The woman walking up the street is dressed very much like one in the background of *La Danse au Moulin Rouge* (believed by some to be Jane Avril), which the artist had reinterpreted in a print only months before. As with many of Lautrec's works, other dates of execution for this print have been suggested, some placing it as late as 1901. Attempts to identify the dog standing in the middle of the street have led to amusing conjectures: it may be Mme Palmyre's bulldog, Bouboule, whose prominence in other Lautrec prints of 1897 ranks it above other candidates. A similar dog appears in one of the *Au Pied de Sinai* prints. The dog's spiked collar is also seen on a dog being led by a young girl in the lithograph *Au Bois,* believed to have been executed as early as 1896, although there is a copy dedicated to Lautrec's cousin (whom, it is said, he wanted to marry) in 1899.

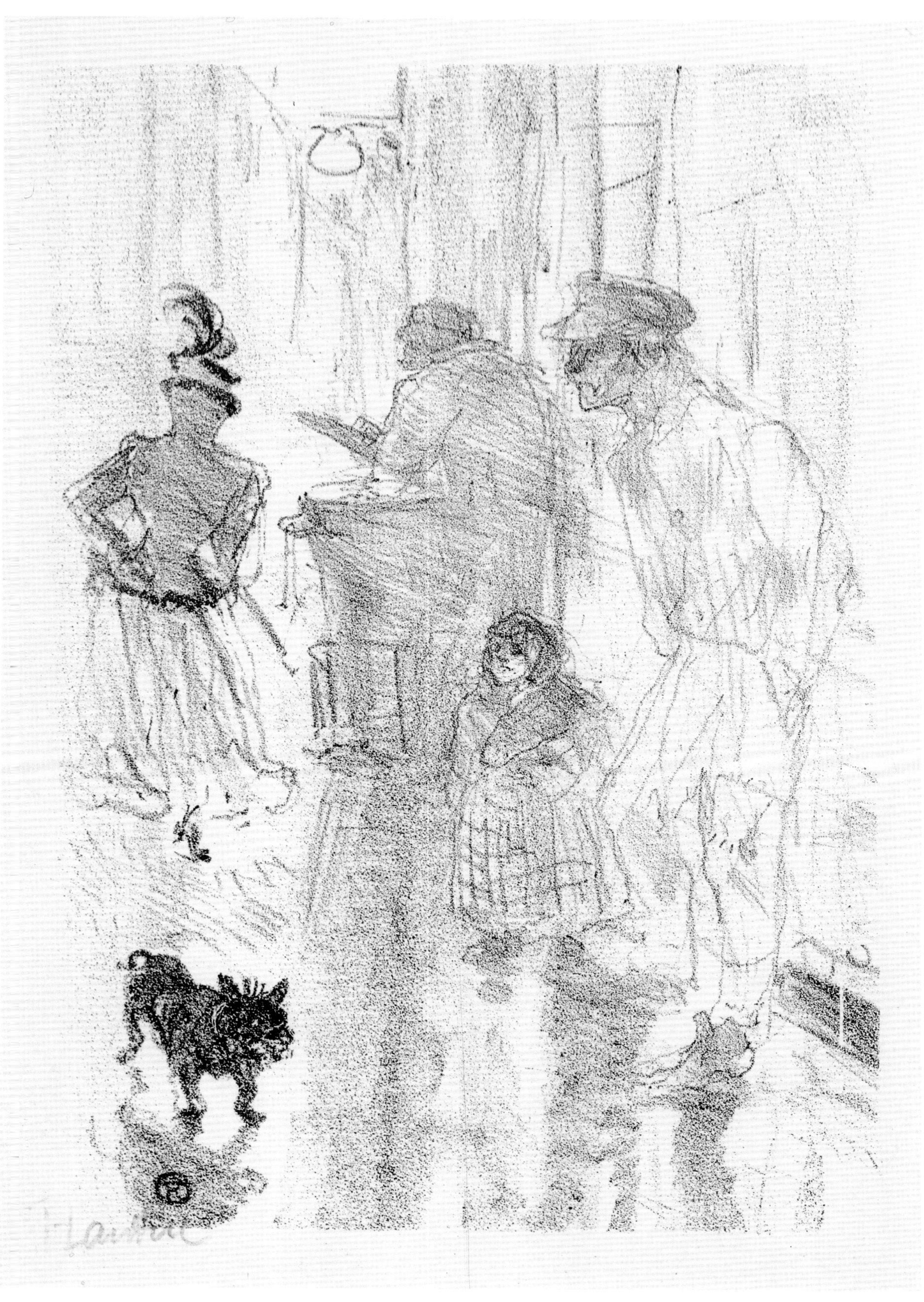

Partie de campagne

1897

Crayon, brush, and spatter lithograph in
  six colors on wove paper
Image and sheet: 15½ × 20¼ in. (39.4 ×
  51.4 cm)
Only state, number 12
Printed by Auguste Clot, Paris
Published by Ambroise Vollard in the
  second *L'Album d'estampes originales
  de la Galerie Vollard*
Inscribed lower left in pencil, *No. 12*
Wittrock 228; Adriani 228; Delteil 219;
  Adhémar 322

Ambroise Vollard invited Lautrec—together with Pierre Bonnard, Maurice Denis, Edvard Munch, Odilon Redon, and Édouard Vuillard—to create color lithographs for *L'Album d'estampes originales de la Galerie Vollard*. Vollard, who was to become the major Parisian dealer of contemporary art, later published albums devoted to each of the French artists, with the exception of Lautrec. In one of his few prints that focus on outdoor activities, Lautrec fills his landscape with fresh air, daylight, and lively movement. Running down an empty road is a trap drawn by a single horse driven by a woman, her top-hatted coachman sitting to one side. A collie chasing the trap provides a further indication of movement. In a contemporaneous lithographic sketch, Lautrec pictured a two-horse cart with the same occupants. Various opinions place the location of the scene near the Natansons' country home in Villeneuve-sur-Yonne, though nothing on the low horizon is recognizable. Neither of the figures have been identified, but it is probable that the collie belonged to the engineer J. Robin-Langlois, since his dog is the only one of that breed depicted by Lautrec in several prints during the following year. Although Lautrec first wrote about Robin, as he was called, in 1893, they may have known each other since childhood. By the end of 1897, when this print was completed, Lautrec's capacity to control his drinking had vanished, and a year later, on the verge of his breakdown, he frequently found a haven at Robin's apartment. This last major print before Lautrec became totally incapacitated could be a metaphor of his decline: helplessness in the apparition of an unknown woman driving to an unknown destination.

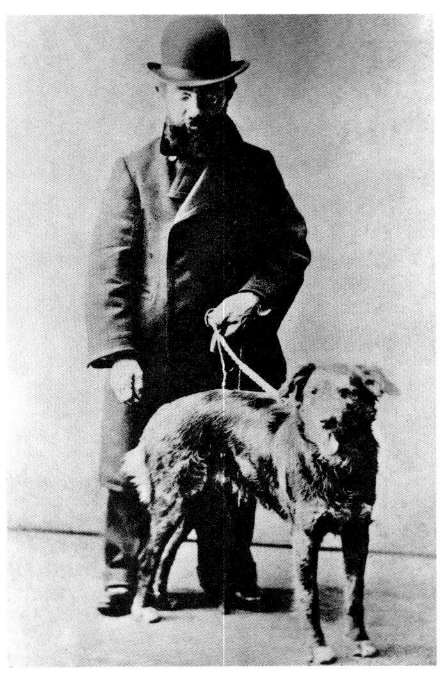

Toulouse-Lautrec with his Dog,
photograph. Private collection.

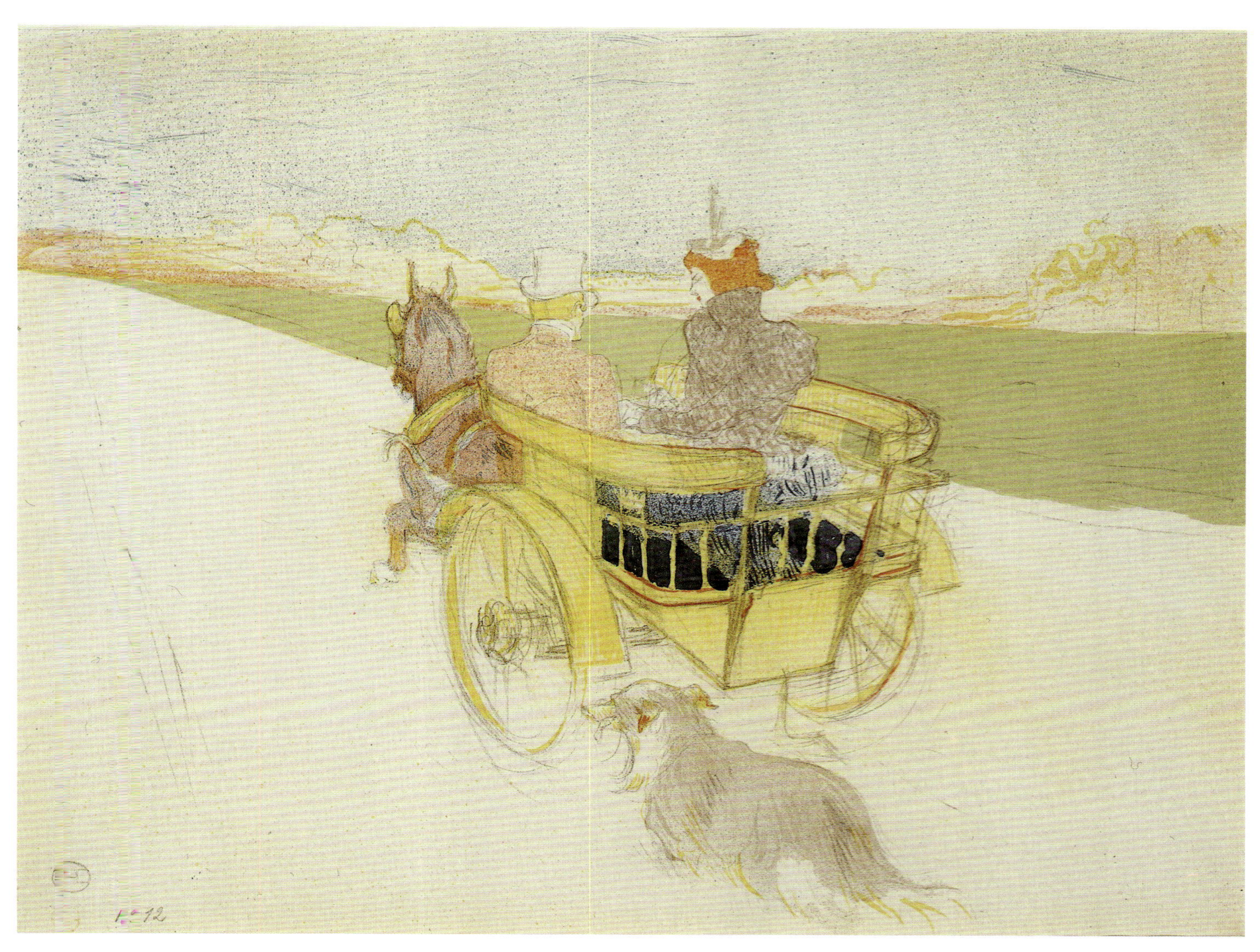

65

Le Bon Graveur: Adolphe Albert

1898
Crayon lithograph on wove paper
Image: 13½ × 9½ in. (34.3 × 24.1 cm)
Sheet: 18¾ × 14 in. (47.6 × 35.6 cm)
Only state, number 34
Published by Boussod, Manzi, Joyant
  & Cie
Signed lower left in pencil, *HTLautrec;*
stamped, *34;* with blindstamp lower
  center of Goupil and Cie (Lugt 1090)
Wittrock 297; Adriani 304; Delteil 273;
  Adhémar 301

Adolphe Albert was one of three brothers, all of whom were involved in Lautrec's life in one way or another. He and his brother Joseph studied at Cormon's studio; Adolphe became a printmaker and Joseph a painter and a prominent figure in Lautrec's painting *Moulin de la Galette*. The third brother, Henri, was the Paris representative for the German magazine *Pan* and probably introduced Lautrec to Julius Meier-Graefe, who commissioned the print *Mademoiselle Marcelle Lender, en buste* (cat. 29). Adolphe, familiarly called Dodo, invited Lautrec to exhibit at the Salon des Indépendents in 1889. The printmaker also had Lautrec's work included in the Salon des Peintres-Graveurs in 1893, the year he married Renée Vert, a milliner Lautrec used as a model. The lithograph shows Adolphe drawing on a lithographic stone, typically set at an angle. Lautrec shows him working with his hat on, light streaming in from a window at his side. It is not known whether it was Lautrec or Adolphe's idea to imitate the composition of Rembrandt's etched self-portrait of 1648.

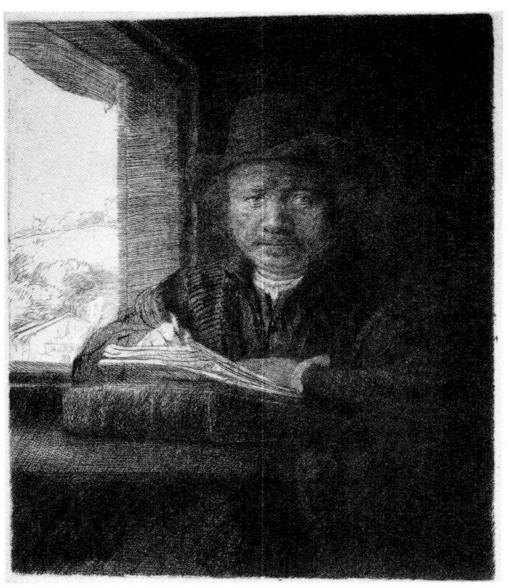

Rembrandt van Rijn, *Rembrandt Drawing at a Window*, 1648, etching, sheet 7⁷⁄₁₆ × 5⁵⁄₁₆ in. The Metropolitan Museum of Art, New York, gift of George Coe Graves.

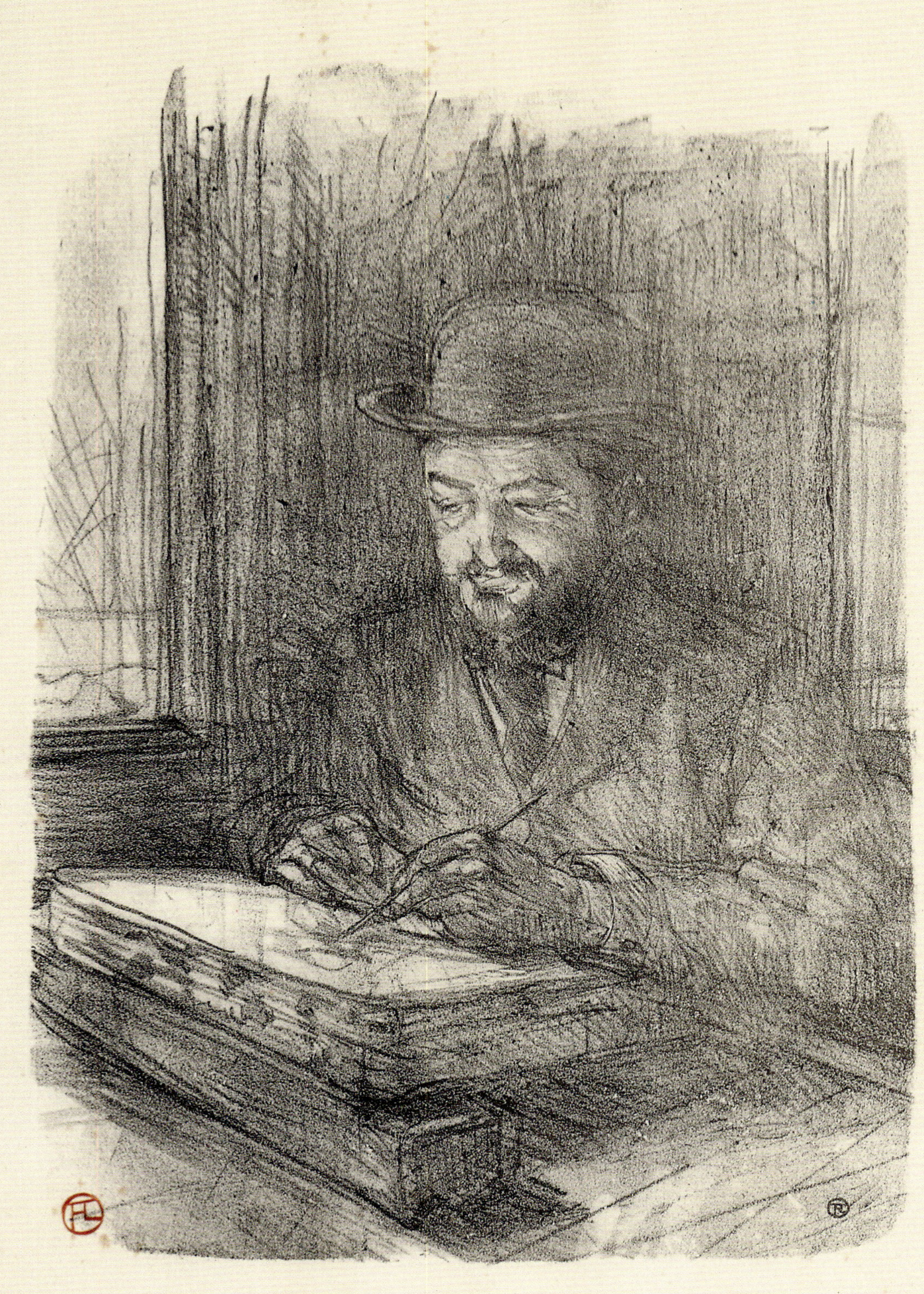

66

Le Jockey

1899
Crayon lithograph in six colors on
 China paper
Image and sheet: 20¼ × 14⅛ in.
 (51.4 × 35.9 cm)
Second state
Printed by H. Stern, Paris
Published by Pierrefort, Paris
Inscribed lower right in pencil, *193hm*
Wittrock 308/II; Adriani 345/II; Delteil
 279; Adhémar 365

In May 1899, Lautrec left the clinic in Neuilly, somewhat before the completion of his treatment, having convinced everyone of his intention to remain sober. Around that time, he accepted a commission from the publisher M. E. I. Pierrefort to prepare a series of lithographs about horse racing. In 1898, during his precipitous slide into the state that had put him into the clinic, he had made several lithographs of horses housed in the livery stable downstairs from his apartment run by one of his drinking companions, Edmond Calmèse. While recovering in the clinic during April and early May, Lautrec had been allowed to take outings in the Bois de Boulogne, where he visited the Longchamps racetrack. He prepared four lithographs for the series, which was to have been titled *Courses* (Racetracks), but only *Le Jockey* was completed and published, first in black-and-white, and then in color. Again, as he had in his painting of the Cirque Fernando and his poster *Babylone d'Allemagne,* Lautrec depicted the horses from the rear. The tradition of showing races from the spectator's side had been broken two decades earlier by Édouard Manet in his *Races at Longchamps,* when he showed racehorses head on. Lautrec's image has a close association with Degas's many sketches and paintings of racehorses, which showed them and their jockeys in every possible aspect. Lautrec's contribution was the depiction of movement. By exaggerating the perspectival view of the main horse and emphasizing the power of its massive haunches, he produced the impression of great speed. The other three prints planned for the series exist only in proofs and show three phases in the preparation for a horse race: *Le Paddock, L'Entraîneur et son jockey,* and *Le Jockey se rendant au poteau.*

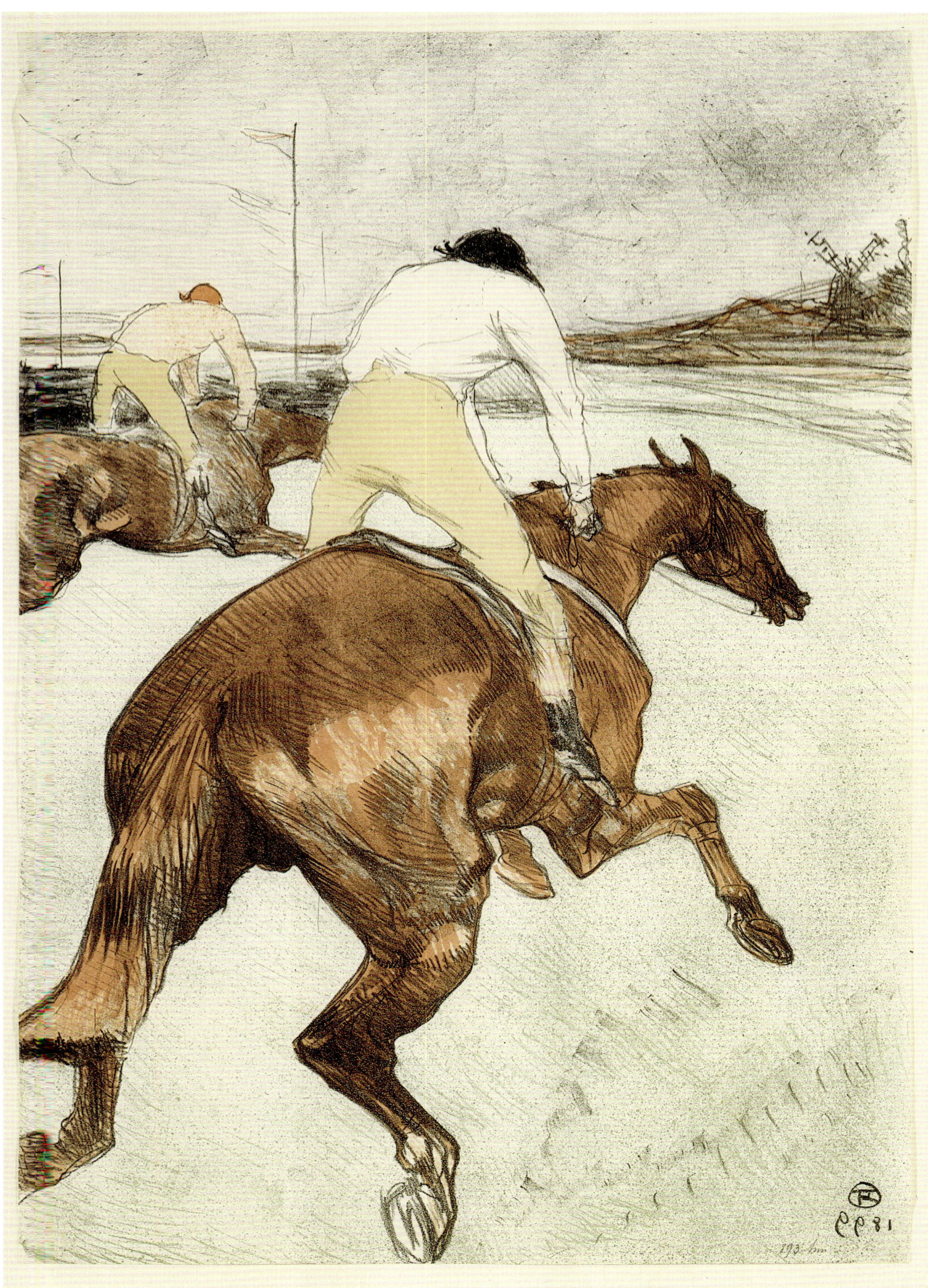

67

Petite Fille anglaise: Miss Dolly, au Star

1899

Crayon lithograph
Image: 8¾ × 6⅞ in. (22.2 × 17.5 cm)
Sheet: 17¾ × 12 in. (45.1 × 30.5 cm)
Printed by Malfeyt, Paris
Inscribed lower left in pencil, *à Calmèse*;
 signed in pencil, *HTLautrec*
Verso: stamp in dark purple ink,
 COLLECTION CROSS (not cited in
 Lugt)
Wittrock 324; Adriani 351; Delteil 274;
 Adhémar 367

In the summer of 1899, Lautrec and his companion Paul Viaud de la Teste made an excursion to Le Havre, the usual jumping-off place for ships to London and Bordeaux. Even though Viaud was there to keep Lautrec from drinking, they regularly found entertainment at the bars frequented by the many sailors who came ashore between trips. British sailors were drawn to the Star, where English women performed in their language. During Lautrec's last visit to the port, he sketched several of the performers. Two lithographs resulted, one of which documented the antics of the lively barmaid Miss Dolly. As Lautrec's health declined, his works alternated between extraordinarily complimentary portraiture and incisively rendered caricature. On this visit to Le Havre, he made two oils on wood: one a flattering portrait of Dolly and the other, made into this lithograph months later, showing her as a character in performance, wearing a sailor's hat and carrying a shoe. This example of the print was dedicated to his neighbor Edmond Calmèse, depicted a year earlier by Lautrec in his realistic manner.

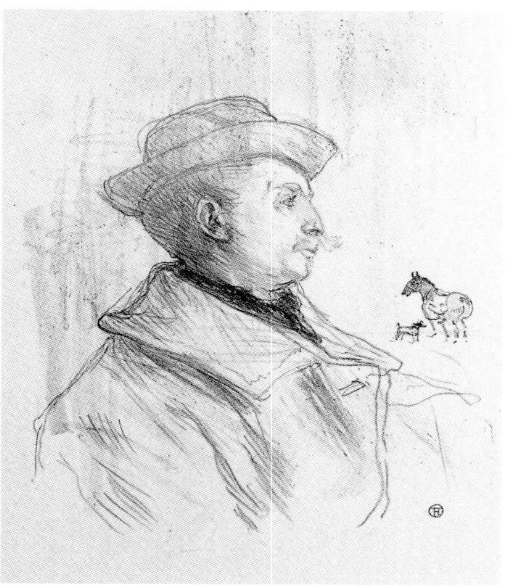

Henri de Toulouse-Lautrec, *Calmèse*,
1898, lithograph, sheet 21⅝ × 17¾ in.
Bibliothèque Nationale, Paris.

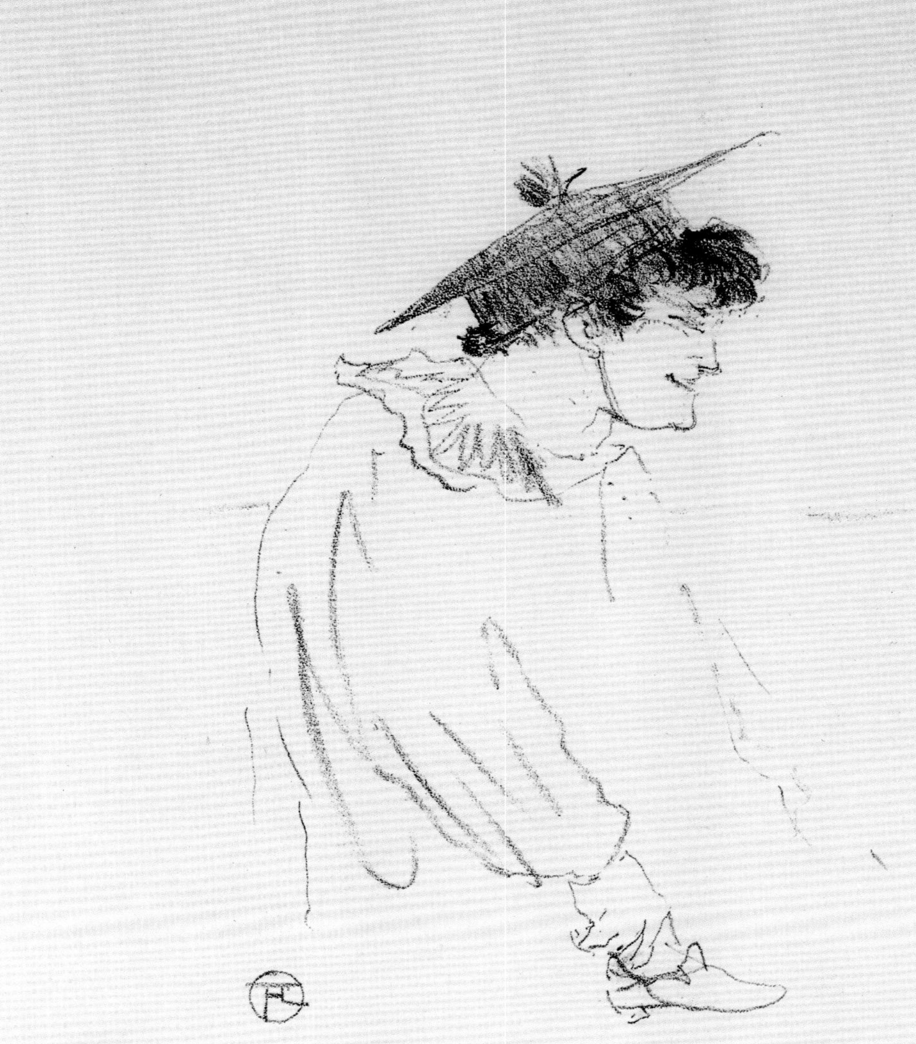

Jane Avril

1899
Brush lithograph in four colors on
  wove paper
Image: 21¼ × 14⅛ in. (54 × 35.9 cm)
Sheet: 21¼ × 14¼ in. (54 × 36.2 cm)
Third state
Printed by H. Stern, Paris
Commissioned by Jane Avril
Wittrock P29/B; Adriani 354/III;
  Delteil 367/II; Adhémar 323/II

Among Lautrec's friends who stood by him during his spiraling descent into alchoholic oblivion was Jane Avril, who owed a certain bit of her fame to Lautrec's pictures of her between 1892 and 1896. This poster, like his earlier ones, was commissioned by her, but according to her memoirs it remained unpublished. There has been speculation that Lautrec's longtime printer Henri Stern, whose name is on the poster and to whom Lautrec dedicated a water-colored version of its first state—"to Stern, with the emotion of a first debut"—may have been given more responsibility in its creation than usual. The small poster is based on a wildly drawn swaying figure in a long dress ornamented its entire length with a serpent. In the second state of the print, limited to twenty-five copies, Lautrec added a remarque of a snake in the lower corner. The composition's charm derives from the paper-doll-like figure placed on an unprinted background and the manner of coloring the serpent portion of Avril's dress. The variegated or rainbow effect of the serpent was accomplished by placing three globs of ink (yellow, blue, and yellow) on the surface from which the printer inked his roller, rolling over the inks several times to meld the edges, and then inking the stone with that one roller. This rainbow technique (applicable to other printing mediums as well) became popular during the late 1960s and into the 1970s when artists—notably Jasper Johns and Andy Warhol—used it in their prints and the rock music industry plundered its magical symbolism on album and magazine covers.

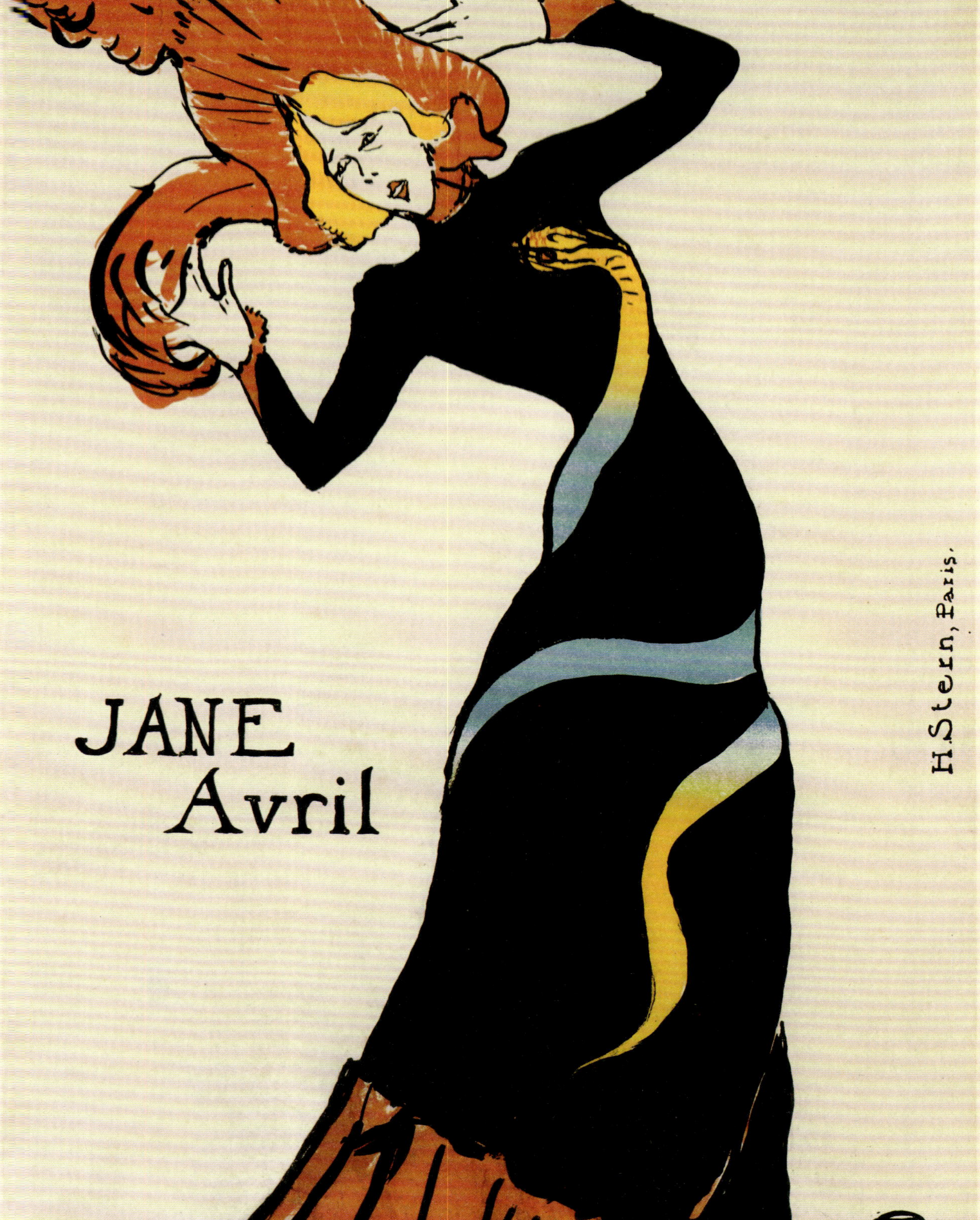

JANE
Avril
H.Stern, Paris.
1899

Selected Bibliography

Aitken, Geneviève. *Artistes et théâtres d'avant-garde: Paris 1890–1900.* Pont-Aven: Museé de Pont-Aven, 1991.

Bouret, Claude, ed. *Toulouse-Lautrec: Prints and Posters from the Bibliothèque Nationale.* Bilingual. Brisbane: Queensland Art Gallery, Australia, 1991.

Boyer, Patricia Eckert, and Phillip Dennis Cate. *L'Estampe originale: Artistic Printmaking in France 1893–1900.* Zwolle, Netherlands: Waanders Publishers, 1991.

Castleman, Riva, and Wolfgang Wittrock, eds. *Henri de Toulouse-Lautrec: Images of the 1890s.* New York: The Museum of Modern Art, 1985.

Cate, Phillip Dennis, and Patricia Eckert Boyer. *The Circle of Toulouse-Lautrec.* New Brunswick, N.J.: The Jane Voorhees Zimmerli Art Museum, Rutgers, The State University of New Jersey, 1986.

Desloge, Nora, ed. *Toulouse-Lautrec: The Baldwin M. Baldwin Collection, San Diego Museum of Art.* San Diego: San Diego Museum of Art, 1988.

Feinblatt, Ebria, and Bruce Davis. *Toulouse-Lautrec and his Contemporaries: Posters of the Belle Epoque.* Los Angeles: Los Angeles County Museum of Art, 1985.

Frèches-Thory, Claire, Anne Roquebert, and Richard Thomson. *Toulouse-Lautrec.* London: Hayward Gallery; Paris: Galeries Nationales du Grand Palais, 1991.

Frey, Julia. *Toulouse-Lautrec: A Life.* New York: Viking, 1994.

Gelfer-Jørgensen, Mirjam, ed. *Toulouse-Lautrec Posters: The Collection of the Danish Museum of Decorative Arts.* Rhodos: International Science and Art Publishers, 1995.

Hoffman, Werner, ed. *Pariser Leben: Toulouse-Lautrec und seine Welt.* Hamburg: Hamburger Kunsthalle, 1985.

Huisman, Philippe, and M. G. Dortu. *Lautrec by Lautrec*. London: Macmillan and Co., 1965.

Ives, Colta. *Toulouse-Lautrec in the Metropolitan Museum of Art*. New York: The Metropolitan Museum of Art, 1996.

Murray, Gale B., ed. *Toulouse-Lautrec: A Retrospective*. New York: Hugh Lauter Levin Associates, 1992.

Schimmel, Herbert D., ed. *The Letters of Henri de Toulouse-Lautrec*. New York: Oxford University Press, 1991.

Stuckey, Charles F., ed. *Toulouse-Lautrec: Paintings*. Chicago: The Art Institute of Chicago, 1979.

Catalogues Raisonnés of Toulouse-Lautrec Prints

Adhémar, Jean. *Les Lithographies et pointes séches de Toulouse-Lautrec*. Paris: Arts and Métiers Graphiques, 1965.

Adriani, Götz. *Toulouse-Lautrec, the Complete Graphic Works: A Catalogue Raisonné, the Gerstenberg Collection*. London: Thames and Hudson, 1988.

Delteil, Löys. *Le Peintre-graveur illustré, X–XI: H. de Toulouse-Lautrec*. Paris: Chez l'auteur, 1920.

Wittrock, Wolfgang. *Toulouse-Lautrec: The Complete Prints*. London: Philip Wilson Publishers, 1985.

Catalogues of Collectors' Marks

Lugt, Frits. *Marques de Collections (Dessins-Estampes)*. Amsterdam: Vereenigde Drukkerijen, 1921. Reprint, San Francisco: Alan Wofsy Fine Arts, 1975.

———. *Marques de Collections (Dessins-Estampes) Supplément*. The Hague, Netherlands: M. Nijhoff, 1956. Reprint, San Francisco: Alan Wofsy Fine Arts, 1988.

Photographs of the Stein Collection, except the *Elles* series, are by
Peter Harholdt, Baltimore. Photographs of the *Elles* series are
courtesy Christie's Inc. All other photographs courtesy owners of the
works illustrated, except the following: pages 14, 94, and 142, courtesy
Zimmerli Art Museum, Rutgers University; pages 16 top, 21 top, 42,
44, 72, and 80, © 1998 The Museum of Modern Art, New York; pages
17 top, 92, and 116, © 1997 The Art Institute of Chicago, all rights
reserved; page 18 top, by Hervé Lewandowski, © Réunion des Musées
Nationaux; page 20, Jean-Loup Charmet; page 36, © 1997 Board of
Trustees, National Gallery of Art; page 38, © 1984 The Metropolitan
Museum of Art, New York.

The text of this book was set in Fournier, a facsimile of a face cut by
Pierre-Simon Fournier (1712–1768), French printer and punch cutter.
The display type was set in Golden Type, designed in 1890 by William
Morris, based on the faces of Nicolas Jensen (ca. 1420–1480), French
printer and punch cutter.

The book was printed on Premier Silk 150 gsm by Balding + Mansell,
Norwich, England.